Portraits of Pride

Portraits of Pride

Chinese Historical Society of Southern California
Los Angeles, California
2005

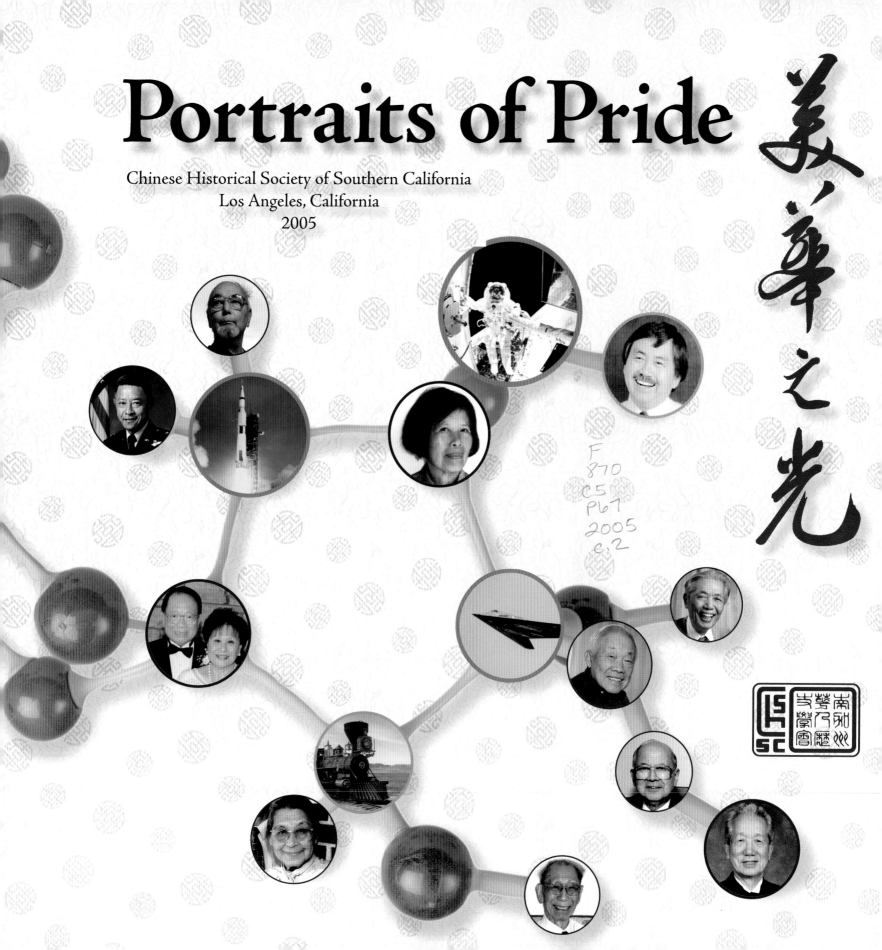

Publisher
Wing Mar: Project Director
Chinese Historical Society of Southern California (CHSSC)
415 Bernard Street
Los Angeles, CA 90012-1703
Website: www.chssc.org
Email: chssc@earthlink.net

Manuscript
Wing Mar: Editor-in-Chief
Joyce Mar: Lead Editor
Edgar Wong: Principal Editor
Frank Bupp: Review Editor

Artwork
Jason Jem: Book design, production manager and selected portrait photography
Yvonne Chia: Cover design

Printed in China by C&C Offset Printing Company

Copyright © 2004 by the CHSSC

ISBN 0-930377-98-2

Library of Congress Cataloging-in-Publication Data
Portraits of Pride.
    p. cm.
 ISBN 0-930377-98-2
 1. Chinese Americans--California--Biography. 2. Chinese
Americans--Biography. 3. Scholars--United States--Biography. 4.
Scientists--United States--Biography. 5. Professional employees--United
States--Biography. 6. California--Biography. I. Chinese Historical Society
of Southern California.
 F870.C5P67 2004
 979.4'004951--dc22
                        2004019691

Prologue

The volume you hold in your hands is a treasury of true-life stories of early 20th century and World War II generation Chinese Americans. For almost three decades, the historians of the Chinese Historical Society of Southern California (CHSSC) have breathed life into Chinese American stories in numerous publications; Portraits of Pride is no exception.

Again, we stand upon the shoulders of our predecessors to document the life struggles and career achievements of 38 Chinese Americans. On the cover, we depicted their portraits with their common bond of Chinese heritage. The icons symbolize their wide range of careers including, but not limited to, healthcare, science and defense. Many of the stories contain poignant moments and even personal discoveries. It is noteworthy that this project began as a photo exhibit capturing only a very brief glimpse into the lives of seven men and women during Asian Pacific American Month in 1999.

Readers will recall, or learn, of the harsh environment endured by the early Chinese immigrants and often by their offspring in adjusting to American life. They had to overcome the obstacles of racial discrimination in naturalization, schooling, housing and employment. The Chinese Exclusion Act of 1882 and the words used in the California Constitution of 1879 served to institutionalized the discrimination that profoundly impacted the lives of Chinese Americans for decades.

Yet, in painful moments, people of good will (frequently at risk to themselves) such as teachers, mentors, friends and neighbors, helped to open doors for these Chinese Americans to integrate into the community and workplace. As their experience comes to light in these stories, the reader will surely discover that these 38 Chinese Americans were true pioneers. If these stories seem familiar, that is because they are the untold stories of your friends and neighbors.

We have included two new features to this book: an historical appendix and CD version. The additions will increase your reading enjoyment by providing an easy access to supplementary educational material via the Internet.

To fulfill our education mission, the CHSSC will distribute 1500 books with CDs to various libraries as a public service. Visit the last page of the book for the details of our "Free Library-Book Program."

Pleasant reading.

Wing Mar M.D.

馬榮賢

Project Director

Contents

Note: In the CD version of this book, each item is a hyperlink directly to the article

Senator Diane Feinstein was elected to the U.S. Senate in 1992. Her career has been one of many firsts:
- first woman President on the San Francisco Board of Supervisors
- first woman Mayor of San Francisco
- first woman elected Senator of California and the
- first woman member of the Senate Judiciary Committee.

Her concern for the Asian American community is demonstrated by the following speech, *The Growing Web of Suspicion of Asian Americans*, on the June 21, 2001 proceedings of the 107th Congress as recorded in the Congressional Record:
"We all need to work together to raise awareness about the positive contributions all Asian Americans have made to every aspect of life here in the United States, and of the sacrifices they have made in defense of this country …."

DIANNE FEINSTEIN
CALIFORNIA

COMMITTEE ON APPROPRIATIONS
COMMITTEE ON ENERGY AND NATURAL RESOURCES
COMMITTEE ON THE JUDICIARY
COMMITTEE ON RULES AND ADMINISTRATION
SELECT COMMITTEE ON INTELLIGENCE

United States Senate

WASHINGTON, DC 20510-0504

http://feinstein.senate.gov

Tribute
By Dianne Feinstein
United States Senator

I would like to thank the Chinese Historical Society of Southern California for distributing this book free of charge to public libraries statewide. I look forward to Book II with the interesting lives of people of other disciplines and different age groups, but beginning with the eldest seniors in Portraits of Pride is appropriate.

Credit has been given to the Chinese for building the railroad and reclaiming farmland throughout the Valley and building other infrastructures of our great state, but it is time to put individual names and faces on our hard-working and creative Chinese Americans, who have contributed to our communities and our economy for the last 150 years in so many other ways. The 38 individuals in this book are from the generation who spoke English and bridged the cultures. They overcame nearly insurmountable obstacles and trail blazed for the future generations.

From the humble laborer in the California fields to the halls of Congress, we all must take lessons from these stories of Chinese Americans. This series of books will give long overdue recognition to those who have chosen to attain their dreams and share their capacity in this land of opportunity. They are loyal and dedicated citizens who have earned their civil rights fighting discriminatory laws, and they deserve our admiration and trust.

About the Editor

Finding two words that describe our flinty editor and fearless fundraiser—yet a compassionate physician and loving family man—is difficult in English. But doing so is simple in Chinese: Wing Mar.

Dr. Wing Mar is a retired family physician who had practiced in Southern California since 1956. He has been a member of the Chinese Historical Society of Southern California since its founding in 1975. In 1999 he chaired the committee to pay off the Society's mortgage on Bernard Street. He and others then felt that it was time to publish a book about the achievements of under-recognized Chinese-American men and women; the result is this publication: Portraits of Pride.

Wing was six months old in 1924 when he arrived in Seattle, Washington, from Toishan in Guangdong Province, China. His childhood was spent in Stockton's Chinatown, where he attended neighborhood schools as well as the obligatory hours of Chinese School. Activities at the Chinese Christian Center and at the YMCA were a part of his early years. During the depression he spent time helping with the struggling family businesses. He would later discover that he was the son of a "paper son"—a subject discussed in the stories herein. Upon honorable discharge from overseas duty in the Pacific, he attended the University of California at Berkeley and graduated from the Stritch School of Medicine at Loyola University in Chicago. After his internship and residency he started his family practice in Torrance, Calif.

In his new community he was asked to give YMCA camp physicals, and later he became a fundraiser and a member of the Board. During his service as president of the Board a new Y building was built. It was then named the Torrance Family YMCA to emphasize programs that were designed for the entire family, a new inclusive direction. Dr. Mar's dedication and tireless support to the Y earned him the highest honor in the Los Angeles Metropolitan YMCA's Golden Book of Distinguished Service in 1968 for "...giving his time, talent and substance to help build an outstanding program..."

In 1978 when geriatric medicine was in its infancy, Dr. Mar's compassion for elderly patients compelled him and a few other physicians to found a statewide organization, the California Association of Medical Directors (now the California Association of Long Term Care Medicine). Its goal was to help improve care for patients through education of the healthcare team. In 1990 he was appointed chairman of the Little Hoover Commission's Advisory Committee on Medical Quality of Care in Nursing Homes. The Commission published a report, *Inadequate Care, Inadequate Oversight*, which made specific recommendations on the Medical Quality of Care in Nursing Homes for the State.

His enthusiasm and interest in the Chinese-American experience are no less significant than his past medical and community accomplishments. Portraits of Pride brings a new dimension—of a hard-nosed manager/editor—to this truly humble man. Wing Mar resides in Torrance, Calif. with his wife, Joyce, whose support he acknowledges as being central in his lifelong community and professional involvement.

A Prelude to the Portraits

by Edgar Wong and Frank Bupp

Great Expectations

Mighty oaks from little acorns grow is an appropriate opening thought for describing the Chinese in America in the 20th century. Immigrants and those born here have achieved their American dreams in a fertile land of freedom where the economic, occupational, social and political environment was most challenging and often harsh. In this place, Chinese family beginnings were of family roots and values, of respect and obedience, and of traditions and culture—laying a firm foundation for life in this new land called Gold Mountain (Gum Saan).

The more-common-than-not pattern of individual upbringing was based on achieving lofty expectations—yes, great expectations! Success was achieved through hard work and unabashed nurturing until about school age, and then through strict discipline: mostly one-way communication (from parent to child, and very few spoken words at that), a strict study and chore regimen (schedule memorized by rote, no memo slips on the fridge), minimum encouragement (perhaps an occasional nod, but no hugs and kisses), and occasional admonition (a stare or a "konk" on the head) … yes, you who have been there know well the drill.

Thus, fulfillment of ancestral family expectations (some noble, some not) became a universal covenant—a lifelong obligation and payback to one's profession, school, community, parents, and roots. The process automatically continues along traditional Chinese values and behavior—usually on a subconscious level; and when expectations go unfilled, a powerful built-in sense of guilt sets in—and this on a very conscious level.

It is from these basic family beginnings that the Chinese Americans have grown and flourished—like the proverbial mighty oaks—to become full participants in the American way of life. They have many stories to tell—stories that are sentimental for the senior readers, inspirational for the younger readers, and interesting for all—stories that we present with pride. The spirit of Lady Liberty would have been proud of her "huddled masses" in California's teeming shores, far away from Liberty Island and her lamp beside the golden door.

Little Stories

"Great fortunes depend on luck; small fortunes depend on diligence." Great fame or small fame … which stories to tell first in our Historical Society's hall of fame? A number of famous Chinese Americans are already nationally or internationally recognized, and deservedly so. Those who warrant our initial attention are our ordinary citizens, who go about their daily lives as silent minorities, largely unnoticed and unsung. Seen among the many faces of Chinese Americans in Southern California are the entrepreneurs in public places like malls, shops, and restaurants; less visible are the workers in private places like offices, cubicles, and laboratories. It seemed appropriate, then, to begin our portrait series with the lesser-seen faces, and the pages that follow present their stories.

This is the first in a series of publications heralding Chinese Americans; this first volume presents the portraits of more than thirty individuals. For this first book, the portraits were chosen almost at random from an admittedly narrow circle of friends of the Chinese Historical Society of Southern California (CHSSC), who were readily accessible for providing detailed biographical information. The portraits are presented herein in their order of completion.

Portrait Attributes

In the mid-to-late 19th century, the Chinese in America were judged to be "unassimilable." A century later, the Chinese Americans were hailed as the "model minority"—a stereotype that has invited scorn as well as praise. The publicized academic and occupational achievements have tended to obscure the fact that these successes were results of lifelong sacrifice and work diligence (or perhaps from simply good fortune). Thus, to get a more complete and better-balanced view, most of the stories herein have emphasized the life-journey—the life struggles along with the career successes—believing that the journey is as enlightening as the destination (achievements). It is hoped that this collection of remarkable journeys will inform and that the shared knowledge might bring our multi-ethnic communities a little closer together.

While the individual stories are about personalities, most include connections to important events of the era (some historic and some not). The racially controversial events are reported forthrightly as valuable lessons learned (without laying blame or expressing malice) to maintain the Historical Society's continuing non-advocacy role. With this ensemble of words—non-controversial, non-advocacy, clinical objectivity, and historical society—one might easily conclude that the stories are necessarily antiseptic and archaic, all destined for early storage on bookshelves and dusty archives even though the book has a nice cover. Not so!

Besides being good recreational reading, the stories are suitable as forum material for discussion groups. These oral histories have been carefully fact-checked and are considered suitable educational material. Some parts will be especially family-relevant when, say, your kids or grandkids ask, "Was great-grandfather a guest (detainee) at Angel Island?" or, "Did great-grandmother have dainty bound feet?" or, "What was our ancestor's true name apart from their false-paper (gah gee) identity?" or, "How come so many Chinese lady ancestors have the same middle name (Shee)?" So why not compare your answers to the versions herein. You most certainly will find them engaging.

A Word about Words

The writing of each portrait involved a person representing the profilee (the subject or the relative of the subject) and the profiler (the author). Of course, storytelling based on recollection of past, undocumented events (some decades ago), might lead to unintended inaccuracies by the two sources. Hence, our interviewing-and-reporting process was conducted in an iterative manner, involving several rounds of independent fact-checks by both the profilee and the profiler.

Upcoming Series

Our individual and collective memories of the golden past are, sadly, fading. Rightly, there is a growing sense of urgency for documenting a minimum set of representative faces beyond the first set. In this information age, it would be almost irresponsible not to make a concerted effort in finding, documenting, publishing, and heralding the next set of Chinese American stories, for it is so relatively easy to do. These thoughts have been in the back of our minds during the busy work of researching and writing the first series of portraits for this Book.

All of the portraits herein are about men and women born before World War II. These individuals have balanced gracefully between two cultures—retaining their Chinese heritage and fitting into the mainstream American culture—and achieved their American dream. For successive generations, this Americanization is unquestionably lessening their ethnic identities and traits. Might they take life easier and lower their expectations? We shall see.

Thus, it is our fervent hope that this initial publication will serve as a model and a catalyst for others to submit their biographies for subsequent editions of this portrait series. Our ultimate goal is to present a comprehensive family of portraits that is representative of Chinese Americans of both genders, from all walks of life, and from various age groups. In our future publications, we especially look forward to the inclusion of papers from our younger generation—for they are the pioneers of the 21st century—who are now in their life-journey facing a different, yet still difficult, set of diversified challenges.

Commentaries

by Members of the Chinese Historical Society of Southern California

The individuals depicted in Portraits of Pride truly are in a "class of their own." We know about the early Chinese pioneers who came for the gold rush, worked on the railroads and farmed the rich soil of California. These early Chinese faced uncertainty and danger in a foreign land but were not deterred from their mission—to provide for their families in China and in the United States. Unfortunately, we seldom were able to put a name or a face to these thousands of early Argonauts.

And, now, thanks to Dr. Wing Mar's Portraits of Pride, we see the next generation building upon that same ingenuity and then some. We can put names to their faces; we learn that regardless of birthplace or where they spent their childhood, many in cities and states clear across America, this generation excelled to a higher degree than would be expected of any second generation ethnic group much less Asians. As youngsters they learned the lessons the early pioneers learned—hard work, frugality and the need to strive for the betterment of the family.

Highly educated and imbued with high levels of curiosity and a "can do" attitude, the heroes of Portrait of Pride did not allow a glass ceiling be a part of their psyche. Yes, the prejudice they faced at various times in their lives became momentary incidents but it did not deter their visions. Collectively, it seemed, they elbowed their way to the table and became leaders in the field of medicine, research science, engineering and the likes. Governments and top companies sought their expertise and communities and organizations recognized their achievements. To them we owe our thanks for raising the bar not just one more notch but ever so high that the third, fourth and fifth generation, those who have been endowed with so much more opportunity, can shoot for the stars.

Sylvia Sun Minnick
Author of SAMFOW: The San Joaquin Chinese Legacy
and The Chinese Community of Stockton

As immediate past-president of the Chinese Historical Society of Southern California, I watched the Portraits of Pride team—drawn from our multi-talented membership—make great efforts over the weeks, months and years to finally realize this magnificent volume. These chronicles of the achievements of Chinese Americans in various spheres of society—physicians, scientists and others—write a great chapter in the history of Chinese Americans, American migration and America itself. I wish to praise the PoP team's ambitious educational and public service initiative of placing 1,500 Portraits of Pride copies on the shelves of libraries and institutions in these United States and Canada; and, to acknowledge the generosity of the project's sponsors who—by their continuous support from its inception—made this possible.

Linda Wong Smith
President (2003-2004)
Chinese Historical Society of Southern California

As the long-awaited Portraits of Pride sees publication, I extend my congratulations to Dr. Wing Mar, the visionary who conceived this book, and to his team for their wonderful work. The stories portrayed here shed new light on health, science and engineering careers which became available to Chinese Americans during the Great Depression and World War II. Readers will learn how family, hard work and tradition played a role in the achievements of the book's profilees. Portraits of Pride is a thoughtful and entertaining work for young and old.

Kenneth L. Chan
President (2004-2005)
Chinese Historical Society of Southern California

Acknowledgements

by Wing Mar, Editor-in-chief

A surprising number of people volunteered their time, talent and substance to produce this book. The tasks were many and the list includes names of donors, interviewers, writers, researchers, proofreaders, book designers, graphic artists, calligraphers, photographers, advisors, editors and friends. Much of the work was done through the Internet when the technology was accessible. Edgar Wong, my editor, who also acted as my ombudsman, furnished the technical support. He kept the editorial staff moving along by following a work plan. We were able to make our deadline because we had the wholehearted cooperation of the individuals and their families highlighted in this book.

Major support from generous donors encouraged us to move forward. Our thanks to L.P. Leung for his lead gift and also to Adrianne Chen, Howard (Toby) Louis, Dorothy and Eugene Louie, Wendel Wye, Joyce Mar, the Li Foundation and Drs. Milly and Steve Liu. While these were significant gifts there were many other donors who supported this publication and we appreciate their participation as well.

As a measure of our involvement, Edgar Wong and I logged on more than 1600 e-mails during the 20 months of this project. Over the last 18 months our core team met 11 times over dozens of cups of coffee at Pete Chinn's Jolly Jug Café in El Monte, California.

Our core team contributions:
- Randy Bloch, from the CHSSC, was the administrative support for the project.
- Frank Bupp was an editorial consultant.
- Bill and Natalina Chew guided us with their publication experience.
- Yvonne Chia designed the book cover and dust jacket.
- Pete Chinn was responsible for managing the production and delivery contract.
- Louise Colbert has been the information technology consultant.
- Jason Jem was responsible for the management and production of the book's final layout and design.
- Susie Ling was the guide for this book to be as historically accurate as possible.
- Joyce Mar had the final look for accuracy and flow.
- Eugene Moy brought his valuable historical, marketing and publication expertise.
- Elaine Woo, journalist, spent countless hours doing copyediting.

To those of you who inspired me by your confidence to pursue this project I am grateful. For all the time, talent and creativity brought forth by the volunteer team there are hardly enough words to express my gratitude. I have tried to remember all who helped in so many ways, but I am sure that I could have forgotten someone—many thanks to you.

Portraits of Pride has been a real team effort:

Linda Chong ✦ Gilbert Hom ✦ Jack Hom ✦ Carolyn Sauvage-Mar ✦ Gayle Mar-Chun ✦ Stanford Mu ✦ Howard Hew
Qian Deng ✦ Yep Wong ✦ George Lew ✦ Lionel Sauvage ✦ Edwin Kwoh ✦ Franklin Mah ✦ Ben Nakayama ✦ Calvin D. Lee
Nadine Soo Hoo Levy ✦ Jeff Quan ✦ Christin Li ✦ Dolores & Delbert Wong ✦ Margie & Al Lew ✦ Kyra Woo ✦ Icy Smith
Anita Wong ✦ Don Nakanishi ✦ Angi Ma Wong ✦ Lynne Wang ✦ Judy Chu ✦ Sumi Fujimoto ✦ Robert Elorreaga ✦ Ed Escovar
Eddie Chen ✦ William Chun-Hoon ✦ Gene Lam ✦ Russell E. Lowe ✦ Christine Mei ✦ Johnson Yee ✦ Marjorie Lee ✦ Ann Lau
Mike Eng ✦ Marcella Low ✦ Tom McDannold ✦ Charlie Woo ✦ Kenny Yee ✦ George Y. Lee ✦ Betty and S.H. Gaw ✦ Bill Yang
Leland Wong ✦ Bill Forrest ✦ Bill and Yvonne Liu ✦ Ken and Josie Mar ✦ Jeffrey Mar ✦ Jem Lew ✦ Ella Y. Quan ✦ Betty & James Fong
Otto Snepple ✦ Ron & Deanna Toy ✦ Rose Marie Lee ✦ Eugene Cooper ✦ Lester Kim ✦ Henrietta Yuan ✦ Al & Shirley Foung
Hayward L. Fong ✦ Montgomery Hom ✦ Pete Chinn ✦ Karen Lee Buell ✦ John Tsao ✦ Betty Yeow ✦ Spencer Chun
Charles Wang ✦ Stanley Chun ✦ John Gault ✦ Sue Chow Hoy ✦ Collin & Sue Lai ✦ Kelli Allen ✦ Cy & Betty Wong ✦ J. Charles Ferrari

Portraits of Pride

美華之光

Allen Gee

Hard Work Gets Results

as told to Edgar Wong
with an introduction by Wing Mar

Born in Patterson, Calif., Allen was an outstanding chemistry student at the University of California at Berkeley. Patterson was a very small town … maybe a thousand or so, somewhere "out there" in California's San Joaquin Valley. It was hot and dusty in the summer, bleak and damp in the winter. There was no interstate system then, no central irrigation project, no Apricot Capital of the World. In fact, there was no refrigeration, no air conditioning and no central heating—just hardworking folks trying to make a living.

We were residents at the same fraternity house at UC Berkeley where he patiently helped us with our studies in physical chemistry. And we weren't the only ones. Allen seemed to help nearly everyone in the fraternity house. As the years have gone by, we find that Allen is generous and patient in all that he does, not just tutoring.

So it is yet another remarkable story of a Chinese American who grew up in stark circumstances but who would go on to two of the United States' most prestigious universities to become a successful scientist. Following is a glimpse into Allen Gee's life as told through a series of stories that were transmitted to the editors via e-mail. They are presented nearly verbatim with some italicized historical material inserted where appropriate.

Family

I was born in February 1924 in Patterson, Calif., which I called home until I left for college. My wife is Mary Wong, who grew up in Fall River, Mass. We have two children: Everett (wife Donna Gee and five children) and Beverly (husband Manu Daftary and two children).

My father was born in 1880 and was married by being matched around 1900. His wife (and later my mother) gave birth to a daughter who died in her first month and later, a son. Soon after, my father left for Mexico; he traveled steerage and when not seasick he enjoyed dining with the Chinese cooks. He landed on the Mexican coast and found his way to a Chinese laundry in Mexico City. Around 1906, he arranged by means of some underground railroad to board a fishing boat up the coast to San Francisco. There he worked at various laundries that provided two meals, $5 per week, and space to spread his bedroll under the ironing bench for the night. During World War I (1914-18), he took a job at a U.S. Army camp near Pittsburg, Calif. It was about 1920 that he took over a small hand laundry in Patterson. (Chinese hand laundries were one of the first types of businesses associated with Chinese immigrants.)

photo by

My mother was born a Fong in 1882. And, because she was the first child of a needy family, she did not have her feet bound until her early teens. She remained in the village with her son until 1922, when she arrived in the United States through Angel Island under an assumed identity as someone else's wife due to harsh immigration laws. I have no idea how my parents greeted each other after an 18-year separation.

Regarding my mother's bound feet, binding feet of very young girls (starting at ages 3 to 8) was a millennium-old practice in China until it was outlawed in 1912. The feet were wrapped tightly with cloth to hinder normal growth; all toes, except for the big toe, were broken and wrapped under or over the foot. The dainty bound feet, as today's high heels, were to promote graceful movements like ballerinas in ballet shoes on Pointe (or sexy movements like models in a runway-walk with buttocks-out and back-arched). For my and her family, feet binding was a source of unwarranted shame and ridicule.

Possibly because of their long separation, my parents were basically silent people. For the first decade they seemed to open their mouths just to argue. In the next decade during the 'big depression' they argued less and worried more. For their last decade together they learned to quietly share their thoughts and in their own way fulfill the American Dream.

My father was semi-literate and my mother was completely illiterate. Neither spoke much English. I did not learn English until the first grade.

By contrast, my wife Mary's father, Frederick Wong, came from China as a student in 1916 to attend Adelphi College in Vancouver, Wash. Later he went to Massachusetts to enter the restaurant business and also to establish and distribute goods from the Oriental Chow Mein Company, known throughout the New England area.

Mary's mother's family has been in California for several generations. Her grandfather was the keeper of the Joss House in Weaverville (now a state monument) and her uncle received an appointment to the California Highway Commission from Gov. Ronald Reagan.

Education

It's said that education begins at home. My father always told me that he wished he had spent more time in school and less time plowing the fields with his pet water buffalo. Shortly after my birth he took out a $2,000 endowment policy for my future college education. He owned just two books: a red hardcover English-Chinese dictionary and a bound pamphlet that might have been his first Chinese reader entitled (in loose translation) "Three-Character Verses," with its familiar first verse: "Man's Beginning." My father frequently quoted the last line to me when I was ready to hit the books: Hard work gets results; play does no good (a recipe for a dull boy). I recall that my father told me that for whatever reason I was named for the 4-year old in line 10—"Gah Yung" (phonetically in my Toisan dialect). The "Gah" character in Chinese means family. My father, and to some extent my mother, had committed this pamphlet to memory. We received the daily Chinese Times through the mail and the Sunday San Francisco Examiner was given to us by a neighbor and we used that solely for wrapping paper.

Father's bound pamphlet: This traditionally silk-stitched bound booklet was found in many Chinese homes of the era. A Chinese character version of the "Three-Word Chant" written by Wang Ying Lien in the Sung Dynasty, Southern Sung Period (1127-1279), can be seen at website: www.chinapage.com/3words.html.

My father tried to prepare me for the first grade by memorizing the pamphlet as well as the alphabet from the dictionary. He tried to teach me numbers with the aid of an abacus. I remembered being intrigued by adding the numbers 123456789 repeatedly eight times and got the digits in reverse order (with a small adjustment: minus one, plus ten). There was no talk about verbal or social skills.

When I entered the first grade there was word recognition but very little memorization and no abacus. I did have my first two friends, Jane, my after-school friend, whose father ran the local water district, and Billy, my occasional weekend friend, whose folks had a restaurant. Jane and I enjoyed inventing childhood games as we walked home. Billy usually wanted me to play catch or to help him build things with wood and hammer.

Grade school had been uneventful. After my freshman year in high school my father decided that I should learn some Chinese with the hope that I would accompany him to the village of his birth for his retirement; Chinese would also help for my possible employment there as well. He brought a tutor to Patterson to teach the five Chinese children in town. That did not work out well, so he arranged for me to live in San Francisco Chinatown for my final two years of high school.

In San Francisco, I stayed at the Chinatown YMCA. I tried to enroll at Lowell High but ended up in Galileo High. Chinese school in San Francisco was a disaster; they first put me in with the sixth graders but I couldn't pick up the dialect. They finally put me in their adult education class. Galileo High may have started my interest in science. There was the observatory (although few clear nights) and, uppermost, Mrs. Murphy, who spent extra time in teaching me chemistry. I also spent many a weekend at the DuPont and the General Electric exhibits at the World's Fair Grounds on what was Treasure Island.

Perhaps a third of the Galileo High student body lived in Chinatown. During the noon hour they seemed to congregate in several tightly knit groups and talked mostly in Chinese. I don't remember making a single friend there. At the YMCA, however, there was a group from Hawaii attending San Francisco Junior College; they sometimes invited me to join them. This was my first experience with a group of mixed races that seemed so open with each other. I also accompanied a stage-door-Johnny to meet a waitress who performed in a Chinese opera and to the Forbidden City nightclub to meet a chorus girl.

After just one year and perhaps because of the impending war, I returned home to Patterson Union High and graduated in 1941. Years later I learned that Jane, who moved to San Francisco for training to dive in the Olympics, graduated from Lowell High that same year.

When I first entered UC Berkeley I majored in civil engineering because my father thought China needed work in transportation. I went into the Army in 1943; when I returned to UCB on the G.I. Bill, I switched my major to chemistry. As I was about to graduate from Berkeley, Professors Hildebrand and Latimer recommended that I should continue with graduate school in the Boston area. I went to MIT (Massachusetts Institute of Technology) and wrote my doctoral thesis in the area of protein chemistry.

Career

When I was a teenager, hardly anyone worked for money; we just helped each other with chores so that they could come out to play sooner. I remember helping bag candy or potato chips from bulk and distributing posters for the next movie.

My first paying job was the Army, which sent me to Aberdeen Proving Grounds in Maryland for basic training. I spent a year in rocket R&D mainly as a "go-fer" to two scientists. On occasion Major Edwin Hubble (the astronomer), who headed the Ballistics Research Laboratory, would drop by. I was then sent "overseas" to the territory of Alaska (before statehood) where I handled Army Signal Corps messages. The war was a common subject of conversation. I met an older soldier regularly in the latrine because he would take his morning break at the same time that I did. He would talk about the Battle of the Bulge (December 1944), and he would seem very knowledgeable about the European theater of the war. He turned out to be Dashiell Hammett, the renowned writer of such novels as The Maltese Falcon and The Thin Man.

When I finished at MIT in 1951, the job market was not very good. I took my only offer to join the National Bureau of Standards in Washington, D.C. where I stayed in the academic-like atmosphere for seven years. I did a little work on the effect of fluoride on bone and tooth enamel (still a controversial matter). Most of the time was spent on developing analytical methods. The infamous 1950-1954 Joseph McCarthy investigations into Communists in government added some turmoil while I was there.

In 1957 DuPont began recruiting for increasing their fiber production. I helped put in the process controls for their second Orlon plant and their first Lycra plant. At first Lycra was just to be a better latex; we certainly didn't foresee how the use would take off. Partly because DuPont had yet to accept minorities in its line organization, I accepted a position with Texas Instruments (TI) in Dallas in 1959. TI was exciting but too disorganized for me to accomplish much. Also because of the Dallas climate, I took the next job to work on the space program in California.

When I joined Hughes Aircraft in 1961, I was assigned to a group that made custom chips to demonstrate feasibility of projects like phase-array radar that doesn't require a rotating antenna. Hughes became the prime contractor for the Lunar Surveyor and the Early Bird that was the first stationary communication satellite. Some people in a lab found that if the surface of the moon were covered with a certain thickness of volcanic pumice or (yes) green cheese, the reflection from radar waves would be greatly reduced. We therefore had to upgrade the system for sensitivity as well as to increase the reliability in an environment of high vibrations and wide temperature swings.

Old timers in the early days of radio remember the crystal set which used a "cat's whisker" as a detector. The Doppler system used basically the same device to receive the reflected signal. We thought that with newer semiconductor theories we could greatly improve the performance of the Doppler diode. After much trial-and-error, we made significant improvements even though none of the theories seemed to fit.

Before the first moon shot we had many long monotonous meetings on the many possible modes of failure. When the first shot landed successfully and pictures were sent back, we felt more relieved than excited. Shot No.2 failed but there was no investigation. Five of the seven Lunar Surveyors landed successfully, so we had set a standard for sending

Receiving an award for the successful Lunar Surveyor project

vehicles to another planet.

Because Hughes Aircraft had the policy of getting as many patents as possible for cross-licensing purposes, I filed for over 10 patents during my career there but only had one issued, circa 1968.

Affiliation
While in college I was elected to Phi Beta Kappa and Sigma Xi. Later, I served on the Salvation Army Advisory Board for 20 years. My professional memberships included: American Chemical Society, New York Academy of Science, American Institute of Chemists and the Electrochemical Society.

Retirement
I retired in 1974 at age 50 because of disability from arthritis and asthma. Mary went back to work; and we managed to send our children through college. Years later I did receive an interesting employment call from a retired Nationalist Air Force General Shek (meaning stone) who wanted me to consider teaching science in Beijing. His recruiting slogan, "A Chinese is always a Chinese" aroused very mixed feelings for me. Because of the climate and Tienanmen Square incident (1989), the matter was dropped.

Retrospective
I recalled some adverse events, some traumatic and some funny; I write them here for human interest. For me, these events were yesterday's life tribulations and are today's life lessons.

In my first year of school there was a single incident of rock throwing with racial chanting, but the bus driver nearby put a stop to it. During the war years when I changed to my civvies (civilian clothes), I received some yells as though I was Japanese.

In 1941 my faculty advisor drove me to Modesto to interview for one of the two $300 scholarships offered. She told me I had the best record and possibly the greatest need, but I was turned down.

In 1944 I was perhaps the only ROTC (Reserve Officers Training Corps) student washed out of Army OCS (Officer Candidate School) after four weeks. The only other non-white in the class came up through the ranks, received his commission and returned to his all-black organization (the US Army was segregated then). Ironically, I tutored him in map reading.

For peer group influence I must give credit to my first friend Jane. She was a star pupil and member of a middle-class family. She told me how the families avoid the local summer heat by staying at the beach at Pacific Grove. For an after-school snack she showed me how to use an ice pick to chip the ice from the icebox to make the milk colder to go better with the goodies in the cookie jar. There were the after-school birthday parties (at first I did not know what birthday meant). Then we moved on to the next school (Patterson's four-year system for elementary, middle and high school) where we all made new friends. Fast forward to the eighth grade: Jane's family planned a large party on her 13th birthday for her coming out. According to prevailing social customs, non-white minorities were not invited. I didn't feel the pains of rejection until most of my friends talked of the fun they had at the party and thought that I must have been there. The coming of age function worked out as designed in this case. Even though Jane and I were in the same small classes in high school, we never stopped to talk to each other again.

Epilogue

Allen's life achievements and values are rooted in the Chinese American experience of 20th century America. As a minority, Allen overcame numerous social adversities and institutional discrimination by exercising the simple values of work and family—values that he learned from his parents. In fact, his father thought that "family" was so important that he gave his son the name "Gah" to serve as a constant reminder.

Allen received his B.S. from UC Berkeley and Ph.D. from MIT

John B. Lee

Husband, Father, Friend

By Keith J. Lee, Ken P. Lee and Karen Lee Buell

John Lee's professional legacy is well known and honored in both the aerospace and the health care industries. A snapshot of John's multifaceted career is shown in the "Career Biography," below, which is reproduced from a display at the Autry Museum of Western Heritage as part of the exhibit of the Chinese Historical Society of Southern California. This display also included significant technical memorabilia from his distinguished aerospace career.

Career Biography

Early in his career, John Lee worked with mainframe computers and later on was one of the first to recognize the enormous potential of personal computers, the Internet, and email. Lee was utilizing and discussing HTML (Hypertext Markup Language) years before the general population knew about its potential power. During his career, Lee developed the most reliable database for the F-2 program for the Stealth Bomber, which was used in the Gulf War and the war in the Balkans. Utilizing his database and talent for software cost estimation, Lee was instrumental in assisting Northrop Corporation in winning a $1.5 billion contract from the United States Air Force. This contract provided work for over 500 technical people during a 10-year time span. In the late 1980s, Lee was a consultant in devising a mobile database system that brought continuity of medical care to the aged at home and multi-level nursing homes. Lee's management protocol is still being used in the long-term health care field. John Lee's creativity, technical know-how and tenacity enabled him to leave legacies in aerospace and the health care industry.

Family and Faith

John Lee's professional legacy has earned him an honored place in two industries, and yet he was reticent about his professional achievements being publicized (and he would have been shy about his biography being published). Despite the demands of a two-profession career, John always found time to be a great husband to Rosemarie, his wife, a kind and cherished father to his three children, and a good friend to all who knew him. Indeed, the life and character of John is best described not by his career achievements, but rather by his love of family and his Christian values.

Knowing that John would like to be remembered as husband, father, friend and Christian, we have compiled three short narratives touching on his human side. His family and friends contributed these little stories, and they are presented below. They are written in John B. Lee's memory on the 10th anniversary of his passing in September 1992. These short stories, plus the epilogue written by his children, will give an insight into how John earned his way into our hearts. But first, a note from John's Pastor:

"I was privileged to be John's pastor and share in the spiritual growth of both John and Rosemarie. John's steadfast commitment to God and His word was an amazing thing to watch. It encouraged and edified everyone he was around. John was always willing to volunteer for any job that needed to be done around the church. Nothing was too small or insignificant to him, even when John faced his greatest challenge in life—cancer—he never stopped growing, or being involved. I will remember John as one of the greatest examples of humility and strength I have ever known. He was

a great father, great husband, great friend, great Christian and a truly great man."

Pastor John Long,
Monterey Park Four Square Church

1. The Potluck Gang

Borrowing an introductory phrase made famous by a KCAL veteran news anchor—"From the desert to the sea to all of Southern California"—the best meal in town on a given Saturday was at our potluck group's quarterly dinners. These dinners were held at one of the homes, in rotation, amongst a dozen or so families. Our typical "menuscript" (a word coined by John Lee) consisted of home cooked dishes of various regional cuisines: Cantonese, Mandarin, Shanghainese, Szechwan, Taiwanese, and occasionally other Asian foods (except Chop Suey). This potluck series started in the 1950s after our college days and at the mutual beginnings of families, careers, and investment groups in Southern California. Happily, over the ensuing decades, the dinners and fellowship have continued into our golden years.

I recall one potluck dinner (circa 1980s) that was held at George Lee's home in Rancho Palos Verdes. John and Rosemarie came to dinner with John's co-worker, whose wife was away for the weekend. Realizing his Caucasian friend's unfamiliarity with Chinese food, John was attentive in explaining each dish in detail at the dinner table. Afterwards, his friend commented on the extreme contrast between John's Saturday feasts versus his daily fare at work. He said that at their mid-morning coffee breaks, John would unpack his brown-bag lunch and eat it as a snack; and at noon they would go out to lunch together, frequently to the Price Club (now Costco) for his favorite kosher hot dog and drink combo. That's right, a kosher hot dog at the Price Club! Before the next tale—of their mid-afternoon snacks—could be told, John hurriedly poked his friend with his elbow and then glanced over to Rosemarie with a sheepish grin. Rosemarie returned with a tiny little smile, paused, pointed to John, and then laughed! While John was blushing as his secret was now revealed, our entire table (Betty

and Larry Fong, Joanna and Bill Sheng, Sue Hoy, Judy Woo and my wife, Theo) burst out laughing too. It was a fun moment that is long remembered. Tom Woo missed the entire episode because he was at the buffet table getting more food. To John: thanks for the fond memories and a hearty "bon appetit" from your fellow gourmands.

Richard Jiu, Pi Alpha Phi Fraternity Brother.

2. The Timepiece

It was Christmas 1953. John was living in Haddonfield, N.J., working for RCA in Camden. I was stationed at Newport, R.I., attending the Navy officer candidate school. On Christmas Eve, as bachelors away from home are wont to do, John and I met in New York City to celebrate the holidays. We started with a dim sum lunch on Mott Street in Chinatown; then, we went to see a Broadway show matinee, "The King and I" (starring Yul Brynner); later, we went to a dinner show featuring "Christine Jorgensen Sings" (recipient of the first gender reassignment surgery). After the evening show, we walked to Times Square to join the holiday crowd in greeting the arrival, at midnight, of Christmas morning. That evening was cold.

Arriving at Times Square early, we decided to stop in at one of the all-night jewelry stores to get warm. An energetic salesman greeted us and convinced me that the watch that I was wearing was unsuitable for the Navy; he showed me a suitable watch (round-faced, sweep-second hand, shock-resistant and water-proof). He then turned to John in hopes of selling another watch. John said that he acquired his watch (with a carton of American cigarettes) in Germany during WWII and that the watch runs okay; but, he said the band was old and, pointing to the Speidel band rack, said he could use a replacement. The salesman took John's watch to find a match, but then he discovered that the watch was a Vacheron Constantin! He called for the floor salesmen and the backroom jewelers to examine this unique watch-of-watches (none had ever had the pleasure of seeing one). Naturally, the salesman was reluctant to put a Speidel band on John's watch; but he painfully did so. By the way, in addition to

the military discount (I was in my sailor uniform) he gave us an additional "Lee discount" for the privilege of showing the watch to the staff. Years later, John's watch was lost in a home burglary, as was mine earlier this year. Today, I still have vivid memories of this truly unforgettable Christmas in Manhattan with John Lee. He was an extraordinary guy (as steadfast as his Speidel band) and with a heart of gold as superb as his Vacheron Constantin timepiece. I still miss him.

Edgar Wong, brother-in-law

3. The Medical Legacy

Most of our avocation activities are done at sites such as the golf course, the jogging track, the bowling alley, the TV room or wherever. For John, it was at his computer room. It had built-in bookcases (full of esoteric software), a computer workstation (full of sophisticated computer hardware) and an ergonomic chair (where he spent many happy hours). John's passion for the computer went well beyond the norm for an aerospace electrical engineer. John became intensely interested in the medical field, especially in cancer research. He generously assisted USC cancer researchers with analytical studies. John volunteered many hundreds of hours in this critical research; yet, he found time to make innovations in my medical duties.

For a large managed care organization with tens of thousands of patients and multilevel care facilities (hospitals to nursing homes), manual data management was a daunting task. For me, John provided an invaluable computer tool for contemporaneous data management in my daily geriatric care activities. My patient database was printed daily (computer data sharing was not widely used then) and the printouts were distributed to the team of physicians, nurses and telephone operators that were on-duty while I was off-duty. These "heads up" data were particularly useful. Patients in unstable conditions were highlighted to alert expected emergency calls. The terminal and futile cases were flagged to denote continuing comfort care and pain control. This patient database tool afforded a seamless continuity in our quality medical care. It is noted that John's original work was the forerunner of today's healthcare management tools, and I'm proud to have been closely associated with John and his data management software. John is a pioneer (in both engineering and medical fields), and I appreciated his kindness, patience and selflessness in helping the elderly. Thanks, John.

Wing Mar for the medical community

An Epilogue by the Lee Children

Reading the above "sentimental journey" stories was nostalgic and parts of the three stories form new remembrances. Our three individual stories are best

combined into a common one—life lessons from Dad:

Conversations with our father were usually brief. It wasn't that he was uncaring or disinterested in us as children; it was just that he was the kind of man who knew that a parent's actions, rather than words, were what mattered most. Over the course of his brief 66 years on Earth, his quiet example taught us many valuable lessons in life:

- Material possessions, in the grand scheme of things, are not very important.
- Always pay our bills on time and never owe anyone anything.
- Follow-through is the key to getting any job done.
- Worry is a waste of time and energy.
- Patience is a virtue.
- It is important to keep challenging ourselves at work and to take the initiative whenever possible.
- Babies are wonderful gifts from God; they should be cuddled, held and loved as much as possible.
- Take pride in being Chinese.
- True love and friendship, the kind that lasts a lifetime, requires endurance and forgiveness.
- Never hold on to grudges.
- Chinese food is, by far, the best bargain and the tastiest choice of any world cuisine.
- People can change and grow no matter what their age. They can develop an even deeper love for their life partners and forge a greater connection with their faith.

And so much more. Even after all these years, we still have brief "conversations" with our father that are, not surprisingly, much like they were so long ago. A quiet "good job" or a gentle "holy cow" still finds its way through to our collective hearts. Our father, unassuming and reserved, is still with us , guiding us gently by his deeds. And for that, we will always be grateful.

Much love,
Karen, Keith, and Ken Lee

Edgar Y. Wong

Friend, Mentor
and
Noble Thinker

By Frank E. Bupp

> *A plaque given to E.Y. by his colleagues at TRW was engraved with this tribute: "Awesome range of knowledge; creative insight and imaginative approach; aggressive and dedicated pursuit of excellence; ... fierce loyalty and mature judgment... extraordinary tireless logical planner; concern for welfare of subordinates ...."*

I was engaged in negotiating a teaming agreement between two major U.S. corporations. The stakes were high; we were targeting a contract in excess of $1 billion dollars. But the negotiations were stalling, and I called my company headquarters seeking assistance of someone of the "highest caliber" to help close the deal. They sent E.Y.

When E.Y. arrived at my hotel, I immediately sensed both admiration and despair. Standing before me wasn't the hard-edged, flinty, high-powered corporate executive I expected. Instead, here was a man that was clearly compassionate, friendly and approachable.

We spent the next hour or so discussing the status of the negotiation, our corporate position and some of the technical details. We were working from a couple dozen viewgraphs that I had prepared for the negotiation. That we only took an hour or so was clear evidence that E.Y. was a "quick study," as the subject matter was complex in both its breadth and depth. And then, to my amazement, E.Y. crafted a single, hand-drawn chart that summarized the entire contents of the negotiation. The key feature of this single chart was that it not only covered the entire scope of the impending procurement, clearly and objectively showed the advantages to be gained by both parties in a teaming arrangement. My despair of just a short time ago had completely dissolved.

The next morning at the negotiation session, the other party arrived in force—three or four vice presidents and a technical team. After the introductions, E.Y.'s single chart was presented. What followed was a couple of hours discussion, all centered on E.Y.'s chart—and guided by E.Y. And then it happened: We had a handshake on the teaming agreement. EY's perception and insight, his ability to graphically portray not only the complexities of the situation but also how the two teaming partners would "split" the pie, and the benefit to both parties, was extraordinary.

From that point, E.Y. and I became closely associated both personally and professionally: personally as true friends, professionally as my mentor, and E.Y. always as the noble thinker. Thus, I am delighted to write E.Y.'s profile and honored to submit this profile to the Chinese Historical Society of Southern California (CHSSC) for their inclusion in the Portraits of Pride series.

Upbringing

During the recent national dialog on "Character Counts," E.Y. and Howard Setzer (a mutual friend originally from North Carolina) compared views regarding character and core values. They exchanged thoughts on their own upbringing to see if their difference in ethnicity (Asian versus Occidental) or their regional upbringing (East vs. West Coast) had mattered. These thoughts were my source material for the following insight on E.Y.'s character development in his early years:

E.Y. was born Edgar Yuen Wong in Los Angeles, Calif.

on June 8, 1929. His parents were Jen and Him Wong, and both had immigrated to the United States from Guangdong, China. The children born to the Wongs were Esther, Edgar, Louise and Rosemarie. The Wong family has a long tradition of morality, respect, loyalty, cultural and Christian values, and E.Y. was instilled with these values as part of his early family life. He was an inquisitive and obedient child and worked many boyhood jobs in the family laundry business where he was inculcated with a strong sense of personal responsibility and work ethics.

E.Y. was an accomplished student and enrolled in the California Institute of Technology where he earned a Bachelor and a Master of Science degree in 1952 and 1953. The Caltech years were formative for E.Y., and not only did they prepare him scholastically for the future, but they were also instrumental in shaping his core values, imparting a strong sense of honor, virtue, nobility, citizenship, and friendship. After college, he served as an officer in the U.S. Navy and it was here that he developed a strong love of country, patriotism, duty, and leadership. These worldly values, combined with his family values from his positive upbringing, defined E.Y.'s character.

Career

For their upcoming 50th Caltech Class Reunion, E.Y. and Brij Seoni (his classmate from India) exchanged mini-resumes to update each other on their civil engineering careers. In lieu of my summarizing E.Y.'s lengthy resume, I'm using this mini-resume from his electronic mail archives:

Dear Brij … Thanks for updating me on your professional activities since our Caltech graduation in 1953. My career path took me to a vastly different (geographic and engineering) area than yours. I started my four-year career in the U.S. Navy Civil Engineering Corps at Pearl Harbor doing public works maintenance. Our classmate Mel Smith was in the Navy also. After this service, I spent seven years doing research work on the effects of nuclear weapons (atmospheric and underground detonations) for the Atomic Energy Commission. After the Russian Sputnik, I joined TRW and spent 30 years working on government programs including ballistic missiles (ICBMs), strategic defense (Star Wars), nuclear waste disposal (Nuke Dumps), a variety of so-called classified projects (Black Programs), and business acquisition (Proposals). Classmate Gus Soux was at TRW too. My work was initially in engineering and then later in management. In 1992, I retired from TRW and subsequently worked a year for the Taiwan National Space Agency as a consultant in their organization staffing and space program startup; and, then finally in Las Vegas as a management consultant on government contracts. I'm a registered engineer in California and Nevada. Like you, I traveled around a bit, but not along the civil engineering route that we were trained for in school. Evaline and I met and married in Honolulu during my Pearl Harbor tour of duty; our three kids are: Jeff (Colorado), Mark (Los Angeles), and Debra (Manhattan). I'm known as 'EY' because there are so many Ed's around the workplace…

Edgar

Recognition

Over his career, E.Y. was at the core of many developments that were vitally important to our national interest. To those of us who were in the space and defense industry, we were very honored and proud to make whatever contribution we could. None of us ever expected any form of acknowledgment other than "job well done." But for E.Y., a tandem of recognition was received from unexpected and unusually special sources:

In 1983, President Reagan announced his Strategic Defense Initiative (Star Wars) vision for an impenetrable shield against weapons of mass destruction delivered by incoming ballistic missiles. Ten defense contractors were selected to perform architectural studies on the makeup of such a system. The New York Times was interested in publishing an in-depth article on the challenges facing the nation's quest for an impenetrable shield. From the list of ten missile-defense contractors, several contractors, including TRW, were selected for interviews by the Times. On January 2, 1986, they published a front-page article, "Star Wars Task is Testing TRW," and featured E.Y. as the central figure.

More than a decade later, the CHSSC selected that New York Times article as one of their several displays at the Autry Museum of Western Heritage's exhibition on the Chinese-American community in California. E.Y. told me that the CHSSC selection (and not the New York Times selection) was his "15-minutes of fame." He truly values this recognition from his Chinese-American peers.

Tribute

To add my heartfelt salute in this profile, I'm borrowing material from yet another source. No finer tribute can be paid to E.Y. than that on an engraved plaque given to E.Y. from his colleagues at TRW:

"… *awesome range of knowledge; creative insight and imaginative approach; aggressive and dedicated pursuit of excellence; dissatisfaction with the status quo; mature judgment and fierce loyalty; dependable, tireless and energetic performance; extraordinary logical planner; concern for welfare of subordinates …*" Now that says it all.

Our Current Interaction

E.Y. is now "officially" retired. He travels extensively worldwide with his wife, Evaline, and together, they also regularly visit family and friends. And E.Y. still gets those phone calls today, calls from friends, former supervisors, peers, and from those he's mentored over the years. Many are seeking his advice, but some are also "calls of inquiry" on his availability for work. Today, family, faith, wellness, and cyberspace activities occupy his mind and body. He continues to develop all the right values. Oh! Yes, we still maintain our daily contacts through the internet in sharing thoughts and ideas on the events of the day. And, yes, E.Y.: still my friend, still my mentor, and still noble thinker.

Dateline: October 2002. Author: Frank Bupp is a retired aerospace executive and lives in Las Vegas, Nevada. He is a writer-activist for good government and better education.

Dora Ames Lee

"I will be a Doctor"

By Karen Ng

The year was 1919. Gen. Pershing was traveling through Tucson, Ariz., on a troop train. Six-year-old Dora was awestruck by the sight of the Red Cross nurses in their gray uniforms and headdresses emblazoned with a red cross on a white hatband.

It was a defining moment in the life of Dora Lee, one that would shape her future. The year was 1919. Gen. Pershing was traveling through Tucson, Ariz., on a troop train. Six-year-old Dora was awestruck by the sight of the Red Cross nurses in their (then) gray uniforms and head-dresses emblazoned with a red cross on a white hatband. Dora turned to her mother and said, "I want to be a nurse like them." Dora's mother told her that nurses have to take orders from the head nurse. Dora replied, "Then I will be a head nurse." Her mother said the head nurse has to take orders from the doctor. So Dora responded, "I will be a doctor then." To many, it might seem a fanciful boast from a mere child. But from that moment forward, Dora Lee set forth to make that boast a dream—and the dream a reality.

Faith and Determination

To understand the source of Dora's faith and determination, one needs only a glimpse of her family history. Dora's father, at age 13, went to sea on the U.S.S. Albatross of the United States Fish Commission. His mother had died just one year earlier. He took a post as a cabin boy with Professor Aggazzi of Harvard who was heading an expedition on marine biology study of the Pacific Basin. "During those days this exciting opportunity was open to all the young boys who wanted to travel and see the world," Dora explained. He crisscrossed the globe but was always glad to return to San Francisco to be with his father.

In 1898, he took a leave from his sea duties to take his ailing father back to his village in Guangdong Province China. It was on this trip that Dora's father decided to find his bride. He asked the pastor of the Chinese Baptist Church for a letter of introduction to take to the Poi To Girls' Baptist Academy. The principal introduced him to a student, the girl who would become Dora's mother; Dora's father was 20 and her mother was 16. After a brief courtship, Dora's mother accepted a marriage proposal from Dora's father. Their mutual consent of marriage was not like the customary unilateral 'arranged' Chinese marriages common in those days.

Dora's father returned to America to resume his duties onboard the U.S.S. Albatross while Dora's mother remained in Guangdong to continue her studies with the encouragement from her new father-in-law. Eventually, Dora's father sent money and the immigration documents to bring her mother to San Francisco. The year was 1902—the beginning of this Lee family in America.

Dora's parents were both devout Christians and that faith was passed on to Dora. She said of her childhood, "We were taught that our life was given to us by God and we should serve and love others as shown by the example of his son, Jesus Christ." In fact, Dora's middle name, Ames, was given to her to honor the missionary who taught her father at the Chinese Baptist Church School in San Francisco. Dora's faith has been central to her service in her church and in the community.

Her parents placed the same high priority on education for their children, for both their sons and daughters. That was not the norm for parents in the early 1900s, much less Chinese parents. "You know, we were very fortunate to have been born to parents who appreciated the value of a quality education for all," she said. Dora took full advantage of her educational opportunities. She graduated from high school with the highest honors and went on to the University of California at Berkeley, as did her two brothers and two sisters. "My parents instilled in us a sense of academic achievement. They were frugal, so we could all attend college without any scholarship assistance," Dora said proudly. No doubt that Dora's determination in her life's work came from her seeming inherited single-mindedness.

Medical and Community Service

Dora received her medical degree from University of California at San Francisco Medical School in 1937, an uncommon accomplishment during the Great Depression era, but even more remarkable for a Chinese American woman. Dr. Lee interned at the former Stockton State Hospital and then externed at Boston Psychiatric Hospital (now Massachusetts Mental Health Center). She was interested in psychiatry and the Boston Psychiatric Hospital had a good program. "I learned about developing human relationships and had a chance to learn about other viewpoints and gain other experiences from what I obtained on the West Coast." After a year at Boston Psychiatric, she was asked to take a year of psychoanalysis to finish her residency in psychiatry.

But Dr. Lee had other priorities: "I had a different goal in life and wanted to begin practicing medicine to start helping people right away." So, in 1939, Dr Lee returned to Stockton to start her private practice. Dora Lee chose Stockton

While Dr. Lee says she didn't experience [overt] discrimination against her in school or in her work, she did see—and was deeply troubled by—the injustices against Native Americans when she lived in the Southwest and against African Americans in other parts of the country.

because she was familiar with its medical needs—she knew that Stockton needed a doctor like her. "I opened my office close to the County Courthouse so I was able to help many non-English speaking immigrants with various language, health, economic and social needs," she said.

Her medical practice during World War II was the most hectic; it was when most of the doctors in town were drafted into the military service. Dr. Lee delivered babies at all hours, assisted in emergency operations when called and cared for an office full of adults, children and the elderly all day long.

Dr. Lee's professional life was filled with service to others and a determination to help wherever and whenever she was needed. Besides her dedication to her patients, Dr. Lee was instrumental in promoting the medical profession in her community. She was elected president of the San Joaquin Medical Society in 1946. And for 30 years, from 1958 to 1988, she served as secretary-treasurer of the medical society. For her decades of service, in 2001, the society honored Dr. Lee with its Lifetime Achievement Award.

Her involvement in civic and community organizations was also extensive. In 1965, the local Chinese Cultural Society named Dr. Lee Outstanding Member of the Stockton Chinese Community. Two years later the Stockton Quota Club named her Service Woman of the Year. That year she became the first woman to be appointed to the Stockton Parks and Recreation Commission. Dr. Lee was an early supporter of the Chinese Methodist Church (now St. Mark's United Methodist Church). She served as a Sunday school teacher, youth club advisor, choir director, organist and church board member. In recognition of her tireless efforts on behalf of the church, Dr. Lee received the Bishop's Award in 2000. It is the highest award a lay church member can receive.

While Dr. Lee says she didn't experience discrimination against her in school or in her work, she did see—and was deeply troubled by—the injustices against Native Americans when she lived in the Southwest and against African Americans in other parts of the country. Dora Lee redoubled her personal efforts in not practicing any such discrimination. Her upbringing and faith taught her to accept all people with Christian love and charity. "I value openness and acceptance of all people whatever their color, education, achievement or social class," Dr. Lee emphasized.

Wong Family Life

Paralleling her illustrious career and busy volunteer work, Dr. Lee with her husband applied their loving care in raising a family. It was in 1946 that she married Richard Wong. Richard was in the quartermaster corps, assigned to the China-Burma-India theater during World War II. After the war, he returned to Stockton and worked as an assistant manager at the National Dollar Store. He eventually turned his passion, photography, into a profession. He became a well-known commercial photographer in Stockton. Mr. Wong died at age 61.

The Wong family was blessed with two sons: Richard Lee, a clinical laboratory scientist, chemistry department supervisor at Dameron Hospital in Stockton, and Robin, who followed his mother's footsteps and became a physician. Dr. Robin Wong joined his mother's practice in 1980 and a year later she turned over the entire practice to him, knowing that Robin would continue her life's work. For four decades Dr. Dora Ames Lee was a dedicated family doctor,

serving the health care needs of the Stockton community. Her volunteerism continues today as she devotes herself to helping many non-English speaking Chinese immigrants from overseas.

And more than fulfilling that bold boast made by a six-year-old girl long ago, "I will be a doctor."

Wing Mar assisted Karen Ng in the interview and research.
Post script: Dr. Dora Lee passed away on June 4, 2004.

Lois Wong Chi

An Award-Winning Professor and Researcher

By Edgar Wong and Susie Ling

In a short paper on high achievers, interspersing the subject's achievements along with the subject's history can easily overshadow the subject itself—becoming a story more of the deeds and less of the achiever. To avoid this story-telling pitfall, Lois Chi's deeds are presented separately from her story as follows: a brief list of her career achievements first (at the top) and followed by her life story second (at the bottom) ... like frosting on a cake.

A Chronology of Professor Chi's Achievements

1962: Conceiver and cofounder of the Chinese American Engineers Association of Southern California with her engineer husband Henry (later expanded to include both engineers and scientists forming CECASC), and together with her husband Henry, a joint recipient of its Achievement Award a decade later, and Lifetime Service Award at CESASC's 34th anniversary convention.

1966: Principal Investigator for the first research grant awarded to California State College Dominguez Hills (CSCDH). Her research was on the study of endemic tropical parasitic infection of the liver causing schistosomiasis, or "snail fever". At that time the California State Universities and Colleges were principally for teaching. Research was not supported or encouraged. One had to find his or her own time for research.

1969: Cofounder of the Chinese American Faculty Association of Southern California (CAFA), recipient of Distinguished Service Award in 1993.

1972 and 1979: Recipient of the Outstanding Professor Award from the California State University Dominguez Hills (CSUDH).

1974: Appointee by HEW Secretary Caspar Weinberger into the National Advisory Council of Infectious Diseases which had a global health role in evaluating and giving direction to research studies in the U.S. (Defense industry readers might remember Mr. Weinberger as the Secretary of Defense in the 1980s).

1978 – 1986: Director and Principal Investigator for the first multi-project institutional grant MBRS (Minority Biomedical Research Support) awarded to California State University Dominguez Hills (CSUDH) for the research study of endemic worldwide parasitic infection of the liver by schistosomiasis and other biomedical research. This program is still going on after Lois' retirement with a new director.

1979: First woman recipient of the State Outstanding Professor Award—given to two educators by the California State University and Colleges Foundation Board of Trustees—in the statewide system of over 30,000 faculty members.

1978 – 1985: The implementation of the first minority biomedical research grant at the CSUDH campus had resulted in the yearly acceptance of a record number of applicants (average of 10 to 12) into medical, dental, and pharmaceutical schools due to her dedicated tutelage.

Roots in Fuzhou

The 1911 Revolution profoundly devolved China from its millennia of imperial rule to a provincial state. In the tumultuous political transition, provincial warlords used the military to manipulate institutions to their advantage. By the 1920s, social evolution turned the traditional Confucian familial practice to more modern forms of which one of the more prominent was Christianity. Lois Chi's father, Leland Wang (1898-1975) was an official Chinese scholar of the state and a navy lieutenant stationed with the Chinese fleet at the Fuzhou Naval Base. Disenchanted with the politicization of the navy, he left his government posts to pursue a nobler calling.

Leland Wang's intellectual and spiritual beliefs led him to become an evangelist for preaching the gospel to all the people, rich and poor. Along with his evangelical success, Mr. Wang became the president of the Chinese Foreign Missionary Union serving overseas Chinese in the Philippines, Singapore, Indonesia, and other South Sea islands as well as the United States, Canada and Europe. In 1949, Dr. Leland Wang received his Doctor of Divinity (DD) degree from Illinois' Wheaton College (known today for its Billy Graham Center). His wife, Ada P. Wang (1897-1989) attended the Wa Nun Christian College and became an evangelist, so their union was a perfect match. Together they raised a family of six children.

photo by Jason Jem

Coming to America

Lois Wang was born in Fuzhou and at grade-school age moved with her family to Hong Kong. After high school, her father was able to procure financial aid for Lois to follow her sister, Joyce, to Wheaton College. Lois boarded the last sailing of the American President Line's S.S. President Pierce to San Francisco before World War II. Lois recalls her trip vividly: "I was assigned a dining seat at a table with foreigners who all looked like businessmen. I was so timid that I would forgo salt and pepper, and even the delicious-looking rolls and butter, rather than asking for them in broken English. At the dining table we were asked to circle our orders on the daily menu. I caught sight of "thousand island" on the menu and then circled it with confidence, thinking it would be a thousand goodies piled up like an island. Instead, a big head of lettuce was served with some dressing on top. In China we knew better not to eat raw vegetables—it was left untouched. I waited for the thousand islands to arrive, but they never came."

Overcoming culinary, cultural and linguistic adjustment problems, Lois excelled and went on to obtain her bachelor's degree at Wheaton College and her master's and doctorate degrees in biology at the University of Southern California in Los Angeles. After graduation in 1953, Dr. Chi besides teaching, continued her research, now full-time, on the parasitic infection of the liver, intestine, and bladder from schistosomiasis.

Researcher in Tropical Diseases

Throughout the annals of military medicine, parasites have afflicted military personnel from skin exposure to all types of parasites (e.g., schistosomes) found in various marshes, rivers, streams, and rain forests. The Armed Services formed the Commission on Parasitic Diseases of the Armed Forces Epidemiological Board (AFEB) to work on parasite detection, prevention and control. For laboratory and field studies, the commission was empowered to use both military and civilian assets. Dr. Lois W. Chi was teamed with Dr. E. D. Wagner to be the principal investigators at the School of Tropical Medicine, Loma Linda University, to study snail species, the vectors of tropical diseases for the U.S. Army.

Field studies of the amphibious snails took them to Japan, Taiwan and the Philippines. They were the first to differentiate between male and female snails, a principal discovery in parasite control. (They found that the eggs produced by the female worms, not by the worms themselves, is the cause of the human body's schistosomiasis reaction). The team of Chi and Wagner published results of their five-year study in seven scientific papers dated from 1954 to 1959. The research has been invaluable in finding medical protocols for helping an estimated 200 million people around the world who have the disease and 120 million who are symptomatic. After completing her service as a research fellow at Loma Linda University, Lois served in the Department of

TropicTopics

OCTOBER, 1955

Volume 6, Number 4

Dr. Lois Wong searches for snail eggs in a field near Kofu, Japan. See story on page 2.

Edward Wagner Photo

PUBLISHED BY
SCHOOL OF TROPICAL AND PREVENTIVE MEDICINE
College of Medical Evangelists
LOMA LINDA, CALIFORNIA

Biology at Immaculate Heart College in Los Angeles for 10 years as associate professor and research director.

A footnote on Lois Chi's Army assignment: Senior civilians traveling under military orders were given a virtual rank of Major and received privileges commensurate to this military rank—addressed as "sir" or "ma'am"—stayed at the officer's quarters and ate at the officer's dining room. Lois recalls, "Although I became accustomed to eating raw veggies in the U.S., I was still careful not to order a 'thousand island' salad at the officer's mess hall overseas."

Educator at the California State University

The California state college system includes separate entities: the California State College (CSC) and the California State University (CSU). From the Higher Education Act of 1960 to just two decades later, the college system became the largest in the country; the CSU entity now has 44,000 faculty and staff and 409,000 students at 23 campuses—with 13,000 students at CSU Dominguez Hills. The Dominguez Hills campus evolved rapidly as follows: a California Community College in 1960, a CSC in 1966, and a CSU in 1974. Dr. Lois Chi joined the college in 1966 and recalls (with unabashed pride): "I joined CSC Dominguez Hills the first day the college started on its present site, where the cattle and horsemen still roamed on the campus grounds, and no one thought much of it. Believe it or not, I was the one who taught the first class on the opening day of CSCDH in September 1966 at 7:30 A.M. The remaining classes of that first day were scheduled to start 8:00 A.M., so I was first by half an hour."

At CSU Dominguez Hills Dr. Chi continued her laboratory research in parasitology and tropical medicine and published more than two dozen papers. She retired after 25 years, but her commitment to education and students did not end. Dr. Chi with her husband, Henry Chi, endowed scholarships—at CSU Dominguez Hills, Chinese American Faculty Association and Chinese Engineers and Scientist Association of Southern California—to be used for student research in biology and biochemistry.

Life with Henry Chi

Another lifetime partnership developed during Lois' graduate studies. Her husband, a structural engineer in private practice, Henry Chi, reveals: "I met Lois when I was a young graduate student at USC. During a football game that we both attended, she got so excited she started hitting her neighbor. Fortunately, I was sitting next to her. Our romance bloomed, eventually leading to a partnership of marriage for 48 years now. My wife, Lois, is a shy, timid, kind little girl (I remember her that way), but she has an iron determination and persistence with a loving, tender heart. We are very lucky to have three great kids: Lanie, David and Joycelyn."

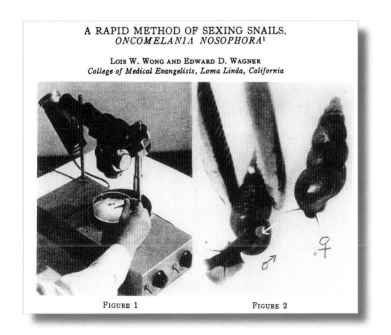

A RAPID METHOD OF SEXING SNAILS,
ONCOMELANIA NOSOPHORA[1]

LOIS W. WONG AND EDWARD D. WAGNER
College of Medical Evangelists, Loma Linda, California

FIGURE 1   FIGURE 2

A devoted wife and mother—and a role model for all—Dr. Chi has succeeded in her endeavors. She was a researcher who has helped schistosomiasis sufferers worldwide and an educator who has been a mentor to all her students. Still an avid traveler, musician (hand bells and a little harp), dancer (ballroom), and family activity coordinator, Lois Chi is characteristically active in her retirement.

Commenting on her long list of career achievements, she reflects: "I credit much of my success to my parents—my role models—for their dedication to others and their value in education. I guess my strong will—Henry calls it "iron determination"—came from experiencing and surviving life in China's new beginnings and in America's coming of age." Well said.

Wing Mar did the initial interview on Lois Chi.

Tung-Hua Lin
Scientist-Engineer-Professor

By Bill Chew and Wing Mar

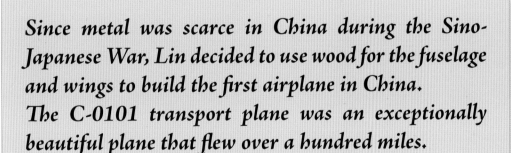

Since metal was scarce in China during the Sino-Japanese War, Lin decided to use wood for the fuselage and wings to build the first airplane in China.

The C-0101 transport plane was an exceptionally beautiful plane that flew over a hundred miles.

In 1937 Tung-Hua (T.H.) Lin received his master's degree in aeronautical engineering at M.I.T. During his studies, Lin also visited U.S. aircraft factories and received first hand knowledge, which became extremely valuable. Upon his return to China from the United States, the staff at the aircraft factory in Nanchang, China quickly recognized Lin's talent, knowledge and ability. He was asked to design airplanes as a national priority due to the loss of so many planes in the Sino-Japanese War.

China. The Mitsubishi G3M medium bombers were completing their missions with almost no opposition from the Chinese.

Already by the autumn of 1937 the command staff of the Japanese air forces considered the enemy's aviation completely destroyed. At this time, Russian military aid was given to China through a mutual assistance and non-aggression act. Soviet air advisors and Chinese pilots flew the

China's first domestically designed and produced airplane C-0101

At the beginning of the war, the Japanese air units surpassed the Chinese in numbers and quality, and also in the training of their flying and technical personnel. In spite of its heroism, the Chinese Air Force suffered enormous losses. The Chinese fighter groups flew antiquated planes, such as the Curtis Hawk III biplane, the British Gloster Gladiator and the French Dewoitine D-510.

The Mitsubishi A5M4 Type 96 and the Nakajima Ki-27 Japanese fighters completely dominated the sky over

Polikarpov I-15 biplane series, which later evolved into the I-16 model. They provided some positive effects but were still outclassed by the Japanese fighters.

In September of 1940, the Japanese unleashed the new, sleek mono-wing aircraft, the Mitsubishi A6M Zero that completely destroyed the Chinese Air Force. It was not until the advent of the American volunteer group, better known as the Flying Tigers, headed by retired Army Air Corps advisor Claire Lee Chennault, who finally helped to alter the balance of air power in China.

As the war progressed, Lin led his colleagues, who were graduates of Chinese colleges of engineering, in the challenge of designing and producing the C-0101 Transport Plane that could be modified into a light bomber—a first. A new manufacturing facility, three stories high, was built in a nearby mountain cave (Haikongdong Buddha Cave), which was safe from the Japanese bombing. Since metal was scarce, Lin decided to use wood for the fuselage and wings. Lin, and the team were excited because they relished the challenge of designing, fabricating, inspecting and testing the first aircraft made in China. At the same time they felt proud that they were accomplishing these feats for China during a time of conflict.

The Haikongdong Buddha Cave was in a remote area surrounded by hills. The neighboring area was covered with big rice fields. The Japanese bombers were unable to damage such a cave since the ceiling was made of solid rock more than 100 feet thick. From spring to summer, there would be all kinds of rare wild flora turning the valley leading up to the cave into a place of rare beauty. Lin and his wife, Jiang, lived nearby until 1944.

photo by Jason Jeri

The new aircraft, the C-0101, was exceptionally beautiful in its design and color, polished and painted bright blue. The landing gears were installed under the wings, and they could be retracted backward into a short cabin of the engine, giving the body a smooth silhouette. On its maiden flight between Chongqing and Chengdu on November 18, 1944 with seven passengers aboard, it marked the success of the first Chinese plane to be designed, tested and flown in Chinese aviation history. Only recently was a full scale replica of this airplane on display at the Chinese Aviation Museum in Beijing, Professor Lin had every reason to be proud of his part in this historic event and had lived up to the motto in China, "Save China through Aviation".

Engineer-Scientist-Professor: *Hope, Fate and Destiny*

World War II was nearing its end not long after Lin's successful production of his prototype plane. The Chinese government was hoping to expand and further develop its aviation industry. The plan was to co-produce jet planes with the McDonald Airplane Company in St. Louis in 1945, but negotiations did not produce an agreement. Rather, the Chinese technical and business delegation finalized an agreement with the Gloucester Aircraft Company in England, so Lin left for England. Two years later his family was able to join him there. However, the Communist revolution swept across China, and the Chinese-English collaboration with Gloucester was ended. Lin and the engineers in the partnership were asked to stay in England and work with Gloucester Aircraft since their working relationship had become very cordial and productive. However Lin remembered his student days in the United States and had adopted enough of American culture and attitudes that he made another important family decision: to bring his family to the U.S. to find employment. He arrived in New York with his pregnant wife and two children. Because he could not get a security clearance he was unable to work for Boeing Aircraft where he had applied and where he had hoped to bring his expertise and experience to the aircraft industry. Instead he accepted a teaching position at the University of Detroit. All his colleagues there were very friendly. Within a year the university raised his monthly pay from $300 dollars to $400. With the University of Michigan only 30 miles away Lin enrolled at the University of Michigan where he was able to study for his doctorate in engineering mechanics. He obtained his degree in 1953 at age 41. Teaching and research was now his destiny.

With his new degree Lin become a professor and he excelled in his research and teaching. After he taught at the University of Detroit he joined the faculty in the School of Engineering and Applied Science at UCLA in 1955. In 1978 he retired as a professor emeritus at UCLA. In the early 1970s the technological interest was in applied mechanics, fracture mechanics, plasticity and micro-mechanics of fatigue crack initiation. Lin has always been and continues to be at the forefront of this technology. His accomplishments in the field included the development of the physical theory of plasticity, inelastic structure analysis, and micro-mechanic theory of fatigue. The importance of this work provides present day engineers with the theory and understanding and with tools for analyzing structures;

thereby predicting with a degree of certainty the possible failures due to transient and complex loads on dynamic structures such as aircraft, turbine blades and railways. His work has increased the reliability and safety of buildings, aircraft and rail transportation.

In 1990 he was elected to the National Academy of Engineering. In 1991 an international meeting was held in Beijing; the entire meeting was filled with presentations given in his honor. The meeting was attended by scholars of engineering mechanics from China, United States, France, Germany, Japan and Russia. Lin's research and writing had become well known among his colleagues around the world. During the meeting, most articles and papers given by colleagues and former students were on plasticity of metals, inelastic structures, material fatigue and other subjects of his interest. This symposium was a way to show their respect for his scholarly work. At age 80 Lin received the Theodore von Karman Medal of Civil Engineering for his contribution to the aviation industry. His three letters of congratulation by the Presidents of MIT, University of California and University of Michigan reflected on his distinguished service to his profession and the nation. In June, 2001 the engineering societies held a special symposium in San Diego to honor his 90th birthday.

Professor Tung-Hua Lin came from a prominent scholarly family in Fuzhou, China. Starting with his great-grandfather, was a long line of scholars who took and passed the Imperial Examination at many different levels. T. H. Lin's father, Lin Ruoqing, passed the first entrance examination of a scholar at the county level and became a "xiucai". With the abolishment of the royal examination he lost his chance to take the "Juren" examination, which is the next level for a scholar of middle rank. However, he was famous for his memorizing powers. Lin heard that at one time his father was asked to recite a 700-Chinese character article, with the promise that he would be treated to a big banquet if he could do it. After only reading it over two times, he earned his banquet meal easily.

Reflecting on his long career, Lin feels that making life safer for society through engineering gives him much satisfaction. Becoming an academician rather than an engineer-industrialist has allowed him to teach and inspire many to continue with research pursuits in engineering. He feels deeply indebted to his wife, Jiang Ruiyi, who counseled him wisely, raised two sons and a daughter and worked so hard to create a home where Lin could concentrate on his work. Widowed now, he is proud of his adult children. He has a son who is a professor in the physics department and director of the solar laboratory of UC Berkeley. His physics department has successfully launched a satellite orbiting the earth and is exploring the propagation of solar energy. Another son won the Sloan Fellowship from Princeton University in mathematics and is teaching at UC San Diego. The daughter is a teacher in Michigan. The Lin family continues with the lineage of five generations of scholars.

Shiu Chi (Ray) Lau

Lau

A Tale of Two Destinies

By Pat Lau

His enzyme inhibition method for the measurement of micro amounts of organo-phosphate insecticide residues in crops was selected by the American Chemical Society in its American Official Agricultural Chemists manual as the official method to be used by American agricultural chemists.

Ray Lau's journey from Hong Kong to the United States had its roots in his father's life work and philosophy and led him ultimately on a quest to improve human conditions through science and social activism. Their lives, separated by a generation, geography, and geo-politics, have embraced Confucian principles and American democracy. These are their stories.

The Father: Lau Hey Shing in China

Ray's father, Lau Hey Shing, was born to a farmer in Hang Hew Village, Toi Shan District, Guangdong Province, China. Lau Hey Shing's name meant "ambition to succeed"—and this proved prophetic. He loved school, particularly the teachings of Confucius. Lau Hey Shing's parents cultivated rice, raised chickens and vegetables. Farming in China then was especially hard. As a young man, Lau Hey Shing had to look beyond the family farm for his future.

In 1906 Lau Hey Shing joined fellow Chinese villagers in Australia or "New Gold Mountain" to seek his fortune. Unfortunately, there was no gold to be found. Instead he peddled rattan goods from China by day and washed dishes at night. It was in Melbourne that a Chinese herbalist, Mr. Pon, noticed the hard-working Lau Hey Shing and arranged a marriage with

his third child, Edith. She was Australian born and came from a family of 12 children.

In 1910 Lau Hey Shing's cousins opened The Chinese Merchant Bank in Hong Kong and the trustworthy Hey Shing moved back to become treasurer. Having labored on the farm and in the city, Hey Shing became a believer in modernization. The banking business was successful, in part, due to his enthusiasm for the adoption of modern methods.

Around 1920 Lau Hey Shing and Edith Pon built a new home in the then barren hills east of Hong Kong's Central District, replacing the family apartment, now crowded with their growing family. The location he chose was not easily accessible. He had hundreds of steps made and excavated tons of earth to create their new home. The payoff: a spectacular view of Hong Kong harbor. Lau installed a used generator in the new home; his was one of the earliest Chinese homes in Hong Kong to have electric power. Electricity would be a key to the family's future success.

In 1926 Lau Hey Shing saw a unique opportunity. The Hong Kong Electric Company was auctioning off the old power plant that had been used to supply electricity to Hong Kong residents. The equipment was considered obsolete and room was needed for new equipment. Lau purchased all of the equipment at bargain prices and barged the entire plant to the town of Tai Leung in Shun Tak District, Guangdong Province. Thus the Kwong Jung Electric Company was founded. The company served all the businesses and residences in Shun Tak District (county) until 1941 when the Japanese invaded Southern China and looted and destroyed the company.

The political, economic and social turmoil in China created great hardship and uncertainty for the Lau family. By the early 1940's, Lau Hey Shing's and Edith Pon's eldest son, George, was killed in the Hong Kong volunteer army when the Japanese invaded Hong Kong; two younger sons, Ben and Den, had joined the Chinese army because of the Sino-Japanese war, and Ray had gone to the United States to study. Thus the Lau family never returned to China. The Kwong Jung Electric Company was never rebuilt.

The Son: Ray Lau in America

Ray Lau, born in 1913, grew up in Hong Kong and attended English-speaking schools. He was the sixth of nine children, the second son of Edith Pon. He developed sympathy for the working person and an antipathy towards the British colonists during high school. Ray's views reflected the new intelligentsia emerging in China, a product of new republican thought. While a senior at King's College, he wrote an essay criticizing British colonialism in China. Ray called the British "bandits and robbers." The school administrator turned the essay over to the police, who searched the family house for additional material and questioned Edith Pon Lau. Edith, feeling disgraced, berated her son.

Ray had also written to the Hong Kong English newspaper to protest British inaction regarding the Great Typhoon of September 1937. This devastating typhoon sank hundreds of junks and sampans and killed more than 10,000 people, many of them Chinese boat people. According to Ray's version, the British were aware the typhoon was headed towards Hong Kong but failed to provide adequate warning. His article lambasted the British and accused them of "murderous" behavior. The police once more responded to his hostile writing by invading the Lau household.

During the 1930s, Ray farmed rice on leased land and attended Lingnan University in Canton, China. The nation was in turmoil. The conflict between the Chinese Communist Party and the Kuomintang, and the onset of the Sino-Japanese war wreaked economic and social havoc. The future was bleak, even for a family as well regarded that of Lau Hey Shing. Ray decided to look for opportunities abroad that would galvanize his belief that China should adopt modern agrarian technology.

In 1939, Ray won a two-year scholarship from Lingnan University to study food technology at University of California, Berkeley. The goal: learn modern scientific techniques and processes, return to China and assume a professorship to teach and help propagate new ideas. At that time, China was still an agrarian economy. Chinese agricultural methods were antiquated and crops were highly vulnerable to the vagaries of nature. During the early part of the 20th century, China had experienced terrible drought, floods and massive locust infestation.

Ray spent one year at Berkeley. He transferred to Oregon State College where the food technology program emphasized applied techniques that he preferred over the theory–based curriculum offered by UC Berkeley. After obtaining his masters degree in 1941, Ray delayed returning to China because the Japanese had invaded, sacked, and occupied Hong Kong. Meanwhile, he worked as chief food chemist in charge of quality control for a food company in San Francisco and later, for the Flotill Cannery in Stockton, Calif. The Flotill Cannery ran 24 hours a day, seven days a week, to support the war effort. The work provided the cannery workers, many women from China, a means of support for their families.

While working at Flotill, Ray met and married Lillian (Wai Chuen) Chow, a graduate student at the University of the Pacific in Stockton, (then College of the Pacific) majoring in teaching nutrition and home economics. Lillian, like Ray intended to return to China, where she had hoped to become a teacher. Lillian was also an entrepreneur. While at UOP, she taught in the Chinese school and ran Temple Bell, a Chinese gift shop, to pay for her college tuition. At that time, Lillian had to have an American business partner, as Chinese aliens were not allowed to own a business. Lillian had to overcome many prejudices and barriers, but nonetheless became a successful businesswoman.

During WWII and while working long hours at Flotill, Ray was persuaded to return to Oregon College and complete the research in food hydration he had started. In 1944 he returned to Oregon and earned his Ph.D. in food technology. Ray and Lillian decided to remain in the U.S. because of the post-war turmoil in China.

In the late 1940s, Ray, Lillian and their two daughters moved to Denver, Col.. There, he began his career at the Shell Development Company. At that time, Shell was trying to promote its new Endrin insecticide. In order to do so, a viable quantitative method of analysis was needed. Shell had assembled four analytical chemists to develop such a method, but had not succeeded. Ray was given the opportunity and began his distinguished career of nearly 30 years. Shell transferred its research facilities from Denver to Modesto, Calif. in 1957. Ray remained there until his retirement in 1978.

While at Shell, Ray helped develop original methods for the quantitative analysis of useful insecticides. His enzyme inhibition method for the measurement of micro amounts of organo-phosphate insecticide residues in crops was selected by the American Chemical Society in its American Official Agricultural Chemists manual as the official method to be used by American agricultural chemists. This method was the primary methodology employed for many years and was the prototype for analytical methods using enzymes. It remains the fundamental basis for today's advanced enzyme-based biosensor technology. Ray subsequently introduced fly brain cholinesterase reagent and the results were important: a five to tenfold increase in measurement sensitivity of organic residues.

Modesto proved to be a wonderful community for Ray and his family. Ray and Lillian raised their two daughters, Annette and Pat. Lillian taught Chinese cooking, conversational Cantonese and calligraphy at Modesto Junior College. She also ran a gift shop while Ray worked on his research in analytical techniques.

Outside of work, both Ray and Lillian were active in the Chinese Society in Stanislaus County. As officers, they used their various skills to help other Chinese obtain legal residency in the U.S. Many needed help because of the restrictive policies regarding Chinese immigration. Lillian was active politically and socially. She raised money for political candidates sympathetic towards immigrants. Congressman John McFall was a visitor to their Modesto home and helped Lillian and Ray navigate the confusing immigration system. Lillian was tenacious in pursuing answers despite the many bureaucratic hurdles that discouraged the less educated and the less persistent. Ray's ability to read the fine print, his proper English and excellent writing skills, combined with Lillian's persistence, helped a number of Chinese families.

Ray's family experience in Modesto was a classic American experience. The family thrived despite its immigrant roots and became part of the fabric of American multi-culturalism.

A Perspective

In many ways, Ray's story is not unique among Chinese immigrants. As is true for many Chinese, his story reflects hard work, a belief in education, the generosity of Chinese and Americans, and a strong sense of traditional values. The results, however, are unique.

From his father, Ray learned his love of modern methods as well as his adherence to the Chinese Confucian principles of honor, respect and honesty. He fulfilled his dreams to build a better life for his family, while completing a life's work based on advancing science and human progress.

Edgar Wong and Wing Mar assisted in the research of this biography.

Ko Kuei Chen

陳克恢

A Pharmacologist's Pharmacologist

By Gladys Ikeda and Wing Mar

His success in identifying ephedrine permanently secured his place in pharmacology annals worldwide, and was much appreciated by millions of allergy sufferers. Moreover, his work opened up new avenues for study and research that eventually resulted in the development of alpha and beta blockers, as well as drugs that treat respiratory diseases, nasal congestion, fatigue, obesity and narcolepsy. These contributions led Dr. K. K. Chen to be considered the father of modern pharmacology in China.

The Formative Years

When flowers bloom and pollen wafts through the air, allergy sufferers reach for their medication, not knowing that the person responsible for relieving their symptoms was a young Chinese researcher who later became a driving force in pharmacology. The single individual whose pioneering research yielded relief for generations of allergy sufferers was Dr. Ko Kuei Chen. It was his work as a researcher at Peking Union Medical College in 1924 that gave the world the drug ephedrine for treating the symptoms of asthma, hay fever, and whooping cough. Few others have had a greater impact on uniting different pharmacology organizations and individuals to achieve common goals in the fight against disease.

Born in a village near Shanghai, Ko Kuei Chen came to America in 1918, enrolling at the University of Wisconsin as a pharmacy student with an early objective of studying Chinese medicine by scientific methods. To improve his poor English-speaking skills, he joined a debating society and within two years became a fluent speaker. After receiving his Bachelor of Science in pharmacy in 1920, and two years later earning the first ever Ph.D. in physiological chemistry bestowed by the University of Wisconsin, Dr. Chen returned to China in 1923 to teach pharmacology at Peking Union Medical College.

From the several hundred drugs recorded in Chinese dispensatories, Dr. Chen consulted with herbalists and an uncle, and with intuition and extraordinary foresight, chose to delve into the mysteries of Ma Huang, or ephedra sinica, a well-known Chinese herb. Within weeks, he was able to isolate the active crystalline alkaloid in ephedra sinica. Dr. Chen subsequently charted the physiological action of ephedrine, shown to be useful in treating bronchial asthma, hay fever, and for maintaining level blood pressure in spinal and general anesthesia. His success in identifying ephedrine permanently secured his place in pharmacology annals worldwide, and was much appreciated by millions of allergy sufferers. Moreover, his work opened up new avenues for study and research that eventually resulted in the development of alpha and beta blockers, as well as drugs that treat respiratory diseases, nasal congestion, fatigue, obesity and narcolepsy. These contributions led Dr. K. K. Chen to be considered the father of modern pharmacology in China.

Returning to the United States in 1925, the young pharmacology researcher continued his research and medical education at Johns Hopkins Medical School, where he received his M.D. in 1927. Some of his early studies during this period were published in collaboration with a fellow researcher, Dr. Amy Ling, a doctor who graduated from Case Western Reserve University. Dr. Ling later became his wife and mother of his two children.

A Job Offer He Could Not Refuse

In 1929, while Dr. Chen was an associate in pharmacology at Johns Hopkins, Josiah Kirby, Sr., son of the founder of Eli Lilly and Company, a pharmaceutical firm, recruited him to form the Eli Lilly Company Research Laboratory and become its Director of Pharmacological Research. In a public speech in 1984 recounting his interview with the firm's namesake, Eli Lilly, Dr. Chen reported that "Mr. Lilly said he would give me complete freedom of research, particularly in Chinese material medica".

So began his career in a dream of a position for the innovative research genius. Early during his tenure at Eli Lilly, Dr. Chen and some of his colleagues discovered a medication that was an effective antidote against acute cyanide poisoning. Their experiments proved life saving when one of their colleagues collapsed from accidentally breathing in hydrocyanic acid. The immediate injection of .3 gm sodium nitrite and 12.5 gm sodium thiosulfate kept on hand in an emergency kit reversed the effects of the poison, and the worker fully recovered within the week. "It was gratifying that our own experiments could benefit one of our colleagues," Dr. Chen said years later.

Another study important to the Lilly Laboratories confirmed the analgesic properties of methadone. Dr. Chen's work with methadone led to the development of a compound, d-propoxyphane, that was sufficiently efficient, potent, and had low addictive liabilities and thus could be widely prescribed instead of narcotics such as codeine.

Giving research freedom to Dr. Chen allowed him to spend the bulk of his active laboratory research studying toad toxins. Expressing the skin venom of almost 13,800 toads from 16 species over the years, he and his associates grouped the substances into five classes, obtaining valuable information on the venom's digitalis-like components—aglycones, bufadienolides and cardenolides. Pharmacologists consider his extraordinary series of papers on the structure-activity relationships of over 400 cardiac glycosides and steroid compounds important in enhancing scientific knowledge, even though no marketable drug evolved from those efforts.

The first company to test drugs (screening compounds, isolating and studying active ingredients, standardizing components and testing with animals) the Eli Lilly lab under Dr. Chen defined the pharmacology of dozens of compounds and drugs. Among the drugs whose properties are known through Dr. Chen's work are estrogens, anti-diabetic drugs, anti-thyroid drugs, erythromycin and other antibiotics. Because of his presence and direction, Eli Lilly was able to develop countless synthetic sympathomimatic amine derivatives such as alpha and beta blockers and congeners for a variety of medical conditions. His more than 380 original publicized books, papers and articles cover more than 50 years and include several major review articles and historical papers on Chinese medicine.

Although his own research spanned two continents, his impact went far beyond just his own laboratories. During the 1950s, he was the official U.S. Department of State delegate to the International Union of Physiological Sciences and was an invited guest lecturer for the Japan Medical Congress in 1959. Representing pharmacology on the Drug Research Board sponsored by the National Academy of Sciences in the early 1960s, Dr. Chen played an important role in reassessing the safety and efficacy claims of prescription drugs following the thalidomide catastrophe abroad. In 1964, he chaired the Pharmacology Panel of the Office of Science and Technology of the Executive Office of President. Dr. Chen was a consultant to the National Institutes of Health, a member of the U.S. Public Health Research Training Program and was a professor of pharmacology at Indiana University.

(continued next page)

A Team Player at Work and at Play

But more than anything else, Dr. Chen believed in cooperative efforts, information sharing, and maintaining close communication among researchers in the biologic professions. In his own words, Dr. Chen stated that "…more fruitful results occur as organic chemists, immunologists and physicians collaborate with one another." Dr. Chen credited such collaboration for Lilly's success in the company's development of antibiotics, new analgesics, sulphonamides, hormones, vitamins, and short-acting barbiturates during his career. That credo forms what many of his colleagues consider a major underpinning of his success—a vision and concern that "common goals can be accomplished more effectively by uniting component societies in the cause of fostering knowledge to fight diseases that plague mankind".

Dr. Chen garnered praise for his years of leadership with the American Society of Pharmacology and Experimental Therapeutics and the Federation of American Society for Experimental Biology, as well as for helping to found International Union of Pharmacology. In 1984, the American Society of Pharmacology and Experimental Therapeutics bestowed on Dr. Chen their highest award, the Torald Sollman Award, given in recognition of sustained and significant contributions to the profession.

After his death, tributes and accolades poured in from pharmacologists, biologists and other medical science researchers around the world. They considered him a visionary leader of his profession, credited him with raising the status of pharmacology in industrial and academic research, called him a great forerunner of modern pharmacology and an innovator who worked toward prompt sharing of discoveries among all the subdisciplines of biological and medical science.

Despite spending time on his studies as a young man, Dr. Chen also taught himself to play various musical instruments. As a student in China, Dr. Chen was the leader of a musical group. At the University of Wisconsin, he was a member of the college band. To his children's regret, he put his instruments away when his children were born and thus those talents were never shared with his family. His son, Dr. Thomas Chen of Stockton, Calif., who is well known locally for his love of classical music and his patronage of the Stockton Symphony orchestra, tells of his father accompanying him to symphony concerts when he was home from college.

As a Chinese father in the United States, Dr. Ko Kuei Chen tried to teach his children his native language, a task complicated by the fact that he and his wife spoke different native Chinese dialects. Moreover, they lived in the American Midwest, in a city where his son estimates the total Chinese population then numbered about four dozen residents. Nevertheless, the parents valiantly attempted to impart their fluency in Mandarin, which they both spoke, to their son. Their limited success in doing so did not constrain father and son from taking several cross-country trips from the Midwest to California, where the father opened new vistas and experiences to his young son.

Dr. Ko Kuei Chen passed away in 1988 at the age of 90. He is survived by his wife, Dr. Amy Ling Chen, who at age 100 in 2004 makes her home in San Francisco, with her son, Dr. Thomas Chen of Stockton, Calif. or her daughter, Mei Chen Welland of St. Louis, Mo.

Lawrence Jue

An Update of "My Memoirs"

By Edgar Wong

趙 樹 材

> "I graduated from high school in 1933 and became a happy sign painter making $150 a month. My parents insisted I go to college. Then as an engineer and the Chief Naval Architect, I directed a team in making the navy's first snorkel submarines in the 1940s and later the Sealab for undersea exploration."

Why an Update?

Here today, gone tomorrow. At 81 years of age, I find myself wondering as many people do: "What is the meaning of life? Why was I brought upon the earth?" No one knows for sure. But, as long as we are here, I think that everyone should believe that he or she has a mission here on earth, which is simply: "To make it a better world for future generations." I am a firm believer in this idealistic concept. Let me tell you why.

But wait! I wrote the above opening paragraph eight years ago and my friends at the historical society read my memoirs recently. They wanted me to write an abridged three-page version for this book—a 2004 update of my 1995 document—from the original fifteen-page "My Memoirs." Let me try.

Visit to the Heavenly Gate

In October 1976, my wife Anne and I joined a group of Chinese-American engineers on a 30-day tour of mainland China. On the 22nd day of the trip, we arrived in Beijing, where we climbed the famous Great Wall. The following day, I toured the vast East-is-Red Oil Refinery, and then returned to our hotel for lunch with my fellow travelers.

All of a sudden, and without warning, I was felled by a stroke. I could hear "Larry is sick ... I just pinched him ... he's comatose ... call the doctor!" Strangely, through this whole episode, I could see, I could hear, and I could converse with people. At least, I thought I could as they hurriedly

shoved me into the back seat of a taxi and sped two miles to the Shoudu Hospital. My whole left side was paralyzed by a blood clot in the right lobe of my brain. After three days of intensive treatment by five doctors, and a fine combination of western medicine and Chinese acupuncture, my droopy mouth was straightened and my mobility was restored.

The fourth day was beautiful. While propped up on a pair of pillows, I gazed out the window onto a lovely garden, then I began to doze off. Soon, I was standing before a high stone wall. Behind the diamonds-and-pearls studded gate was a bright blue sky filled with billowing red and orange clouds. "This must be St. Peter's pearly gate to heaven!" I exclaimed to myself. Then suddenly, a voice inquired in Mandarin, "Who is this?" "I am Zhao Shucai (Larry Jue)," I replied. "Where are you from?" the voice continued. "From Beijing," I said without hesitation. From behind the wall came a rustling sound of pages of a large book being flipped by someone searching hastily for the city name. "I am sorry ... we have not resumed diplomatic relations with China ...." the voice explained apologetically. I woke up laughing with tears in my eyes! Anne was in the room and I said to her, "Good thing I didn't tell him I was from San Francisco. He would have opened the heavenly gate and I would have been admitted; and, I'd never be able to see you again."

I recall that during the month-long stay at the hospital, I had prayed many times, unselfishly, to God: "I have no fear of dying, if that is what you want of me. But if I still have a mission in life, I want to serve You." Today, I have recovered the full use of my limbs and faculties. By the grace of the Good Lord, I can speak, walk, run, dance, think and analyze, as well as I ever did. Anne and I even won some trophies at dance tournaments for senior citizens.

Lifelong Community Service

Since my debilitating stroke, I have lived another 19 active years during which I have been able to fulfill my promise to Him. In these past years, I have been called upon to undertake many tough community problems, which in one way or another, were miraculously and successfully solved. Let me tell you about these wonderful challenges that have brought me much self-satisfaction, won many friends and brought our community a better quality of life.

The Chinese American Institute of Engineers and Scientists (CAIES). In 1943, when a friend, quite by chance on Stockton Street, asked me if I were going to the engineers' meeting at the basement of the old post office. I went and to my surprise I was elected president of a newly born organization. Later, I helped in starting the CAIES scholarship program and then headed the investment committee for acquiring the needed funds. Initially, our name was CAIE—the "and Scientists" were added in the early 1970s to form the CAIES of today.

The Chinatown/North Beach Elementary Schools. In 1973, San Francisco woke up to the fact that its elementary school buildings did not meet seismic structural requirements under the Field Act of 1933. The school board declared that the three schools in Chinatown/North Beach could not be seismically upgraded. In response, the CAIES formed a save-our-school committee with me as chairman. To make a long story short, our community activism was successful in saving the Commodore Stockton School Annex (my alma mater in Chinatown), the Garfield School (Telegraph Hill), and the Sarah B. Cooper School (Russian Hill)—at a cost

of $7 million for the seismic retrofit.

The Chinese Cultural Center. In 1964, J. K. Choy gave a talk to the CAIE about his dream of building a Chinese Cultural Center. He was able to negotiate a lease of the third floor of the new Holiday Inn in Chinatown—for a dollar a year. But it was an empty shell, unusable because of incessant noise and vibrations within its confines. I was able to find an affordable engineering solution for mitigating the noise and vibrations from the three large reciprocating Freon compressors running at high speeds. My solution was to remount them on dual concrete slabs and support the slabs on low frequency pneumatic rubber vibration isolators. Since then, I've been called upon to solve other engineering problems.

The Angel Island Immigration Station Barracks. In 1974, the Angel Island Immigration Station barracks faced demolition. Together with the park ranger, several of us worked to save this important relic that was a dark part of Chinese-American history. I wrote the master plan for the rehabilitation of the Immigration Station and it was adopted by the California Parks and Recreation Department. Later, I assisted in the selection of the winning couplet—two sentences of nine characters—from the 65 entries for inscription on the nine-foot tall granite monument.

The Long Kong Tien Yee Assn. of San Francisco. In 1983, I served as the association's national president—and Anne served as the local chapter's Women's Auxiliary chairperson. Together we were proud to plan and execute many fraternal activities. The San Francisco association is one of over a hundred fraternal organizations worldwide for Chinese with surnames Lew, Quan, Jung, and Chew (and its English spelling variants)—the so-called four-family surnames. Over the years, I have helped other chapters with their master planning and in obtaining their federal and state

> *"What you learn is yours to keep and no one can ever take it from you!"*

nonprofit tax-exempt status. I served as chairman of the Ming Yee building restoration committee, which oversaw the million-dollar restoration of the fire-ravaged building at 924 Grant Ave.

The Geen Mun Neighborhood Center. In the 1980s, we saw a growing need for a one-stop service center for the immigrants and the elderly. Together with several others, we were successful in getting Mayor Diane Feinstein to approve a million dollars for its construction. The center housed charitable organizations providing self-help for the elderly, newcomers' service, a nursery and educational services.

Government Service

I was an engineer in the Navy Department, retiring in 1970 after a 30-year career. From 1958 to 1970, I was Chief Naval Architect at the San Francisco Naval Shipyard at Hunters Point. My bosses gave me a free hand in running my sector in the design division, which made it possible for me to make many material contributions to ship design that enhanced the Navy's military effectiveness. Many engineers, technicians and naval officers assisted me in making numerous state-of-the-art ship designs, developmental facilties and design tools.

My design projects included the SSK 241 class submarine killers—the Navy's first snorkel subs in the 1940s. A more publicized project was the Sealab II, built along the principles of a submarine, for undersea explorations. Astronaut Scott Carpenter and his fellow aquanauts have trained in this vessel in the deep Pacific Ocean off of La Jolla, Calif. Jacques Cousteau had praised the ingenious simple ballasting system of the Sealab, having encountered stability and ballasting problems with his undersea habitats. My career brought me three patents: a dehumidifying apparatus, an apparatus for determining circularity of large diameter objects, and a device for supply replenishment of undersea habitats.

Facilities I founded include the Navy's West Coast Shock Test Facility in 1963 at Hunters Point. It was capable of conducting shock and vibration testing of full-size naval machinery and missile systems and shock tests of full-scale combatant ships. Another facility worthy of note is the Explosive Forming Laboratory. Normally, repeated hammer blows are used to pound a heavy steel plate into a dishhead used in the hull of a vessel like the Sealab. Instead, we used a single high explosive force to instantly form the 12-foot diameter, one-inch thick, steel structure.

With the advent of high-speed computers, I was able to assist the Navy in acquiring the computer facilities and developing the design tools (CAD software). Developed were the following: stress analysis of complex ship structures, design of heating, ventilating and air conditioning (HVAC) systems, analysis of complex, three-dimensional rigging systems, and many other analytical tools.

Life Reflections

I have been very lucky to work with my colleagues at CAIES, the great Navy team at Hunters Point, and the many volunteers in community service. I would not trade these experiences for anything—not for all the money in the world! I could never have achieved what I did without the help of a lot of people. My brother Joseph Sunn had always been an inspiration to me. I learned so much from this great genius.

When I graduated from high school in 1933, under my brother's tutelage, I became a sign painter. I made bilingual gold-leaf window signs, metal signs, posters, etc. A sign that I made in 1937 still stands on the front window of the Tai Yuen Company at 740 Jackson St. in San Francisco. I was making $150 a month at a time when many people in Chinatown were lucky to make $50. I had entertained no thoughts or desire of going for higher education. I probably would still be making signs in Chinatown today if my parents didn't urge me to go to U.C. Berkeley, where I earned my BS ('38) and MS ('40) degrees in mechanical engineering. In fact, mom and dad insisted that I go to college, with the sage advice, "What you learn is yours to keep and no one can ever take it from you!"

Most importantly, my memoirs are dedicated to my loving wife Anne; my dear children: Carolyn, Laraine, Linda, and Michael; and my adored grandchildren: Robert, Becky, Stephanie, Brian, Larry, and Scott. I owe them lots of credit for their eternal support. I could not have been engaged in so many lifelong activities without their understanding, inspiration, cooperation, and tolerance.

Yes, every one has a mission in life. No question about it. The stroke that I suffered in 1976 taught me not to fear death, that I must maintain the faith. I thank the good Lord for every day that he permits me to spend on earth. In the final measure, I hope that I have made some contribution to bettering the world in my lifetime. Few may remember Lawrence Sinclair Jue after I'm gone. But I will go with the strong conviction that life has been very worthwhile. And it has been great fun.

The day will come when I will again approach the pearly gates of heaven. When the man asks, "Where are you from?" … I'll reply, "From San Francisco, Sir!" And I will enter those gates with my head held high, for I know that I have done my very best in the fulfillment of my mission on earth.

His daughter Laraine Huey coordinated this July 2003 memoir update by Mr. Jue for the historical society. The original paper "My Memoirs" by Lawrence S. Jue, Copyright © August 17, 1995, San Francisco, California is available for reading at the CHSSC Visitor Center in the Los Angeles Chinatown. Mr. Jue is also listed in the 1988 issue of "Who's Who in California."

As of July 2003, Lawrence Sinclair Jue is living quietly at home in San Francisco with his wife, Anne. He enjoys reading, mah jongg, family association activities, and pondering new ideas.

E. Leong Way

Research Pharmacologist
and
Champion Terpsichorean

Interview by Wing Mar and Ella Leong

Who would have predicted that this eldest son of eight children from a humble immigrant family, whose parents were illiterate in English, would receive some of the highest honors bestowed upon a scientist in drug research?

Professor Way's Career Contribution

Well-known and well-loved Octogenarian Eddie Leong Way is Professor Emeritus of Pharmacology, Toxicology and Pharmaceutical Chemistry at the University of California Medical Center, San Francisco (UCSF). Apart from four decades at UCSF and five years at George Washington University, he took one-year sabbatical visits at Berne, Hong Kong and Gunma Universities, respectively, in Switzerland, China and Japan.

Born with an inquisitive mind, blessed by a sense of humor, this scientist who was "bamboo-switched in the first grade, belt-strapped in the second, and ruler-spanked in the fifth" was salvaged by his seventh grade teacher, Adeline Scandrett. She redirected his restless activities and prevented his being expelled from school when his pranks got out of hand. To this day he has Adeline's picture on top of his old desk. Prof. Way still goes daily to the office, which UCSF granted him in recognition for long and distinguished service.

Who would have predicted that this eldest son of eight children from a humble immigrant family, whose parents were illiterate in English, would receive some of the highest honors bestowed upon a scientist in drug research? While he was proficient in basic research concerned with delineating the metabolic fate of a multitude of drugs, he was especially talented in finding answers to the puzzle of drug dependency and attenuation of pain. Over the course of his active tenure, he headed projects and wrote or edited over 400 articles and books including "The Biological Disposition of Morphine and its

photo by Jason Jem

Surrogates" (with T.K. Adler), "The Fundamentals of Drug Metabolism and Drug Disposition" (with B. La Du and G. Mandel), and "New Concepts in Pain".

Prof. Way has lectured in many countries on problems of drug addiction. These speaking engagements provided the opportunity for local lawmakers to obtain scientific input and opinions in their revisions of drug policies and related legislation. He provided humane and scientifically based insights for addressing the issues of safety, clinical efficacy and abuse, and promoted the needs of education and research. For instance, although politics still play a role in marijuana use, the mass of scientific knowledge generated in recent years now allows increasing advocacy for its medical use and decriminalization for its non-medical use. Much of the data gathered can be attributed to the National Institute on Drug Abuse donating the funds as well as the marijuana for research. As consultant, Dr. Way played a major role in emphasizing the importance of supporting not only basic but clinical studies, as well as providing a standardized plant product as the basis for comparison among different laboratories. His own investigative work on drug dependence is closely related to his study of opiates, or narcotic drugs. These studies are still being pursued by many of his proteges and colleagues in the field.

Even today, many of Prof. Way's research efforts now serve as models for students and researchers to emulate. But perhaps his legacy extended even beyond his impact in research.

With the axiom that "it is a poor teacher who does not learn from his pupils" it is hardly surprising that his mentoring has churned out top-notch fellows and scholars who are raising the bar in the profession and their laboratories.

Prof. Way beams with pride when scientists of Asian ancestry are mentioned, like Chen-Yu Sung, Horace Loh, Ing Kang Ho, Aki Takemori, Kaito Tsurumi, Fu-Shiung Shen, Jim Fujimoto, Nancy Lee, E. T. Wei, P. Y. Law, and many others. These are his colleagues, post doctoral fellows and former students. Remembering his own roots and sensitive to the difficulty for minority researchers to obtain choice positions, he encouraged fairness and diversity in his laboratory.

Prof. Way has lectured in countries heavily burdened with problems of drug addiction. More important, these speaking engagements provided the opportunity for local lawmakers to obtain scientific input and opinions in their revisions of drug policies and related legislation.

Because of his boundless energy and scientific leadership, Prof. Way was elected president in 1976 of the prestigious American Society of Pharmacology and Experimental Therapeutics (ASPET). Capping decades of attracting research grant awards since 1943 which enabled his pioneering studies, Prof. Way received the Nathan B. Eddy Memorial Award for outstanding research in drug dependence. In 1992 he also received the prestigious Torald Sollman Award for lifetime achievement in pharmacology. These commendations acknowledge the importance of Prof. Way's extensive publications on drug metabolism and his concepts on narcotic addition derived from studies concerned with the basic mechanisms involved in morphine tolerance and physical dependence development.

While treasurer of the International Narcotics Research Conference (INRC), he raised nearly a million dollars for professional education. With a flair for philanthropy he was elected president of the Li Foundation of New York, founded by his father-in-law, Kuo Ching Li, the tungsten magnate and philanthropist. One of Way's major public service interests is providing grants to overseas Chinese students for study at American universities. For his global reach and exceptional leadership he received the Gold Medal and Cultural Citation from the Republic of China Ministry of Education in 1978.

Never one to be pigeonholed into the stereotype of a nerdy scientist, Prof. Way is one who lives life to the fullest. He is a terpsichorean champion. Describing his love for ballroom dancing in the Review of Revues (a brief autobiography in a science review journal), he said "nothing was more exhilarating than gliding or stomping in unison on the floor with an accomplished partner to the tunes and rhythms of the big bands." There was also a time when Professor Way enjoyed competing in sports—basketball, baseball, table tennis, and track and field. However, with golden age creeping up, he has taken up golf to supplement his terpsichorean commitments. Students should learn at least this most important lesson of living passionately from Prof. Way.

Currently Professor Leong Way is attempting to write a volume on Pharmacy and Pharmacology for the Joseph Needham series—Science and Civilization in China. It was a revelation for Professor Way to learn about early bioscience in China including: circulation of the blood was described more than two thousand years ago; small pox inoculation used over one thousand years ago; and treatment of goiter with seaweed (naturally high in iodine) was used for at least half a century.

Leong Way's Family Perspective

The discriminatory Chinese Exclusion Act was enacted in 1882 and was not repealed until 1943 after the United States belatedly became an ally of China in World War II. The act denied the right of a Chinese immigrant to become a citizen, hold property, or bring a wife into the country. However, in 1912 my father brought my mother from China to live in Watsonville, California. During the catastrophic 1906 earthquake and fire in San Francisco many government records were destroyed. In the aftermath some Chinese residents rightly or wrongly claimed citizenship by right of birth and it was not possible for the government to support or reject the claims. My father did not discuss such matters with me or my sisters and brothers, nor did we ask.

All eight of us were born in Watsonville. During the Depression, with failure of the family business in the apple industry we moved to San Francisco and lived in the Fillmore district, a multi-ethnic neighborhood bordering Japantown. We did not have many choices because of zoning laws and discriminatory practices even though we were living in a city with a history of tolerance. In any event, we enjoyed growing up there without knowing about the term "ghetto." Although Asian Americans at that time were denied equal opportunity to housing and jobs, public education was open to all—including the Way family. Six of us siblings earned degrees from the University of California; two received doctorates. For me, student life on the Berkeley campus was a happy, encouraging, helpful, rich and unforgettable experience.

My good fortune continued, and during my career I managed to have some great jobs. My final position was at my alma mater, UCSF, where I enjoyed teaching, research and public service for four decades. Happily, after retiring in 1987 my association continues and now exceeds five decades. Without the support of

An opium pipe–a symbol of shame for Chinese and inspiration for Way's drug research and pain relief.

my parents, teachers, and colleagues it would not have been possible to pursue a career of my own choosing and to receive peer recognition. I would certainly opt once more for this career. It was hard for our generation to pursue our dreams in the great depression of the 30's and amid the bias of those times. Many of our generation just passively accepted the acts of discrimination, but now there are many more people of good will who recognize injustice and are willing to fight for reforms. I am ever so glad my father had the vision and courage to find a livelihood in the United States. Although there is room for improvement, this is an extraordinary country with opportunity for those like my family and myself.

Kenow Lou

His Life with Particle Accelerators

By Linda Chong and Jason Jem

Twenty eight years earlier a rude, racist interviewer marred the start of Kenow's engineering career. At his 1983 retirement party, 200 attendees, including department directors, scores of engineers, technicians and clerks, honored him.

From the Farms of Central Valley

With a great amount of understatement, Kenow says, "life had its limitations" for people of Chinese heritage, and even for Kenow Lou who was born in 1917 in Stockton, Calif. which of course makes him an American citizen. Kenow was able to not only rise above these societal "limitations" in America, but he was also able to survive two wars on two continents—Asia and Europe. He then came home to raise a family and became the deputy department head and project manager in America's leading nuclear research center, the Lawrence Radiation Laboratory of University of California, Berkeley.

The young Kenow was inspired by his immigrant father's hard work in dealing with the tremendous environmental and business challenges of farming. His father also made it clear that all his five children had to have very high goals to journey beyond the farms of the Central Valley. However, no one could have imagined the hardships posed by the Sino-Japan War and World War II, which tested his ingenuity and resolve.

As a boy, Kenow enjoyed a simple life in Stockton's farming community. However, his family's journey to America, to become Americans were far from simple. The senior Lou left his home in Guangdong province at the end of dysfunctional, dynastic China to seek a better life in the modern land of opportunity, America. Ironically, after many years of hard labor, saving enough money to marry and bring his wife to the U.S. and raising a family in Stockton, the Great Depression struck. In 1934 Kenow's father had to make the wrenching decision to move part of his family back to Guangdong, where his

prudent investments provided better financial stability for his growing family. After sending part of his family back to China, Kenow's father moved to San Francisco as a reluctant, lonely bachelor, while Kenow's older brother, Wyan, attended M.I.T. to become a naval architect. Unfortunately, it was not long when Japan restarted its drive to conquer China and was bombing Canton. Kenow and his brother Kingdon returned to the U.S. in August 1940 and there were no entry problems since they were U.S. citizens. Their mother, sister Beth and brother Kingget were trapped in Hong Kong when Japan attacked and occupied the city but they eventually made their way back to the safety of their ancestral village and stayed until the Japanese surrendered in 1945. The remaining members of the Lou family were finally repatriated in various passages to the U.S beginning in 1946 and terminating in March 1947 ending 13 years of adventure and hardship. That would have been the ideal ending of this part of the story.

Catch 22 for Mrs. Lou

However Kenow's mother was not a citizen and could not be naturalized because she was Chinese. She left the U.S. in 1934 with permission to be out of the U.S. for only one year. Her overstaying her approved time in China because of many circumstances would only allow her to return the U.S. as a tourist for one year ending on April, 1949 according to the harsh discriminatory laws. Because of these laws Mrs. Lou had to return to Hong Kong for an anguishing and anxiety-filled three years. In 1951 Mrs. Lou's daughter, Beth, persuaded then Senator Richard Nixon to introduce Senate Bill 1028 which enabled Mrs. Lou to immigrate as a non-quota resident. Mrs.

Lou could never become a naturalized citizen because of the discriminatory immigration laws until gradual relaxation of those laws ended in the Hart-Cellar Act of 1965. (The Page Law of 1875, Chinese Exclusion Act of 1882 and the amended law of 1884 barred the entry to the U.S. by wives of Chinese immigrants)

The Lou Story Continues

With another flip of irony, for Kenow, the more secure life in Guangzhou ended in 1937 due to the Sino-Japan war. Kenow survived those war years by working for the provincial highway department and also with the public health department. The highway project was to connect the Burma Road terminal in Kunming and the wartime capital Chongqing, using only conscripted manpower and no mechanized equipment. The public health project was educational, taking public health staff to the countryside to campaign

Tokamak Fusion Test Reactor
Plasma Physics Laboratory, Princeton Univ.

Returning to California in 1940, Kenow was determined to better himself by attending Visalia Junior College and UC Berkeley to study engineering. Unfortunately, with only nine more credits before graduation, war again interrupted his life in 1943. He joined the U.S. Army, serving with Gen. Patton's Third Army. After V-E Day, his division was due back to the U.S. for more training to prepare for the attack on Japan. Fortunately, this time fate was on his side. V-J Day arrived before they were to be shipped off to Asia.

I Found my Dream Job

After the war, Kenow completed his degree in engineering, with help from his bride, Pauline, and proceeded to establish a career and raise their family of three daughters (Robbin, Karen and Monika) and a son (Barry).

for good health and sanitation practices and warn against the recreational use of opium. These projects enabled him to avoid the routes blocked by the Japanese army in 1940. He then journeyed from South China to Guizhou, back through northern Vietnam via the train to Haiphong and then boarded a ship up the South China Sea to Hong Kong. The time spent during the war years living and working with the people in the interior and the refugees were invaluable learning experiences. "It was something I wanted to do and be of some help in the war effort even though it was dangerous and arduous. After being in China for six years and spending time in helping with the war effort, I realized that my contribution was pitifully minor," Kenow recalled. "Better I should continue my education."

Engineering work did not come easily. Once again Kenow faced our country's "limitations". He was encouraged to interview for an opening at Columbia Steel in Pittsburg Calif., after graduation from engineering school at UC Berkeley. His friend's father worked there. Kenow was told the position was filled. His friend could not believe this and called the company about the position and was told to go in for an interview. Kenow Lou was told later that the firm did not hire Asians as engineers. In the next attempt by Kenow an engineer placement officer in a local employment agency told him that the recommendation officer in charge did not believe Chinese could become good engineers. So no referrals of Chinese engineers were to be made at that agency. Fortunately, not everyone subscribed to such racist beliefs and Kenow finally did get an engineering job.

Perseverance for advancement finally paid off. After several years, Kenow was offered "my dream job" at UC's Lawrence Berkeley Laboratory, working on the Billion Electron Volt Particle Accelerator (BEVATRON) and many other high-energy nuclear physics research projects. Some of these projects produced Nobel prizes for scientists and important advances in medical treatments. This engineering work was very rewarding to Kenow. He was challenged because of the contrasting theories of physics, which required different designs and the necessity to build large machines, utilizing enormous amounts of power to control and affect changes on miniscule sub-atomic particles. Armed with experience and knowledge he went on a one-year, research sabbatical to Brookhaven Labs, in Long Island, New York, and earned high praise for enabling the successful transfer of technology to the host Lab.

He was given an exemplary and grateful letter thanking him from the Princeton Plasma Physics Laboratory. Another project he is very proud to have supervised was the design and development of the revolutionary 10 Meter, Multiple-Mirror Keck Telescope, based on top of Mauna Kea, Hawaii.

A Sweet Story

Twenty-eight years earlier a rude, racist interviewer had marred the start of Kenow's engineering career. At his 1983 retirement party, 200 attendees, including department directors, scores of engineers, technicians and clerks, honored him. The Regents of the University of California conferred on Kenow the title of Staff Senior Scientist Emeritus.

Kenow recalls his father's guidance in choosing engineering studies over art courses in high school. His pragmatic choice of engineering was greatly influenced by the Great Depression and the war in China. Now in retirement, he has finally found time to develop his artistic talents, enjoying clay sculpting and stone carving.

Wing Mar, a fraternity brother of Kenow Lou assisted in the interviews and research for this story.

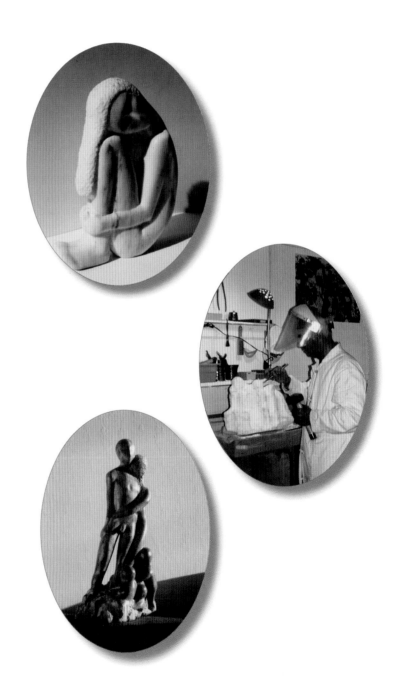

Kingdon Lou

葉景俊

The Navy Was His Second Chance

By Gladys Ikeda

Kingdon Lou made a breakthrough in his work when he was able to identify the presence of a hormone indicating pregnancy…. With this came the first home pregnancy test, called "Daisy Two". Other diagnostic test for conditions and diseases followed.

The Great Depression and
Going West to Canton, China

As a child of two cultures, growing up partly in both with little grounding in either, Kingdon Lou might have been destined to a life of menial work in the Chinese enclaves of Stockton or San Francisco. Yet, with efforts born of his innate intelligence and ability, perseverance, support from his family, plain hard work and some fortuitous circumstances, Kingdon overcame language barriers, financial hurdles and racial obstacles, to chart a brilliant career in immunological research spanning more than 30 years. During the course of his professional life, he received five patents and garnered recognition for several scientific papers he wrote or coauthored.

Kingdon was born in the United States in 1922. In 1934, at the age of 12, he and his siblings, with their mother, were sent back to China while his father remained in Stockton, Calif. In the pattern typical of Chinese sojourners during this era of Chinese migration, the children were to be educated in their ancestral homeland and it was generally intended that the fathers would stay in the United States to continue working to pay for their children's trip and their education and would follow later after the family was settled. Kingdon's father was a successful potato farmer but the potato price fell during

the Great Depression, causing the family's fortunes to fall. Sending the family to Canton to live off the ancestral land seemed the best alternative.

During his teen years, Kingdon immersed himself in learning Cantonese in school but spoke only the village dialect at home. English became a virtually forgotten language. When the Sino-Japanese war worsened, putting their lives in jeopardy, Kingdon and his brother, Kenow, returned to California, in 1940.

As poor young men without job skills or English proficiency, they parted so each could try to make it on his own. Kingdon returned to Stockton to a part-time job as a waiter at a restaurant run by his cousin. In the meantime, he tried but failed to get a high school diploma—his English was so poor that he dropped out of school after two weeks, not understanding the lessons and unable to complete the homework assignments.

In time he drifted to San Francisco where he roomed in an apartment with several other young men from Stockton to find work in the shipyards. Eventually completing a trade school "course", widely recognized at that time as a scam on young immigrants without resources, Kingdon qualified as a journeyman shipfitter's helper. He was hired at Bethlehem Steel for $20-$30 a week, a magnificent sum for a poor Chinese youth in the early 1940s.

Joining the U.S. Navy and the two Wars

Kingdon attempted to enlist in the U.S. Navy shortly after the bombing of Pearl Harbor on December 7, 1941, only to learn that all ratings except steward were closed to "Orientals". Wanting something more, Kingdon waited until September 1942 to join the Navy, when the military finally opened all ratings to Asians. Kingdon requested an assignment as a gunner, machinist, or boatswain, but fate intervened and he was sent to work in the Hospital Corps. "Little did I know that this assignment would be a turning point in my life," he later wrote, "building a foundation which would eventually lead me to a career in the biomedical field." During his months of training with the Hospital Corps, Kingdon studied not only the technical aspects of his assignment but also the English language, educating himself to become proficient in what was to him a foreign tongue. Training in operating room technique, Kingdon qualified as an instrument nurse, working alongside sur-

geons for the balance of his naval career during World War II. During his service, Kingdon escaped death when a kamikaze plane off Okinawa sank the first ship to which he was assigned, the USS destroyer Mannert L. Abele, DD-733. Not long after, the young navy corpsman was transferred to the destroyer tender USS Altair, AD 11. He remained on the Altair, sailing in the Pacific War Zone for the balance of the war, serving as the senior corpsman.

Discharged from active duty from the Navy, Kingdon returned to civilian life in Stockton to a job as a waiter in his cousin's restaurant. He now had a young wife, but his future was still uncertain, even as he enrolled at the local junior college while working early hours at a second job supply-

ing local restaurants with fresh meat and produce. In 1949 his first son was born, and he graduated from junior college and enrolled at the College of Pacific (now University of Pacific).

On a lark, he applied to Stanford University and was surprised to be accepted. It was only with the encouragement of his father and his wife that Kingdon moved to Palo Alto, 85 miles away, to begin studies in biological science at the prestigious but expensive private university. To make ends meet, his family remained in Stockton where his wife was employed, and he took a delivery job for a Palo Alto Chinese take-out restaurant. What he earned barely paid his gasoline costs. The primary benefit of that job was to provide him with a Chinese meal!

The Korean War intervened before he could begin a second year of Stanford studies. Recalled on 72 hours' notice in 1950 to report for active duty in the Navy, the young father was assigned to a combat surgical team with the Marines and eventually ending up as a corpsman up on the USS LST 1040. During the 30-day trip home from Korea, a sailor on another LST suffered an attack of appendicitis, requiring immediate surgery. That particular ship had a doctor but no operating room technician on board. Kingdon, as the only qualified corpsman nearby, had to cross over to the other LST. A line was fired to the other ship; a pulley system with a board creating a bosun's chair transferred him along that line between ships. (To break the monotony of life on board, his mischievous shipmates slackened the line so the bosun's chair skimmed the top of the water, wetting the seat of Kingdon's pants.) For his help with the surgery, which was successful, the crew from the other ship returned him to his own ship with a supply of fresh provisions. Despite their antics, Kingdon magnanimously shared the provisions with his shipmates, who were by then down to eating canned goods.

Stanford University

Kingdon resumed his studies after his discharge, graduating from Stanford in 1952. He was admitted to graduate school, majoring in Medical Microbiology in the Stanford University School of Medicine. His second son was born during his first year of graduate school. For his graduate research topic, Kingdon chose atopy, the condition of hereditary dispositions to serious allergic reactions, because of his own wife's frequent bouts with asthma and his sons' allergies. Kingdon studied by day; by night he had a part-time job at San Jose O'Connor Hospital, where he soon was put in charge of the hospital's lab tech training program.

With a masters' thesis, entitled "Serological Studies of the Atopic Antibodies", dedicated to his wife and sons, he earned his Masters' Degree from Stanford in 1956. The year was momentous for other reasons as well: he and his family were reunited in San Jose after years of separation due to his Stanford studies and Korean War service. Moreover, by this time his work had attracted notice from others, and he was now the Chief Technician at O'Connor Hospital.

The close of his academic career came at a time of significant breakthroughs in the field of immunology. Gamma globulin, the major component of serum protein, was identified as critical in the body's ability to ward off disease. Kingdon writes, "This marks the beginning of diagnostic medicine utilizing immunological reaction and in-vitro reagents." His graduate school experience placed him on the ground floor of such research.

Recruited by Hyland Laboratories, a division of Baxter Laboratories, to conduct research in their fledgling diagnostic laboratory on rheumatoid arthritis as an autoimmune disease, Kingdon was uncertain about taking a new job with an uncertain but promising and exciting future. Once more his wife encouraged him, despite his own misgivings about the sacrifices he was further imposing on her and their sons. Again leaving his family behind, he moved to a rented "shack" in Glendale, in a neighborhood where Asians and blacks were not welcome; unknowingly, he broke the color barrier.

Breakthrough in Diagnostic Testing

Through his research, Kingdon and his mentor, Dr. Roy Fisk, who recruited him to Hyland, successfully developed the first in-vitro reagent to detect the rheumatoid arthritis factor. Kingdon went on to make a breakthrough in in-vitro testing that identified the presence of chorionic gonadotrophic hormone in a pregnant woman. With this came the first home pregnancy test, called "Daisy Two" by the lab's marketing people. Similar test kits with some improvements and modifications are still available in drug stores.

Kingdon and Dr. Fisk also perfected a method of incorporating an antibody in gel medium for quantitation of a serum protein constituent. Due to their work, Hyland Laboratory was the first company to provide the medical community with this important adjunct tool for the diagnosis of disease.

In 1967, Kingdon was recruited by Hoffmann-LaRoche in New Jersey to become their senior scientist in a new diagnostic division in the field of immunodiagnostics. In his move to Hoffmann-LaRoche, Kingdon purchased a home in Upper Montclair in a neighborhood that, until his ownership, was all-white, another breakthrough for the accidental pioneer.

For the next two and a half decades, Kingdon's scientific accomplishments continued to attract notice, and other laboratories and researchers for various projects recruited him. He conducted research and developed tests for blood cholesterol, colon cancer, prostate cancer, HIV/AIDS virus, and plant pathogens. Kingdon also served his community as an Orange County grand juror for 18 months—six months longer than the usual term—writing two well-received reports on education to prevent disease and HIV/AIDS.

Perseverance, Talent and Luck

Kingdon Lou rose from a poor, failing high school dropout to hold five patents, authorship of 12 technical and scientific papers and attain high professional and managerial positions in prestigious immunological research firms. He was listed for two decades in the American Men and Women of Science. His attainment to the high professional and managerial positions in prestigious immunological research companies has been a remarkable ascent of a talented and courageous man. He said he owes his success to the time spent in the U.S. Navy. As Kingdon said, "I was in the right place at the right time even though I did not realize it...."

Wing Mar, a classmate of Kingdon Lou when he returned to the U.S., assisted with the interviews and research of this article.

K. C. Li

Miner, Industrialist, Patriot and Father

By Marie Li Chun

Little could that boy in China know that he would be a significant factor in the mining of wolframite, the refining and application of tungsten - on a worldwide scale and, in so doing, not only bring prosperity to Red Mountain but connect Southern California to the East Coast steel companies. That little boy was Kuo-Ching Li who brought us tungsten, the filament in our light bulbs.

Just a short 100 miles north of Los Angeles is the dusty, dingy mining town of Red Mountain, Calif. It straddles a main, north-south route in California that traverses along the eastern slopes of the Sierras, loosely defining the eastern reach of the Mojave Desert. Today, the town looks much like it did 50 years ago, except that there are only two miners there now, brothers, eking out a living mining wolframite, the ore of tungsten.

Curiously, their mining techniques are not very different from those used by a Chinese boy nearly a century earlier—in a similar mine some 7,000 miles away in China. Little could that boy in China know that he would be a significant factor in the mining of wolframite, the refining and application of tungsten on a worldwide scale and, in so doing, not only bring prosperity to Red Mountain but connect Southern California to the East Coast steel companies. That little boy was Kuo-Ching Li who brought us tungsten, the filament in our light bulbs. At the same time, he was cherished for his love of family and his part in American history. K.C.'s youngest daughter, Marie, tells his life story.

From Changsha to London to New York

My father, K. C. Li, was born in Changsha, Hunan province, China in 1892. He was the second of six sons and two daughters. Although they came from a peasant farming family, K. C. credits his mother who was illiterate for making sure they got a good education.

Dad liked to tell us that he was short (4'11") with bowed legs because of all the hard labor he did in the mines as a child. From the time when he was eight, he would crawl into the tunnel with other child workers. He was one of the lead children who went farthest into the mine, digging the ore by hand. He would hand his bucket of ore to the next child who passed it back to the child behind. When the day's work was done the children would back out the way they had entered because of the tight space.

My father attended Hunan Technical Institute in China. In 1911, he was commissioned by the Qing government to explore tin in southwest China. K. C. surveyed Yao Kang Sein in Wuling's mountain range in Hunan. While there, an innkeeper complained that large outcrops from the mountain would often fall into his back garden. The stones (ores) were then made into effective stoves and other tools. A souvenir stone given to K.C. portended an unbelievable future for him. That "stone" was wolframite, the most important tungsten-bearing mineral.

K. C. took the Empress Dowager's imperial exams for education abroad. The exam was very rigorous, lasting several weeks, and included math, science and history, as well as Chinese classics. He was one of two in China who won that specialized government scholarship. He chose to attend the Royal School of Mines (established in 1851), Imperial College, in London. He learned to speak English in London. He studied under Prof. S. J. Truscott who was dismissive of the wolframite crystal my father had shown him in 1913. "With the discovery that the Germans were effectively using tungsten in the manufacture of ammunition there started the scramble for tungsten. An immediate effect was the rise in price of tungsten to almost $100.00 a unit in the United States. [As opposed to the eight to 10 shillings per unit as quoted by Prof. Truscott]. I lost no time in hurrying back to China," in the foreward from K.C. Li's book, Tungsten, new third edition.

In London, Dad would identify his Hunan souvenir stone as wolframite. K.C. returned to China before World War I and helped establish Yu Hou Tungsten Mining Company. By 1915, the first shipment of tungsten ore from China was delivered to Bethlehem Steel Company and a subsequent shipment was delivered to J. P. Morgan's United States Steel Company. The shipments were assayed and found to be some of the purest wolframite ever mined. China has about 75 percent of the world's tungsten. Tungsten has the highest melting point of all metals and is corrosion resistant. It is used for light bulbs as well as electron and television tubes, x-rays, heating elements and spacecraft. During World War I, Germany manufactured high-speed steel from tungsten.

English and American steel companies quickly followed suit and an army of American mining engineers was sent to China.

K. C. came to the United States about 1915 and established Wah Chang (meaning "great development") Company in 1916. The company began as an importer/exporter of common goods like vermicelli, sesame-seed candy, and other Chinese items. It was always K.C.'s intention to import tungsten but he had to raise the capital. The struggle must have been difficult to raise money and support his family.

Family Man on Long Island

Although previously married with two daughters in China, Dad married Grace Fung around 1915. Our mother was born in Brooklyn, N.Y., to a Methodist minister. She spoke Cantonese. My father spoke Hunanese and Mandarin; they spoke English in our home. Mother was about 18 when she married Father. My eldest sister was born in 1916 in Brooklyn. My parents had four daughters and a son.

Our family moved to Long Island. We five children were raised in a big old house. We were very close. Daddy said, "I want to raise you children in America because I think it is the land of opportunity." He did not want to live in an urban environment. He wanted a place where he could raise his children and his Chinese vegetables. If we got bad marks at school, we had to do extra weeding. I remember I was so young that I couldn't differentiate between weeds and seedlings, so I had to pick rocks. Father thought being useful was very important.

Dad had a sense of humor but he was a strict disciplinarian. Every morning he took the Long Island Railroad train into New York City and his pockets were filled with quarters and dimes for the subway, and three newspapers. We used to steal change from his pockets. One time, Dad got mad. He sent us to a room with orders not to come out until one of us admitted guilt. My older siblings sent me out. I was four. I put out my hand for a spanking, and I started bawling before he hit me. He laughed. That was the end of the punishment.

In the afternoon when my sister, Madeline, and I were in grade school we would cut school and take the train to New York to see the show at the Paramount Theater using Daddy's loose change. For fifty cents, you could see a movie and a stage show. There were Duke Ellington, Count Basie, Nat King Cole – that's how I fell in love with jazz. (Later, Marie Chun interviewed jazz artists on Pacifica Radio KPFK in the mid-1970s.) We would time it so we could see the movie or stage show twice before taking the train to get home before Daddy could find out. My brother swore he took that loose change and learned how to fly at Roosevelt Field! My brother, during World War II became a pursuit pilot with the U.S. Army Airforce serving in the China-Burma-India theater.

There were not any Chinese living near us. But my father laid down the law: we were not to marry anyone but Chinese or we would be disowned. It was only when my sister studied at Wellesley that she brought home some Chinese from MIT and other schools. That was the first time we ever saw any other young Chinese men, much less Chinese women. There were neither Chinese schools nor churches for us. There was no Chinese community. We did have a Mandarin tutor live with us for a couple of years, but we hated it.

Much later, my father relented. One of my sisters fell in love with a white man and she sobbed loudly all during my marriage ceremony. My father sensed what was wrong and he wrote us a long letter saying, "If any one of you wants to marry outside of the race, as long as he is an upstanding and honest citizen, it is okay."

But this was also the era when we would be chased home by kids throwing rocks at us and yelling "chinky chinky Chinaman". We did play with the white neighborhood kids. Most of the kids came to our place because we had a big yard

We did go to some birthday parties. But when we jumped into the neighborhood pool, it felt like everyone else jumped out. Even in college, I remember a lot of the boys looked at me as if I had just gotten off a spaceship.

The business, Wah Chang was in New York City. It grew fast. By 1932, my mother started keeping a guest book of visitors to our house. In 1933, writer Pearl Buck visited. T. V. Soong, H. H. Kung (Mme Chiang Kai-shek's brother and brother-in-law), the writer Lin Yu Tan, the philosopher Dr. Hu Shih, and Mayor LaGuardia were also guests. My mother and father both cooked Chinese food. My father would bring home goods from Chinatown and we would have a Chinese dinner. Before the visitors came, my father would brief us about our guests' achievements, how many children they had and something about their wives. We were expected to converse intelligently. It was excellent training. Afterwards, he would ask us our opinion of the guests. He would always listen to us. He was very open-minded.

My brother, K. C. Li, Jr., was an only son and Madeline's twin. A lot was expected of him. When he was 16 years old, he went around the world aboard a cargo ship. My mother was dead set against it but my father insisted it would be a good education. The sisters were jealous; we were feminists way back then. We all went to Friends Academy a Quaker school. My brother went to Kent School and attended Swarthmore. I went to Skidmore College in Saratoga Springs in 1943.

The Mining Engineer Patriot

My father had to deal with a lot of people: businessmen, politicians, scientists, Chinese, Caucasians, etc. He knew about corruption and politics, but he had to deal with these people. He was very political. He was responsible for Madame Chiang Kai-shek speaking in front of the United States Senate, the first woman to do so. She was able to raise a lot of money for China's defense against the Japanese invasion. Although Dad considered us children Americans, I believe he became a naturalized citizen late in his life. This was because he hated the immigration acts. Immigration officials gave him a terrible time when he came into this country; they gave him a terrible time each time he came from Canada or abroad. He suffered a lot of racial prejudice, as did many Chinese Americans at that time.

My father had invented his own process of refining tungsten. It was much more convenient, efficient, and cheaper. He had his own refining company in New Jersey. Chinese tungsten was very much in demand because it had few impurities. Tungsten was not only used as filament in light bulbs, it is also a highly heat-resistant metal. Before the outbreak of Pearl Harbor, Dad came home from China and told us that something was brewing. He said it was on the level of World War I. He was already talking with Franklin D. Roosevelt. He traveled a lot to Washington D. C. The Axis powers were buying up tungsten reserves; tungsten was an alloy to make steel stronger. In June of 1940, Dad told Roosevelt, "You must do something about this." Cordell Hull, FDR's secretary of state, immediately worked on restricting the flow to Japan of Chinese tungsten housed in French Indochina. The transaction was completed in twenty four hours. Dad also helped the U.S. stockpile tungsten in preparation for our own involvement in the war.

Under K .C. Li's leadership, Wah Chang Corp. grew. The headquarters were in Manhattan, on two floors of the famous Woolworth Building, with plants in Glen Cove, N.Y.; Fairlawn, N.J.; Texas City, Texas; Albany, Ore.; and Huntsville, Ala. It operated tungsten mines in Bishop, Calif.; Lincoln, Nev.; China and Brazil. K. C. Li served as governor of the Commodity and National Metals Exchanges.

> *"You will understand that prejudice has nothing to do with you. It is the problem and insecurity of the bigots."*

Before the war, Dad helped with the China Relief Assn. During World War II, he was an adviser on tungsten to the U. S. government and an adviser to the Chinese Embassy in Washington. He was the Chinese delegate to the Bretton Woods Conference in 1944. He served on the Council of Foreign Relations and the China Foundation for Education and Culture.

In his later life, Dad was involved in exotic metals. He built the first heat shield for the returning space ships. He also built the housing for the first atomic submarine, the Nautilus, christened in January of 1954. Daddy would talk about all this when we were kids. He talked about this energy that would be able to send a ship around the world for a year without needing to refuel. He talked about energy that could heat and light a house for twenty-five years. We didn't realize at the time that he was talking about atomic energy.

When Teledyne bought out Wah Chang in 1967, it was because of the exotic metals plant up in Albany, Ore. By then, Dad was into superconductors. He was into titanium and zirconium. Wah Chang manufacturing plant was established in 1956 to supply zirconium for the U.S. naval nuclear program. It began with 140 employees and a single building on forty-five acres in Oregon. Teledyne merged with Allegheny in 1996.

My father was a fair employer. He was very proud of the fact that his plants were never unionized. The union would come around to organize but the workers were satisfied with their treatment and benefits. My father was a very ethical person. A lot of his engineers and workers were very loyal to him.

My brother was the only Chinese pursuit pilot in the U.S. Army Air Corps during World War II. He flew with the 14th Air Force under Gen. Claire Chennault. When he got his plane, he asked my father what to name the plane. Dad suggested "Spirit of Hunan," but my brother chose "Vicious Virgin." My brother got shot down and was captured by the

Chinese. The Chinese thought my brother was a spy because he looked Chinese but did not speak Chinese, and he wore a pilot's jacket with both Chinese and American flags on the back.

My father had been very hopeful about the communists. He had thought that Mao would be the answer to the corruption of the Chinese government. He was going to return to China himself. He thought he would be safe because he, like Mao, was from the same province and both had started with similar peasant backgrounds. But Dad's best friend, T. P. Hou warned him, "Do not go back to China under any circumstances; your life will be in danger." So my father changed his mind at the last minute. In the 1950s and 1960s, it became clear how unsuccessful Mao's regime was, even though it was very idealistic. My cousins who stayed in China suffered under the Revolution.

My father remained active in American politics through McCarthyism. He was an active leader in Chambers of Commerce. He was a strong Democrat all the way and adored FDR and Adlai Stevenson. We used to listen to FDR's Fireside Chats. One year, I told Dad I was going to vote for Nixon. He said if I didn't change my mind, he would lock me in the attic until voting day passed.

K. C. Li was also a humanitarian and philanthropist. He was asked by Richard Patterson, head of protocol for New York City, to invite Israel to join New York's World's Fair. When Ben-Gurion complained that Israel had no resources, my father said, "You have the Great Salt Sea." He set up the Li Foundation in 1940 with his younger brother. For decades, the Li Foundation's mission has been to "promote friendly relationships between the USA and China by providing support for scholars in China to study in the USA." Each year, twenty scholarships are available for graduate, postgraduate, and postdoctoral students. There were also scholarships established at Columbia University and University of Nevada.

Someone introduced me once as "the daughter of the wealthiest Chinese". I was furious. I was so offended. My father was never about money. He was above all a patriot of China and America.

I remember my father as being strict, as being patriotic, but with a wonderful sense of humor. His ability to network with other people, not only in science, but in business, politics, and for social action was paramount. And he was so proud of being Chinese. He knew we received a lot of prejudice. He must have suffered more. He said, "That should not bother you. You will understand that prejudice has nothing to do with you. It is the problem and insecurity of the bigots." My dad died in 1961 from a heart attack in New York City.

Marie Li Chun, youngest daughter of K. C. Li, who resides in Southern Calif, was initially interviewed by Gayle Mar-Chun. More information from follow up oral history was used by Susie Ling. Some material is also based on Senate Congressional Record No. 46-4 of 15 March 1961, and a forward by K.C. Li in his book, "Tungsten, Its History, Geology, Ore-Dressing, Metallurgy, Chemistry, Analysis, Applications and Economics", (New York: Reinhold Publishing, 1943). Marie Chun has been a friend of the Chinese Historical Society of Southern California since its founding.

Maggie Gee

朱美嬌

Bomber Pilot
and
Atom Smasher

Interviewed by Wing Mar
and
written by Edgar Wong

"Maggie" Gee describes herself simply as a woman who fervently pursued her life passions—undistracted by society's traditional role for women and unhindered by the prejudice against Chinese Americans.

Sitting in her living room in Berkeley, amidst her oriental rugs and art objects from around the globe, Margaret "Maggie" Gee describes herself simply as a woman who fervently pursued her life passions—undistracted by society's traditional role for women and unhindered by the prejudice against Chinese Americans. Maggie tells of her passions for flying, nuclear physics, and politics that have led to three unique careers. She also furnished copies of some memorabilia and a few articles providing historical details for this paper.

A Member of Aviation's List of 100 Most Influential Women and Hall of Fame

Maggie Gee has received two noteworthy awards from Women in Aviation International (WAI). In December 2003, honoring the Centennial of Flight, WAI paid tribute to "100 Women Who made a Difference." The list of 100 is comprised of industry leaders, aviation advocates and pilot superstars. The pilots included: Blanche Stuart (first American women to fly solo in 1910); astronaut Eileen Collins (first women commander of a space shuttle, Discovery, in 1999); Hazel Ah Ying Lee and Margaret "Maggie" Gee (two Chinese American pilots who served in World War II). Earlier in 1993, the WAI inducted the Women Airforce Service Pilots (WASP) group into its Pioneer Hall of Fame—Maggie Gee was a WASP member.

After earning her wings,
Maggie co-piloted the B-17 "Flying Fortress."

Maggie Gee grew up in the 1930s when that generation was fascinated by airplanes. In 1927, Charles Lindbergh made his historic trans-Atlantic flight from Roosevelt Field near New York City to Le Bourget Field in Paris and received a hero's welcome throughout the world. A year later Amelia Earhart became the first woman to fly as a passenger across the Atlantic and in 1932 she became the first women to fly solo across the Atlantic. The Lindbergh and Earhart flights have captured the imagination of the world like few events in history. As a young girl growing up in the East Bay, Maggie recalls spending days gazing up at the airplanes flying out of the Oakland airport, imagining herself piloting the aircraft. Little did she know then that her fascination would someday become reality.

When America entered World War II in December of 1941, Maggie tried to join military units such as the WAC (Women's Army Corps) and the Navy's WAVES (Women Accepted for Volunteer Emergency Service), but she was too young. To help in the war effort, she took a drafting job at the Mare Island naval repair facility in Vallejo, CA. Hearing later of a new organization called the Women Airforce Service Pilots (WASP), Maggie cashed in her war bonds, left her job and moved to Nevada to take flying lessons in hopes of qualifying for the program. The WASP applicants were required to be already in possession

of pilot's licenses and to have a minimum of 35 hours of flight time. Throughout the course of its two-year operation, over 25,000 women applied but only 1,879 were accepted; the WASP training was so stringent that only 1,074 graduated and received their wings.

Maggie Gee was accepted and entered WASP flight training at Avenger Field in Sweetwater, Tex. Except for formation flying and gunnery, the civilian women pilots received training identical to that given to male pilots of the U.S. Army Air force. The principal assignment of the women pilots was to ferry planes from the aircraft factories to stateside air bases for overseas delivery. After earning her wings, Maggie co-piloted the B-17 "Flying Fortress" bombers in training aerial gunners in mock aerial dogfights; she also took pilots aloft to renew their instrument ratings. Maggie Gee finished her service at Nellis Army Air Force Base in Nevada.

By the time WASP was disbanded in December 1944, the women pilots had delivered 12,652 aircraft and flown a total of 60 million miles in 78 different types of aircraft. They had established a safety record that surpassed their male counterparts, and they had proved to have as much stamina and endurance as the men. In the course of this loyal service, 38 women had given their lives. It would be more than 30 years before the U.S. Air Force would again train female recruits to fly.

In the meantime, U.S. military leaders totally overlooked the record set by WASP pilots, who had more than proved that women could and would fly for their country with as much dedication, courage, and aptitude as men. Belatedly, in 1977 President Carter signed a bill giving the WASP war veteran status. In 1979 the Department of the Air Force authorized official discharge papers for the WASPs—Maggie proudly displays her honorable discharge certificate in her home office. In May 1993, a WASP memorial was dedicated at Avenger Field in Texas. A fitting closing—The last sentence from the WAI "100 most influential women" tribute in December 2003 to Maggie Gee read: "Besides her contribution to the war effort, she is still a role model for young Asian women who are interested in aviation."

A Physicist at
Lawrence Livermore National Laboratory

After the war, Maggie went to UC Berkeley for her degree in physics and graduate courses in math. In 1958, she began her career at the University of California's Lawrence Livermore National Laboratory (LLNL), operated for the U.S. Department of Energy. The lab's mission during the Cold War was to develop safe, secure, and reliable use of nuclear energy (i.e., nuclear weapons) for the national defense; later, the mission was broadened to include biomedicine and environmental science.

From the early days at Livermore, computers were the essential tools in thermonuclear explosion (radiation transport) calculations. Supercomputers were in its infancy at the time and Maggie made use of crude, by today's standards, one-dimensional codes to assist in verifying new weapon designs. She often had to extrapolate the results with hand calculations and her woman's intuition. As a result of the immense growth in computing technology—and Maggie's contribution to the laboratory's software development skills—the lab's capability for multidimensional physics models and advanced nuclear warhead designs were enhanced dramatically.

The Navy's Polaris missile program (as well as the Air Force's Minuteman missile program) wanted lightweight nuclear devices so that a single missile could carry as many as 12 warheads to different targets. The Livermore lab's superior computer models for warhead design, the physics validated in atmospheric and underground nuclear tests, were highly successful in developing nuclear warheads for the Navy's Polaris program and later for the Poseidon missile.

Livermore's Magnetic Fusion Program for the peaceful use of nuclear fusion energy was another beneficiary of the lab's computing capability. In fusion, two light nuclei (such as hydrogen) combine into one new nucleus (such as helium) and release enormous energy in the process. One approach to fusion uses a powerful magnetic field to confine a plasma (a gas consisting of charged ions and electrons) for generating energy in a controlled manner. Comprehensive predictive modeling capability for magnetic fusion, benchmarked against ongoing laboratory experiments, became the initial step in Livermore's research and development of magnetic fusion reactors.

After her retirement in 1988, Maggie continued as a consultant working in the magnetic fusion program. Maggie Gee's 30-year service at the prestigious national laboratory had helped to deter nuclear war through making credible the country's doctrine of "mutual assured destruction."

A Pioneer in Political Activism

Maggie Gee's interest in politics and feminism began in the days of Franklin Delano Roosevelt when women pilots were called "aviatrix" and well before the terms "activist" and "feminist" became household words. Ever a socially concerned and responsible person she actively participated in resolving social issues nationally and in her community.

In 1960, Maggie attended the Democratic National Convention and watched John F. Kennedy win the presidential nomination. As a delegate, she attended the Democratic conventions that nominated Michael Dukakis in 1988 and Bill Clinton in 1992. Maggie still remembers vividly her service of more than a decade ago as a member of the 1992 Democratic Party Platform Committee. She recalls contributing to many of the planks in their multi-faceted platform—especially to those that were her special interest.

Some of her favorite causes: (1) The environment—reduce toxic and oil waste; conserve critical resources and protect the environment, forest and wetlands for ourselves and future generations; (2) Civil and equal rights—support the ratification of the Equal Rights Amendment, affirmative action, stronger protection of voting rights for racial and ethnic minorities including language access to voting; and, (3) National service—create new opportunities for citizens to serve each other, their communities and their country.

Today, Maggie continues her love for political service; currently, she is a member of the California State Democratic Party Executive Board and the Alameda County Democratic Central Committee. Beyond party politics, she volunteers her time to community organizations, including city boards and nonprofit organizations in Berkeley.

Steve & Milly Liu

Two Valued and Cherished Gifts

By Wing Mar

The Liu's generosity is legendary. Their donation was the largest the Harbor-UCLA Medical Center Research Center and Education Institute had ever received.

Doctor Steve Liu was threading a cardiac catheter up the femoral artery of an anesthetized dog under the glare of hot laboratory lights. It was 1970. He was carefully measuring the arterial blood pressures and the gaseous blood values while threading the tiny plastic tube up the aorta. Beads of perspiration appeared across his forehead. Dr. Liu was intense in his scientific investigation and was always meticulous in his collection of information. He was fascinated by the cardiac cycle of the normal and abnormal heartbeat. The understanding and the insights derived from research by these early pioneer cardiologists form the basis for our modern treatment of heart disease.

By then Dr. Liu had been doing research in the dynamics of blood circulation for over 15 years and had published papers and books on the subject. He is married to Milly Liang, who is a respected pediatric cardiologist in the South Bay communities of Los Angeles.

Chi Kong (Steve) Liu

Steve Liu's grandfather was an herbalist. During the years before the advent of western medicine in South China, the practicing herbalist—after listening to the medical problem of an ill patient—would make an independent diagnosis of the medical condition by studying the pulse and its rhythm by a gentle touch on the wrist. Another important diagnostic skill was observing the tongue and the general demeanor of the sick patient. Grandfather would then go to the kitchen and return with a brew made from steeping a mixture of specially selected herbs in steaming boiling water. This concoction of medicinal tea (cha)—having a pervasive aroma and a bitter taste—is to be swallowed quickly, followed by eating sweet dried plums for offsetting the bitter brew. Steve Liu never met his grandfather, who died before Steve was born; but as fate would have it, Steve would spend his life working

to understand the human pulse and its implications for life itself in new and different ways.

Steve Liu was the second son of Liu Chock Fan. His older brother was chosen by tradition to run the family pharmaceutical business while young Steve was encouraged to study hard and enter medical school. Steve's father was a successful businessman and one of his products, an anti-diarrhea medication, is still being used in Asia. Chock Fan was active in the underground resistance to free China from imperial rule by the Manchurian dynasty, considered a foreign occupying power by the Han people.

Steve was the top student in high school in spite of his forced relocations during the turmoil of the Sino-Japanese war. After high school, he took the national entrance examination and was admitted to National Central University College of Medicine. It was there that he met Milly Liang.

In 1949, Steve attended Stanford University for postgraduate studies in hematology and cardiology. His first research project was in the hematology department. He helped devise a procedure that increased the yield of blood plasma from 85 percent to 100 percent. This breakthrough allowed Cutter Laboratories (now Bayer) and other laboratories to increase their production of blood plasma for the war effort during the Korean conflict in the early 1950s. In 1953 he gained a research position in Illinois with Dr. Aldo A. Luisada, a noted researcher in cardiac physiology, at the Chicago Medical School. He started to work on various laboratory animal hearts to gain valuable data. While at the Chicago Medical School, Steve—using his Chinese name, Chi Kong Liu—coauthored with Dr. Luisada in 1958 the book, "Cardiac Pressures and Pulses in Right and Left

photo by Jason Ivan

Heart Catheterization." This was the first such book written on this subject in the U.S. and was translated into several languages.

Milly Liang Liu

Milly Liu was born in Meixin, Guangdong, China. Her father was Liang Kwong Ying and her mother was Wong Sim Fong. Milly had one sister and three brothers. Of historical note: Milly's granduncle served as the consul general to the United States in 1888 when he negotiated with the U.S. government for better treatment of the Chinese laborers in this country working on the railroad and in the mining industry.

In the U.S., Milly Liu took her pediatric training at Stanford University and enrolled in the University of Chicago for further pediatric residency training. Later, she became a fellow of pediatric cardiology at the University of Illinois. After four productive years in the Midwest, Milly and Steve were ready to move to California.

Careers in Southern California

Dr. Steve Liu was chosen to be the Chief of Cardiology at Harbor-UCLA Medical Center. He was in charge of the catheterization laboratory and cardiac research center while Milly started her private pediatric practice in the South Bay. In 1963 there was no cardiac research center outside of Harbor-UCLA in the South Bay area. Steve was recruited to set up cardiac units in many private hospitals. He wrote five books, and published 47 articles and 10 scientific abstracts during his 50 year career and retired in 2000. Steve is presently an honorary clinical professor of internal medicine at Harbor-UCLA.

Dr. Milly Liu was the doctor for the children of many physicians in the community. A friend and colleague Dr. Michael Criley noted how grateful he was as a father and a doctor to have Milly care for his four sons. The visits for their

STEVE & MILLY LIU

sons were made non-stressful by Milly's kind and cheerful demeanor, according to Dr. Criley, a noted cardiologist who is the creator of our worldwide "paramedic system". Milly Liu also taught at Harbor-UCLA. She is a clinical professor of pediatrics at UCLA School of Medicine. In 1992 Milly Liu was appointed to the prestigious Board of Visitors of UCLA Medical School. One of the committee's assignments was to assist Dean Gerald Levey in assessing the relevancy and adequacy of the curriculum being taught at the David Geffen School of Medicine at UCLA. Dean Levey acknowledged the value Milly added to the committee with her dedicated participation in all the meetings. Steve was one of the founders of the original Chinese American Physician Society of Southern California that eventually became the Asian Pacific Physicians Assn. of the South Bay.

A Hobby of Note

While attending the weekly cardiac department conference at the UCLA Westwood campus, Steve would encounter the freeway congestion enroute back to the South Bay. To avoid the rush-hour traffic, Steve took an evening course with Duke Hayes, an expert stock market chartist, who taught a stock investment evening class at UCLA in the early 1960s. Steve developed a Midas-like feel for the market pulse. Whether it was the imperceptible telltale blip of an electrocardiogram—or the graph of a stock— they had a profound meaning for Steve Liu. Mr. Hayes who was well versed in fundamentals and technical expertise in the stock market taught Steve well. This sensitivity has rewarded Steve handsomely.

Steve's fascination with stocks continues and his reading of the pulsating market beat is still sharp. Steve and Milly live modestly; and, their two children—Patty and Richard—would be embarrassed if they exhibited their affluence, Milly noted. The couple is proud that they, as immigrants from China, could achieve professionally and contribute so greatly to American society.

Gifts to Posterity

The Lius' generosity is legendary. Remembering their roots in the Midwest and China, they continue to make regular donations to the University of Illinois and to the Chinese heritage scholarships (e.g. the Phi Tau Phi Scholastic Honor Society of America). Here in California, Milly and Steve gave significantly to the new South Bay YMCA fitness center and to the local hospitals. For example, at the 78-acre Harbor-UCLA Medical Center, one can visit the 'Liu Reading Room' at the A. F. Parlow Library. But their major community gift was funding a new medical research center. On May 30, 2003, the 23,000-square foot Liu Research Center was formally opened during a dedication ceremony of more than 500 guests. Earlier in 1999, it was noted by the Harbor-UCLA Medical Center Research and Education Institute fundraisers that the Milly and Steve Liu donation was the largest the center had ever received. "REI's research is world-renowned. We are pleased to help them continue their tradition."

In May 2004, Steve Liu and Milly Liu were honorees amongst 14 Legendary Research Medical Scientists who in 1952 started the Research and Education Institute at the Harbor-UCLA Medical Center (now the LA Biomedical Institute at Harbor-UCLA Medical Center). The event recognized a group of distinguished senior professors with internationally recognized accomplishments in the practice of medicine.

Steve and Milly Liu's most valued and cherished gift of all—of themselves to all that they touched.

Joyce Mar assisted in the interview and writing of this story.

Tom Woo

Networker Extraordinaire

By Edgar Wong with Melanda Woo Koe

From a chop suey restaurant, to architecture and construction, to one of the founders of the Standard Savings Bank.

In life's work, Tom Woo succeeded in part, because of his congenial and jovial approach with people. Even as a schoolboy, Tom was friendlier and larger than most of the boys his age—his many friends playfully nicknamed him "King Kong" after the principal character in the 1933 classic film. Perhaps working with people was a natural for Tom, whose parents gave him the ideal family environment for developing his balance of essential traits. His father was very quiet while blessed with a great amount of common sense and pragmatism. In contrast, Tom's mother was gregarious and artistically gifted. Both parents had a terrific sense of humor that made growing up in the Woo household fun. In this happy setting, they taught Confucian ethics and Chinese family values and they practiced the art of networking long before it became a common tool in the business world. These formative years taught Tom patience and tolerance and enhanced his own Woo sense of humor, which enabled him to network easily in a society that was ethnically varied, socially evolving, and economically growing. A glimpse into Tom's family history and work ventures follow.

were to meet at Promontory, Utah, in front of a cheering crowd and a big band. Grandfather Woo was part of an elite Chinese (and Irish) crew that was chosen to lay the final ten miles of track, completing the work in a record 12 hours. After working in Utah, he returned to China, invested in rice land with his savings, and enjoyed life as a wealthy landowner in his twilight years.

Tom's father, Woo Yet Wo, with his merchant immigration paper, came to America in 1906 and settled in Cleveland, Ohio. As many of the migrant workers then, Yet Wo left his wife Quon Shee (whom he married in 1903) and daughter Sui Sum (born in 1904) at home in China. Father Woo labored variously as a truck driver, laundryman, butcher and cook until he opened and operated a grocery store and a chop suey restaurant with other relatives. He saved enough money to bring Quon Shee to the U.S. and they were blessed with three children—Tom, Robert, and Jane—born a year apart in Cleveland in the mid-1920s. During the 1929 Great Depression, father Woo moved his family of five to Cambridge, Mass., to operate a laundry business. Six years later, he moved the entire clan to the San Fernando Valley to work on a farm. Disliking farming, father Woo moved his family to Los Angeles and opened a chop suey café with an uncle.

The Woo Ancestors

Grandfather Woo Hoo Chiang came to America to work on the Central Pacific Railroad. The first Chinese were hired in 1865 at $28 per month to perform the dangerous work of blasting rocks and laying ties over treacherous terrain during the harsh winters of the High Sierras. On May 10, 1869, the two transcontinental railroad end-sections

Tom Woo's Formative Years

From his birthplace in Ohio, Tom Fong Woo led

a nomadic life. He attended five different schools from Massachusetts to California. He adapted well and excelled in academics (he was valedictorian), in student government (student body vice president), and in sports (baseball, football, boxing and swimming). Like many kids growing up in the Depression era, Tom worked at grocery stores, drugstores, and restaurants. He later worked at the L.A. wholesale produce market as a swamper (a manual laborer) and truck driver when he was a teenager. He found time to attend church and several Chinese schools through the 10th grade where he was especially recognized for his skills at calligraphy. Tom is ambidextrous, which enabled him, with practice, to write and draw equally well with both hands.

Following high school, he was accepted as a candidate for military weather officer training. Successfully completing the first phase of coursework at the University of Oregon in Eugene, the program was abruptly terminated due to the ending of World War II. Tom was reassigned to complete his military service in a meteorological unit at the Army Air Force Weather Station in Hondo, Texas. Subsequently, he attended college at Wellesley's Babson Institute (Wellesley, Mass.), UCLA, UC Berkeley and USC. Tom received certificates in meteorology, cartography and topography and achieved his bachelor's degree from UC Berkeley in architecture with a minor in fine arts in 1950. After graduation, he settled down to one location but not to just one field of endeavor.

Tom (right), his younger brother Robert and sister Jane

The Tom Woo Family

Christmas 1953 was a special day for Tom. At a friend's holiday party he met his future wife, Judy Dan. Judy was born in Shanghai and raised in Hong Kong. Her father Dan Du-Yu (a.k.a. Dan Toa Yee) was a well-known film director and fine artist in China; her mother Yan Ming-Zhu (a.k.a. Ying Sheung Yin) was a popular film actress. Judy worked for Cathay Pacific Airways before entering—and winning—the 1952 Miss Hong Kong pageant. She came to Long Beach, Calif. to compete in the first annual Miss Universe beauty pageant, finishing as the 3rd runner-up. Universal Pictures filmed the coronation and signed Judy to a contract that began with a cameo role in the film "Destination Gobi" (1953). Other film performances to her credit were in "The King and I" (1956), "Pal Joey" (1957), "Spiral Road" (1962), and "Kill a Dragon" (1967). Her television work included appearances in popular shows such as "Perry Mason" (1962) and "Get Smart" (1969). Judy majored in speech and drama at Pepperdine College.

Tom and Judy were married in August 1954 at the Wayfarers' Chapel in Palos Verdes, Calif. They lived in a hillside home in Sherman Oaks designed by Tom to overlook the San Fernando Valley. There, they raised a family of three daughters: Judiann, Melanda, and Becky. Bringing up the girls in a traditional Chinese-American home, Judy continued to balance her acting career with family life while Tom was busy starting not only a career in architecture but also in construction.

Career and Community Work

Tom's diversified background led him to adopt a broad architectural career path in architecture, encompassing both design and construction. He gained a diversity of experience in many types of building and construction techniques through his work at architectural firms. This valuable experience enabled him to obtain his architectural and contractor's licenses. In 1960, he launched his own practice doing "turn key" projects combining single and multi-family dwellings, commercial and industrial complexes, and financial and health care facilities.

His networking with clients and financiers from all over the state led to his eventual participation in the banking industry. Together with five other investors in 1982, Tom became one of the founders of Standard Savings Bank. After establishing its first branch in Chinatown, the bank added five other branches along the so-called San Bernardino Freeway corridor. Today, Tom continues as a director.

He also served the City of Los Angeles as a building and safety commissioner, appointed by Mayor Tom Bradley. Commission meetings were held weekly to resolve public appeals pertaining to the municipal building code. One case involved the Chinese American Museum, and that contact led to Tom's participation on the museum's architectural selection committee for their Garnier Building renovation.

Preserving Chinese language and cultural traditions for the younger generation has been of utmost importance to Tom. He became active in the local cultural association and served several terms as president. Recognizing the need to unify 15 regional Chinese schools he helped organize the Southern California Council of Chinese Schools. For his efforts, Tom was elected the first president of this newly established association.

Judy and Tom

Tom Woo is semi-retired and continues networking with his bank and community-work colleagues. Ever ready for a new venture, Tom is busily honing his computer skills for Internet networking with family and friends. Grandparents Tom and Judy are looking forward to receiving e-mails from their granddaughters Caprial and Alia (now preschoolers) at the busy Koe household.

Ernest K. Lum 林金洮

A Complete Engineer

By Allen Gee

> *From an Hawaiian sugar plantation*
> *to the Apollo program.*

Introduction

Ernest Lum was a third generation Chinese American whose electrical engineering work was recognized by the Apollo astronauts. He grew up in Hawaii in a large church-going family and came to California to attend college, first in Los Angeles and then at UC Berkeley. He noted that, unlike Hawaii, California showed many signs of racial segregation just before World War II. Though mild-mannered by nature he was very active in campus integration, in the promotion of fair employment practices (FEPC), and in protesting the shipping of scrap metals to Japan. He spent the war years working at the Mare Island shipyards and after a few years in Hawaii was employed by the defense industry in Southern California.

The Berkeley campus then and now was a center of student activism. Just before World War II, racism against the Chinese in the Bay Area took many forms. San Francisco had no Chinese streetcar operators. Doctors in Chinatown had only Asian patients and a board-certified specialist would suffer because there were no referrals from the white community. Shell Oil began to hire Chinese graduates as professionals but Standard Oil of California (now Chevron) did not. On campus, social dancing across racial lines was notably absent. Fraternities were far from being integrated, with most of them excluding Jews and non whites. It was in this atmosphere that Ernie fought for equality and got his Chinese fraternity—the Pi Alpha Phi—recognized by the Interfraternity Council.

It should be noted that discrimination against Chinese was not as blatant as Jim Crow in the South, where doors to theaters, drinking fountains and restrooms were boldly marked "White Only" or "Black Only." As late as WW II a socially sensitive Asian getting off the train at Union Station in our nation's capital would immediately face a dilemma and needed to exercise control over more than just his temper. Ernie's oral history follows:

Family

My grandfather, Lum Yan Hoon, came to Hawaii as an independent merchant from Chungshan (near Canton) in 1874 during the reign of King Kalakaua. My father, Lum Kan Nam, arrived from China via Vancouver in 1892 during the reign of Queen Liliuokalani. My mother, Wong Lin, came to Hawaii at the age of two with her merchant parents in 1890. The family had a store at the Kawailoa Sugar Plantation and also leased a rice farm. In 1916, the year of my birth, my grandfather started lotus root farming, with most of the production shipped to San Francisco. I was born on the second story of my folks' dry goods and bakery store built by them in 1897 and located across the street from the resort hotel in Haleiwa on the northwest shore of Oahu. I was the sixth child with seven brothers and two sisters. I was married in Honolulu in 1948.

My wife, Fannie Lee, was a fourth generation American. Her grandfather and great-grandfather came together from China to Hawaii in 1883 and eventually owned a lumberyard. Her maternal grandparents emigrated from China to Japan, where her mother grew up. It was in 1923 (before Fannie was born) that a major catastrophe struck her family. Her mother brought her three young daughters to Japan to visit grandmother. On a day she left her daughters with her grandmother to baby-sit, a major earthquake hit, killing the three young girls. In 1946 Fannie graduated from Armstrong Business College (in Berkeley), where my younger sister also studied. In 1981 she retired from her job as administrative secretary for five consecutive school principals of the local Laguna Beach High School.

Fannie and I are blessed with four children. Wesley, Allan and Lorna were born in Hawaii; Randy arrived after we settled in Laguna Beach, Calif.

Education

My first schooling began in Haleiwa elementary and the local church. I eventually moved to Honolulu for the higher grades and to attend Chinese language school. I graduated from McKinley High in 1935. I spent the next year completing the high school equivalency for Chinese. Since I had a strong interest in radio and electronics and University of Hawaii had no such course, I took a boat to Los Angeles in 1936 to attend the National Technical School. I started classes at UC Berkeley in 1938 and obtained my BS in electrical engineering in 1942.

Career

Since I graduated from UC just after Pearl Harbor and was rejected for the draft because of color-blindness and

NASA

despite my ROTC training, I had no difficulty finding work in the defense industry. I worked for Mare Island Shipyards during the war and then went back home to Hawaii. In 1955 I returned to California to begin a 27-year stint in the aerospace industry.

During my first year at Mare Island, I was designing naval degaussing (to prevent steel hulls from activating magnetic mines) and electrical systems. Along with Lawrence S. Jue, I helped improve the snorkel system used by submarines to run the diesel engines while submerged. Then I was transferred to the radar design section to ease the backlog on war-related projects, which involved radar installations as well as a Combat Information Center to coordinate major operations.

At the end of the war in 1945 I returned to Honolulu. When the Korean War broke out in 1950, I rejoined the war effort by helping to reactivate the Pearl Harbor Naval Base. I hired and trained engineers on naval system designs. In short order we converted an older submarine to a snorkel type, re-outfitted a sea-going floating drydock and took many vessels out of mothballs.

In 1955 I returned to California to work for North American Rockwell for the rest of my professional career. I designed much of the test equipment used in planes, missiles and space systems.

In 1958-62 I worked in research and development to develop a supersonic (Mach 3) bomber to replace the aging

B-52. Only three were built, but much of the design work went into the B-1 (1983) and then the B-2 stealth bomber used in the 1990s.

In 1962-66 I was assigned to the Apollo project, which turned out to be most exciting. I did some electrical work for both the Saturn rockets and the Apollo modules that carried the astronauts to the moon. Much of my work was to design tests and test equipment for systems to operate in unknown environments with mission reliability. For this work I received a certificate of recognition signed by 28 astronauts.

From 1967 to my retirement in 1982 I worked for the electronics division in the new technology of integrated circuits and mini-computers. I had the primary responsibility to coordinate the numerous test programs and supply the needs of R&D projects.

Childhood

I had pleasant memories of my first home in Haleiwa and of the rice and lotus root farm nearby. I had such chores as plowing the field with a water buffalo and helping to prepare food for the farm hands that came mostly from Japan and the Philippines. Playtime included hiking, catching frogs, fishing, hunting with homemade bow and arrows, and surfing with redwood logs. When I moved to Honolulu at age seven, I had less time for recreation because Chinese school took away two hours six days a week. I did play on the baseball team in junior high and pitched and won the championship game one season.

Community/Activist

At Berkeley, being a center of student activism, I immediately joined groups to help solve problems of discrimination obvious to me with my Hawaiian upbringing. I was a member of the Student Body Welfare Council, staff secretary of Stiles Hall YMCA, and a member of Pi Alpha Phi founded by Chinese students. I worked to get the Japanese and Chinese student clubs recognized as on-campus activities and my fraternity recognized by the Interfraternity Council. I helped in removing discrimination in student housing and in student hiring by the registrar at the beginning of each term. I organized several boycotts of restaurants and clubs for unequal treatment of students and their employees. These activities I began as a student and continued after graduation when I held a full-time job at Mare Island. On some weekends I served as advisor at the San Francisco Chinese YMCA. At the end of WWII I helped entertain Japanese-American GIs stopping over in San Francisco enroute home to Hawaii.

In my years in Laguna Beach as my children were growing up, I had been active in sports as well as the PTA. I recovered from two serious auto accidents—once in Hawaii just before the Korean War and again late in my retirement. I liked to shop, to cook for family and friends, and to garden for exercise. Fannie and I met the beach crowd when we opened a coffee shop near the Laguna Beach Hotel for several summers in the 1960s. We also did much traveling in the states and back to Hawaii.

Wing Mar and Linda Chong assisted Allen Gee in writing the life story of Ernie Lum, who passed away Oct. 2, 2002.

Steve & Ella Leong

Our Successful Partnership

By Edgar Wong

梁冠華　蔡月嫦

> *"Many of us need to expand our knowledge of the business we are in … not only in the narrow technical areas we are involved in, but also in the less technical areas. For engineering, this includes manufacturing, construction, operation and maintenance. Actual experience in these fields is even better. All this background leads to a more balanced and broader-based individual, which improves the chances for promotion to middle and upper management."*

At the Fall 2002 meeting of the Chinese Historical Society, a special filming was made of the evening's program. The setting was similar to a Larry King or a Charlie Rose television interview—sitting across the table were the host, Dr. Wing Mar, and the guest, Mr. Steven Leong. Steve, in his customary business suit and trademark bow-tie, answered the interviewer's and the audience's questions for over an hour. It was a memorable show and worth a revisit.

For this book's interview, two changes were made: (1) the scope, from 'My Life Story' to 'Our Life Stories' and (2) the venue, from a public stage to a private home setting. The interviewer is one of the historical society's editors—abbreviated "Ed" below. Steve and Ella Leong's stories and reflections follow.

Ed: Thanks for consenting to do this encore interview with Steve and a new interview with Ella ...

Steve: Oh, wait! In the last interview I forgot—at the beginning—to introduce my wife of 60 years: Ella Toy Leong... I'm still learning... (turning to Ella and smiling).

1944

Ed: Greetings to you two. In the film, Steve speaks of athletics—in contrast to academics—as being the most important factor in his formative years. That's pretty unique for a Chinese kid from your era.

Steve: Maybe so. My competitive spirit came from being the fifth born, the second son of eight kids and living altogether with an extended family in Watsonville, Calif. When I was six, my father's apple drying business failed two years before the 1929 depression—an inauspicious beginning of the Leong tradition of being ahead of the times. Our family was forced to move to San Francisco in 1927. It was near our San Francisco Chinese school that I discovered the Boy Scouts, the YMCA, and later competitive athletics (especially tennis, track, swimming and basketball). Often at home, table tennis contests with my four brothers determined who was to be the dishwasher-of-the-day. Thus, my competitiveness is a residual of coming from a large family and from an early passion for sports. Moreover, college academics were a major four-year grind for me—I had labored overly hard to achieve the reasonably fair grades expected of me.

Ed: Nonetheless, all eight siblings are over-achievers—six with college degrees, including two PhDs.

Steve: Yes, I'm the academic black sheep of the family. One out of eight isn't bad.

Ed: All this family success came from?

Steve: Our parents. They were the brave and adventuresome pioneers that came to America without much education, English language proficiency or any particular skills, fortified only by their will to work and stoical acceptance of low pay, hardship, intolerance. They raised families and even scrimped enough to send funds back to the relatives in China. In today's idiom they were awesome.

Ed: Your siblings' surname is 'Way' and yours is 'Leong.' They, or you, used an immigration surname?

Steve: No. My father's name was Leong Man Way. And, when he enrolled my oldest sister in school, he stated his name and the school officials erroneously named her Lily Way, rather than Lily Leong. It wasn't until World War II that we went back to Watsonville to get the proper documents for making a legal changeover to Leong. By then, my brothers had published papers under their old name and they elected to continue using it. I wasn't famous so I made the changeover.

Ed: Ella, your turn to tell us about your upbringing days?

Ella: Oh, that was so long ago. But okay, here goes. I was the 10th in birth order, fifth daughter in a Bakersfield family of five boys and six girls. My traditional-minded parents strongly favored customs from their Cantonese background. After school hours, we had duties in the family restaurant. After graduation from high school and junior college, I attended UC Berkeley only briefly.

Ed: What do you remember best about growing up in Bakersfield?

Ella: During my earlier days in Bakersfield, seasonal festivals were observed by our Chinese neighborhood. One recollection was a August 15th "Full Moon" festival. Roast pigs, cooked foods, watermelons, other fruits were laid out

Our companionship is like yin (moon) and yang (sun)—opposites working in harmony and balance—it worked quite well for our lives.

on a candle-lit closed street. At a gong signal young people grabbed the goodies and ran home with them. In general, parents saw the "Americanization" of their children but tried to imbue native language, customs, beliefs and ideas they grew up with and brought to the new country. There were clashes! Appreciation came later—much later. And Chinese food is still the best.

Ed: Yes it is. Now, tell us about your first meeting, the courtship and marriage with Steve.

Ella: Do you really want to know the gory details of how Steve and I met? This takes me down a 1939 memory lane. On one of my visits to the Bay area, we had glimpses of each other at a UC vs. USC football game in the Berkeley stadium. My brother-in-law, who was in the same Boy Scout troop, arranged a meeting for that evening. It turned out to be Steve at the stadium! We went to see Tommy Dorsey and I recall hearing "On Treasure Island," the song … or was it being at Treasure Island, the place—I forget which. Later, sporadic correspondence and occasional meetings led to a 1943 wedding, then our settling in Los Angeles. While Steve went to his job at Douglas Aircraft, at his urging, I enrolled at UCLA and graduated in 1944 with a BA degree, at which time Steve earned his PhT (Putting her Through). And as they say, the rest is history.

Ed: What were your hectic activities during the family years?

Ella: I worked at Marinship, a wartime Liberty shipbuilding yard in Sausalito. I completed UCLA after marriage to Steve, and worked at UCLA library. Then I became a mom to two daughters—Marsha and Cindy. I took care of family and home during Steve's frequent and often-lengthy business trips, a number of times on overseas assignments. But, our domestic work was nothing compared to our parents' workload of raising eight and 11 kids—struggling to make ends meet during the depression. We have automatic dishwashers now, while they only had the tired hand of the loser of a ping-pong game. (Incidentally, Steve's overseas assignments took him, in no particular order to, Taiwan, Spain, Germany, Sweden, France, Italy, Korea, Japan, Mexico, Saudi Arabia, and New Zealand).

Ed: Back to Steve, give us a quick overview of your distinguished engineering career.

Steve: After 1941 UC Berkeley graduation, I was employed at Union Diesel Engine in Oakland, followed by a government assignment in Arizona to train the first groups of Chinese Air Force Cadets from China in World War II period. I was their ground school instructor. My next position was at Douglas Aircraft in Santa Monica, after which I joined the Bechtel Corporation. Little did I suspect it then, but 32 years later I retired from Bechtel, my last assignment there being the manager of international power operations.

By the way, it was during my early Bechtel days that I built our home.

Ed: A good summary. After all these years, you're still excited about buying a lot and building a house back in 1949. Please tell us a bit more.

Steve: Yes. Apart from my family, there were two major milestones in my life. My "song hay" (double happiness) is my career at Bechtel and our building of our first—and current—home. Back then, I made a $3,000 offer on a lot in West Los Angeles, and the offer was promptly rejected because I was Chinese. A colleague at work heard about my predicament and he generously offered to buy the lot and sell it to me—he offered $2,700, and the owner accepted it. Thus, the kind deed was done. I put up $6,000 for the building material and completed building the house in less than a year. Primarily Ella and myself did the work with some help from others (only the roof and fireplace were contracted out). I was young then and was able to work two full-time jobs; the self-satisfaction had minimized the long 80-hour work week.

Ed: In your film interview, in stark contrast to your home-building enthusiasm, you seemed pretty subdued about the magnitude of your Bechtel career accomplishments.

Steve: I feel extremely fortunate for being at the right company, working for the right boss, facing the right opportunities, and all at the right time. In 1947, when my first and only boss at Bechtel hired me, there were less than 100 employees at the Vernon, Calif., office—I was the only Chinese. The post World War II economy developed an insatiable need for cheap energy and we, at Bechtel, were in a unique position to satisfy this growing need with fossil-fueled and nuclear-fueled power plants. From 1947 to 1979, our Vernon office grew exponentially to more than 5,000 employees for serving the energy marketplace. This growth allowed me the opportunity to use my competitive skills gained from sports to become an engineering manager of 1,700 of our office professionals. Of course, hard work and a leadership bent contributed to my success with the Bechtel team. I retired after working for the same boss 32 years.

Ed: Some of our readers are young professionals and potential managers ... any words of wisdom for them?

Steve: Certainly. First, we must understand the requirements for a manager. Managers are primarily responsible for the work of others, and must organize and lead them in accomplishing a common goal. Among the more significant requirements for managers are leadership, ability to communicate and knowledge of the business. We could develop leadership abilities through participation in outside activities that provide opportunities for leadership development,

"It has been fulfilling years because our parents took that slow boat from China and settled in our "Gum Saan" (Gold Mountain). We would like to openly acknowledge our eternal gratitude for their remembrance: to Mr. and Mrs. Leong Man Way from Steve with respect and to Mr. and Mrs. Din Toy from Ella with love."

such as community, social and political organizations and events. We could improve oral communication by joining Toastmasters' Clubs where there is plenty of oral communication practice. Many of us need to expand our knowledge of the business we are in… not only in the narrow technical areas we are involved in, but also in the less technical areas. For engineering, this includes manufacturing, construction, operation and maintenance. Actual experience in these fields is even better. All this background leads to a more balanced and broader-based individual, which improves the chances for promotion to middle and upper management.

Ed: Good timeless lesson. Ella, you were a Bechtel-wife of many years. What are your thoughts?

Ella: I think the domestic engineers operate pretty much with the same broad knowledge and good communication principals. I believe the ability to communicate is the key to leadership—and a key to a happy home as well. As part of the Bechtel family, both Steve and I still look back on his work experience with much pride. He is grateful for his opportunities that provided broad experience, career growth, and lifelong friendships. I credit the post World War II environment—the opening of the opportunity door wider to all—for having enriched our corporate and retirement lives.

Ed: Steve's retirement from Bechtel in 1979 ushered in your golden era. My final question for this interview: What is your daily life like for each of you? You have the last word.

Ella: Playtime! Less work and more play … indeed, less is more. I attend senior citizen programs, do some traveling, pursue needlework hobbies, stay in touch by email, and keep track of an ever-growing clan.

Steve: Showtime! We recently had installed a cable TV service with gazillion channels of sports—24/7—but I'm not a couch potato yet. I still love doing home construction projects, helping in community work, dabbling in the San Francisco family business and playing a few rounds of golf.

Leongs: The house we have lived in and enjoyed was built with our own hands, from the foundation up, built over half a century ago. Our companionship is like yin (moon) and yang (sun)—opposites working in harmony and balance—it worked quite well for our lives. The Yin-Yang has been our logo, all these years. Being absolute opposites, we often have entirely separate conversations—even simultaneously to save time—and neither one heard what the other has said, but we knew what was said. For us, this unique art form of companionship and communication has been our hallmark for all seasons. Well, it's winter in our lives now, but it seems like late fall… and we are content. It has been fulfilling years because our parents took that slow boat from China and settled in our "Gum Saan" (Gold Mountain). We would like to openly acknowledge our eternal gratitude for their remembrance: to Mr. and Mrs. Leong Man Way from Steve with respect and to Mr. and Mrs. Din Toy from Ella with love.

The video that motivated this interview is available for public viewing at the Visitor Center of the CHSSC. Please ask for "Steven Leong, Speaking at the Chinese Historical Society, October 2, 2002" (50-Minutes).

Gaing Wing Chan

A California Family Legacy

By Wing Mar and Edgar Wong

> "When I was a boy, I read about how Thomas Edison couldn't help his ailing mother, even though he was an engineering genius and very wealthy. That inspired me to study medicine."

Gaing Chan was born in 1922 in Oroville, a small town just 70 miles north of Sacramento, Calif. Today, Dr. Chan is retired and still resides in West Sacramento. Gaing and Lily Chan visit China regularly and Gaing enjoys his woodworking hobby in his fully equipped workshop. His family background is rich in California's 19th and 20th century history. Three notable examples of the Chan family legacy follow.

Grandfather Chan: Pioneer Entrepreneur in Oroville

Decades earlier in 1870, Gaing Chan's grandfather, Chin Kong You, immigrated to Oroville from Toishan, China, to seek his fortune in Gold Mountain. Known as the Gold City, Oroville's history runs deep with gold. Beginning in the Gold Rush of 1849, Oroville (called Ophir City until 1855) was a boom town known throughout the West. With streets filled with miners and laborers, Oroville became one of the largest cities in California. By 1863, a Chinese temple was built by local Chinese, to serve a community of 10,000 Chinese with separate chapels for Taoism, Buddhism and Confucianism. When the railroad was completed in 1869, thousands of railroad workers were laid off. Most of the laid-off workers on the western portion of the transcontinental section were Chinese and they began their migration to California in quest of work—and gold—adding to the Chinese population in Oroville.

With his savings from a decade of hard labor, Elder

Chan opened the Fong Lee Company of Oroville in 1870, a little store that became a large conglomerate. The store was a major supplier to the mining, lumbering and farming industries; it was also a large provider of consumer goods—including Chinese medicines and herbs—to customers. Their broad services included assaying and buying gold, acting as an employment agency, offering language translation services, and providing overseas mail services.

A depression hit California in the 1870s and many white Californians blamed the Chinese for the hard times. Strong anti-Chinese sentiments led to acts of violence and the enactment of discriminatory laws in cities throughout the state. Californians in 1879 adopted a new state constitution that contained strongly worded anti-Chinese provisions. Three years later in 1882, the United States Congress passed the Chinese Exclusion Act prohibiting further Chinese immigration.

In this increasingly hostile political and social environment, Elder Chan was able to survive—and even prospered—due in part to his unusual ability to maintain friendships with officials and business people including George C. Perkins. Mr. Perkins owned a transportation enterprise known as Goodall, Perkins and Company, just one block from Grandfather Chan's Fong Lee Company. Neighbor Perkins eventually went on to become a California state senator, the 14th governor of California, and a United States senator. Elder

Chan became a successful and respected businessman in spite of the unfriendly era.

Today the Fong Lee Company is listed in the National Register of Historical Places as Building #82002173. Also, Oroville's Chinese Temple is also listed and open to the public. In the temple, there are the Tapestry Hall displaying the extensive tapestries, costumes and puppets from the Chinese Opera Theatre and the Chinese Garden containing plants from China.

Chan Brothers and
Fraternity Founders at Berkeley

The Greek-letter college fraternity Pi Alpha Phi began in 1926 with six charter members—two were Gaing Chan's brothers: Wing Cheong and younger brother Wing Chack. One reason for its formation was because all Chinese students had difficulties in finding lodging around the UC Berkeley campus. Three of the founding members stayed in a small apartment behind kindly "Mother" Tusch's house on Union Street near the campus; Mrs. Tusch was herself a victim of racism and was disliked for renting to the Chinese students.

In need of larger living quarters to accommodate the ever-growing student population, a five-room house at 2227 Union St. was rented in the fall of 1929. It was here that the charter members formally formed the Pi Alpha Phi fraternity—fondly known as the "Pineapple Pie." Legend has it that the name was chosen to mean "the Beginning of the Fraternity with Ascending Brightness"—from Alpha (the 1st Greek letter - beginning) and from Pi and Phi (16th and 21st Greek letters - numerically ascending). Actually, the Greek symbol: Pi means longevity (i.e., Phoenix), Alpha means aspiration, and Phi means friendship (e.g., Philadelphia—the city of brotherly love).

In the 1930s, the fraternity was relocated to a rented house at 2420 Bancroft Way and later moved to another rented

house on College Street. During World War II, use of the fraternity was minimum and the few student members and some alumni maintained it. The mid-1950s was the low-membership period with only a few members onboard; these few members got into financial troubles and all were expelled from the fraternity, leaving Pi Alpha Phi with no student members. Drastic remedial action was needed.

Due to the collective efforts of the Pi Alpha Phi alumni, a successful bid of $28,000 was made to buy the Sperry Mansion on Warring Street (from the Sperry Flour estate) for having a permanent fraternity house. In 1956, the alumni raised the down payment of $10,000 ($2,000 in direct donations plus $8,000 in alumni-subscription bonds) and the Bank of Canton financed the remaining balance of $10,000. When the good-faith bonds were due in 1977, they were refinanced for another five years because of insufficient fraternity funds. By the final 1982 maturity date, generous alumni donated the unpaid bonds to the fraternity in a "burning-the-mortgage" ceremony—the beginning of the fraternity's enormous growth.

The legacy of the Chan Brothers, who were among the founders, is the ongoing operation of 10 chapters of the Pi Alpha Phi fraternity. The six UC chapters are at Berkeley, Davis, Riverside, Santa Cruz, Irvine, and San Diego. The four out-of-state associates are University of Michigan, University of Arizona, University of North Carolina and Michigan State University.

Gaing Chan: Medical Patriarch in Sacramento

When he was a youngster, Gaing Chan was very curious about the scientific world. He was fond of reading about the lives and scientific works of Louis Pasteur (1822-1895), Thomas Edison (1847-1931) and Madame Curie (1867-1934). Gaing admired Pasteur and Edison for their inventiveness and he especially admired Marie Curie for her courage in a male-dominated world. Also, Gaing Chan's maternal grandfather was an herbalist in China, so caring

photo by Jason Jem

for the sick had been a meaningful part of his family history. Dr. Chan cites this trio of scientists—and family heritage—as inspiration for devoting his life to medicine.

As one of the many returning World War II veterans on the G.I. Bill, Gaing Chan entered medical school despite fierce competition from over a thousand applicants that year. He was one of only five Asian-American students admitted to UC San Francisco medical school in the class of 1952. He finished his four-year surgical residency at the Southern Pacific Railroad Hospital in San Francisco and then started his private practice in West Sacramento in 1956.

In seven years, Dr Chan's practice grew to the point where he needed and wanted a partner who shared his vision. Dr. Gordon Ma, who just finished his term as chief resident of surgery in the Veterans Hospital in Martinez, Calif. was the perfect match with Dr. Chan. For 35 years, this partnership served the community with their caring medical practice and when they retired their stethoscopes and scalpels, the loss was severely felt. For this was the passing of the golden age of medicine when the doctor-patient relationship operated without a dominating third partner—the insurer.

"Dr. Gaing W. Chan and Dr. Gordon T. Ma" era continues through their children. Most of the Chan children went into medical fields and all are pursuing excellence in their professions, thereby continuing the tradition of the family legacy.

Jason Jem gathered the personal information from an interview with Gaing Chan. Allen Gee was a fraternity brother who supplied other information for this story.

James Bok Wong

A Special Corporate Economist

By Wing Mar

> A mystic predicted his future.
> As an economist, James Bok Wong
> predicts financial futures.

The Soothsayer's Forecast

The grizzled, old, hunch-backed mystic took James's hand after studying the young man's face and head. He peered into the lines on James' palm, looked at James and, in awe, told him that he was special. James had an unusual life-line that ran the full extent of his palm. "You will never have to worry," the mystic predicted. "You will always be helped all through life." The soothsayer was so excited he did not charge James for his service.

This encounter happened shortly after the end of World War II. While on leave, James Bok Wong, a young staff sergeant with the 14th U.S. Army Air Force, flew from the China-Burma-India-theater to Shanghai on his way to his home village near Canton. While in Canton, he met an attractive nurse who was a cousin of one of his fellow soldiers. They fell in love and became engaged. James then continued on to his family village and there he was told by the village elders to visit the village fortune-teller. (James married Wai Ping on August 3, 1946 and brought her back to the U.S. as his war bride.)

When boys reach adulthood it is the tradition in his village to have a session with a fortune-teller who can advise the recipient on his journey through life. This report can be given orally or written in classical Chinese calligraphy. It is to be kept with one's most important papers. James, with a light heart, just wanted to hear the wise counsel and have a picture of his future by the most eminent local fortune-teller.

By that time, James Bok Wong had already been living the prophecy. Born in a small village in China, he traveled overseas to America at age 12, entering through Boston in 1938. His father was living in Canada because, at the time, it was easier to immigrate to Canada from China than to the United States. Fortunately for James' future, he was sent to his uncle's laundry in New York City, with documents of a "paper son" that declared his age as 16. He started attending local schools while working many hours at the laundry where he lived. Not long after, he moved to live with another uncle, who operated a restaurant in Upper Manhattan. Mrs. Supple, a teacher at his new school, recognized an exceptional and unusual mind challenged by a new language. She tutored James, who had arrived in the United States not knowing a single word of English, countless hours after school. Their hard work resulted in James being named class valedictorian at graduation and the principal allowed another student to speak for him since James still did not speak English clearly. Mrs. Supple suggested that James take the entrance examination to the best high school in New York, Stuyvesant High. James scored a perfect 100% in mathematics, while barely passing English, and the school accepted him on that basis.

U.S. Army Air Force

After high school, James Wong was drafted into the U.S. Army. He served with the 407th Air Service Squadron of the 14th Army Air Force, shipping out of Virginia for North Africa, the Mediterranean, then to Bombay, India. He took a train to Calcutta and flew over the Himalayas to Kunming, China. His tasks included repairing and maintaining instruments of P-51 and P-38 fighter airplanes and bombsights of B-24 and B-29 bombers. Even though he wanted and was qualified to be a fighter pilot James was told all Chinese-speaking Air Force personnel were assigned to the ground crew because they were less expendable than the pilots. James survived his extremely dangerous tour of duty, and consequently, the pronouncement by the village fortuneteller only reinforced his deep belief in fate and destiny.

The genesis of the 14th Air Force was the American Volunteer Group (also known as the Flying Tigers). In 1941, an unpublished executive order went out under President Franklin Roosevelt authorizing reserve officers and enlisted men to resign from the Army Air Corps, Naval and Marine air services for the purpose of joining the American Volunteer Group in China. There was a strong sentiment among Cabinet members, members of Congress, the general public and President and Mrs. Roosevelt, that Japan was the invading aggressor and for humanitarian and geopolitical reasons the U.S. should help China.

In 1937 retired Captain Claire L. Chennault went to China at the request of Madame Chiang Kai-Shek to assess the battle readiness and effectiveness of the Chinese Air Force. There was a shortage of trained pilots and only a few aircraft factories that the Italians had built in China. But with the impending geopolitical winds of World War II, the Italian engineers and mechanics left the country. Chennault must have wondered whether the Chinese patriotic and inspiring slogan, "Saving the Country Through Aviation", was realistic. He must have answered emphatically "yes", even though the odds were against him and China, for he agreed to forge a new air force.

Chennault affirmed the belief that aviation could help save China. He repeatedly called for the U.S. to aid China in the form of airplanes. The P-40 airplanes, rejected by the British as obsolete, were secretly sold and shipped to China. At the

same time 100 American pilots and 200 ground crew members formed the American Volunteer Group (AVG). Chennault personally trained the pilots in Burma. They flew the P-40 Tomahawks with the painted tiger face. Beyond their monthly pay, they were given $500 for each destroyed Japanese plane. The AVG compiled one of the greatest records of the war with 286 Japanese aircraft destroyed between December 1942 and July 1943. After the AVG merged into the 14th U.S. Army Air Force in March 1943 they conducted effective fighter and bomber operations, eventually grounding the Japanese Air Force. By the end of the war 2,100 Japanese planes were destroyed. A network of Chinese farmers, using phones and radios were not only saving the downed Flying Tiger pilots, but were also salvaging any aircraft parts for recycling. Dr. T. V. Soong, spokesman for China, said that the AVG was the soundest investment China ever made.

James Bok Wong was part of the legacy of the 407th Air Service Squadron of the 14th Army Air Force.

Education and New Career

When James returned to the United States he applied to the University of Maryland which favored the enrollment of returning veterans who were Maryland residents. James was not a resident but President H. C. Byrd granted him a special competitive admission. James' outstanding scholastic achievement validated the president's decision. He graduated with bachelor's degrees in both agriculture and chemical engineering, ranking first in both the College of Agriculture and the College of Engineering. Three-and-a-half years later, James earned his master's and doctorate degrees from the University of Illinois.

It is James' belief that his guardian angel was always lending a helping hand. He found a job as the senior planning engineer for Dart Industries (formerly Rexall Drug and Chemical Company). Justin Dart wanted the United Drug Company, which he owned, to sell merchandise in addition to pharmaceuticals, so he enlarged the stores and gave them a new name, Rexall. He wanted Rexall to be a multi-national conglomerate. To manufacture the plastics for Tupperware Company that he had just purchased, he wanted to form a chemical-plastics division. James was hired for this new division.

James was asked if he could help the acrylo-nitrile-butadiene-styrene operation in Joliet, Ill., which was losing millions of dollars every year. James was given a year to see what he could do. Using newly developed optimization computer programs, James turned the ABS operation around from loss to profit in 11 months. Justin Dart was so proud of this accomplishment that he reported it at the next annual stockholders' meeting. James was promoted to supervisor of planning and economics and then to manager of long-range planning.

During that period, most large corporations in America had a chief economist. Because of James' leadership ability, his analytical and mathematical talent and his knowledge of the plastics industry, his peer group in his division recommended that he be the chief economist for the organization. Wisely, the corporation, with Justin Dart's blessing, hired James for that prestigious position. Little did they know that they also bought the prophecy: James went on to Harvard and UCLA graduate business schools for the knowledge he needed for his new role. He grasped the possibility of the computer to forecast trends in the business. Gathering input from a survey that he conducted throughout the industries, he came up with a model that predicted the leader price for plastics for the year. His model was accepted as a busi-

ness predictor and price setter. The model was the best in the industry. James was now the business forecaster for the future, an attainment that might even have surprised the village mystic.

Jade Eagle
James Bok Wong

Johnny Hanson, the blond-haired, blue-eyed boy who is destined to be an American hero, finds himself orphaned at an early age and trapped inside China during the dark years of World War II. Beginning with his courageous rescue of a young Chinese girl, Tong May-lee, from a bombed building during a Japanese air raid, Johnny engages in a lifelong love affair with China, her people, and her traditions.

Following the death of his parents, Johnny is taken in by Uncle and Auntie Tong, who raise Johnny as if he were their own son. Here we get to know Big Brother Keung-yan and Little Sister May-lee. Like any dutiful Chinese son, Johnny works hard to bring honor to his family amidst the turbulence of war. He attends school, where he becomes fluent in both major Chinese dialects. The Tongs escape Canton and the ever-encroaching danger of war, traveling to Kweilin.

In Kweilin, Johnny's language skills-fluent in English, Mandarin, and Cantonese-bring him into contact with the famed Flying Tigers group of American fighter pilots and the legendary General Claire Lee Chennault. Johnny becomes Chennault's interpreter and gives the reader a firsthand look at the American war effort in China. Johnny also falls in love with his teacher, the beautiful Wen Tian-hua, by serving as a messenger for an American fighter pilot, Lieutenant Sanford Carter. Tian-hua and "Sandy" fall in love, and when Sandy is killed in combat, Tian-hua faces great shame and rebuke for carrying Sandy's child when they had not been wed. Johnny steps in to save her honor by marrying her, and while the wedding begins as an arrangement it soon blossoms into true love. Johnny, his new wife, and the Tongs travel to Chengtu to build four airfields for the American B-29 Superfortresses. For successfully completing the project, Johnny receives a Jade Eagle from Madame Chiang Kai-shek, making him a national hero. Tian-hua leaves Johnny and her son, Sanford Hanson, also known as Ah San, to return to Kweilin and bring back her family. She is killed in a plane crash, but Johnny only learns this truth a year later when he searches for her.

When the war with Japan ends and the civil war between the Chinese Communists and Nationalists, begins, Johnny hears from his uncle in the States with an offer to attend college. He had been living in Canton with Ah San, Auntie Tong, and May-lee, and had rekindled feelings of love with May-lee. He leaves for the States with Ah San to attend college but not before promising to return and marry May-lee after he graduates.

(Continued on back flap)

From James Wong's book "Jade Eagle"

Retirement and New Challenges

After a successful career working for major corporations, James retired to the Los Angeles area. Thus began a new phase in James Wong's journey through life. He had already raised a family, his three children having earned doctorate degrees and following their own careers. James had always been a presence for his family and they felt secure. He was described as gentle, patient and accepting-an ideal father.

Now his facile mind turned to a more creative pursuit: writing fiction. His latest project has been writing and promoting his successful book, "Jade Eagle." (Again only the fortune-teller could have predicted that the boy who did not know a word of English at age 12 would someday become an author.) It is a poignant and sentimental story of a Caucasian boy growing up in China during World War II, later becoming an American fighter pilot in Korea, and finally returning to China to find his childhood love.

A few years ago, James became a widower. Just as the soothsayer had pronounced: "You will never have to worry, you will always be helped all through life," James met and is now married to Betty Yeow, a successful business woman, who is full of energy and shares his interest in dancing and traveling. In addition, James is president of several organizations, including a charitable foundation that awards a number of substantial scholarships annually to college students. These successful organizations are not aware that they too may be benefiting from James' lucky "life-line."

Joyce Mar and Eugene Moy assisted in the research and writing of this story.

Ralph Fong

Alameda, the World & Berkeley

By Edgar Wong

"*A wondrous journey around the world in 80 years.*"

After an engineering career took him around the globe, Ralph is now retired in Berkeley with his wife, Mary. The short trip from Alameda, his birthplace, to Berkeley took 80 years—his story below.

My Ancestors

"In the 1920s, my parents sailed to America, landing at the "Island" (aye loon). The "Island", of course, was Angel Island, whose immigration station was built in 1910 to enforce the Chinese Exclusion Act of 1882. As was typical for immigrants in those days, our family purchased false papers (gah gee) from Chinese U.S. residents who claimed fictitious sons and daughters to enable "legal" entry to America by others.

Chinese immigrants arriving on the west coast were inspected and those few who passed, by luck or bribe, were allowed to enter directly. Along with the masses, our parents were sent to the less-than-friendly accommodations of Angel Island for detailed interrogations as "guests" (detainees) for weeks or sometimes months. Having memorized their false family oral history (hao gung) well, our parents passed and were released. The old phrase that "all Chinese look alike" must have worked in the immigrants' favor because many paper-family members traveling together—'siblings' and even 'twins'—made it through the halls of visual inspection. If there was a bright side to aye loon, it was that there were no agonizingly long immigration lines, such as were found at San Francisco and Los Angeles airports a few decades later...the result of the repealing of the Exclusion Act and the onset of international aviation.

My grandfather had worked on the railroads in America and saved enough money to go back to China to raise his family. He encouraged my father to go to America to seek his fortune, and for my father's trip, he received false papers of a "paper son" (gee doi) named Ng Yan Pan, the paper-family's oral history, money for passage, and a U.S. twenty dollar gold piece.

My father's true name was Fong Sil Leong, and from all accounts, entry into the U.S. was uneventful. He worked hard, saved all his money, and was eventually able to send for his family that he left behind in the village of Nom On in Toy San. All told, Fong Sil Leong was separated from his wife, two sons, and a daughter for two years, which was considered a short period for most immigrant Chinese families because of finances.

Father lived with his growing family on Pacific Avenue and operated a small grocery store on Park Street in Alameda, Calif. The Chinese could not own property then, so the Pacific Avenue property was purchased in my name when I was two years old. (The California Alien Land Law–Webb-Haney Act–that denied aliens the right to own property was enacted in 1913, declared unconstitutional in 1952, and repealed in 1956.) With barely enough to provide for his family, father opened a small Chinese keno lottery (white pigeon ticket game – pak kop piu) business in the back of the store. Unfortuitously, the store was only two blocks from the Alameda police station, resulting in some gratuities (protection money) exchanging hands.

My mother was from Toy San and born in 1881, surname Gee. She immigrated to the U.S. as the family member of a Chinese merchant. Her name was Gee Shee Fong. (Note: Shee means nee or born; hence, Gee Shee Fong means "born Gee, married Fong." Or, Mrs. Fong Gee Shee is equivalent to Mrs. Smith nee Jones.) She gave birth to me in October 1923. Following me came three more brothers. Mother didn't speak English, but she managed the household and brought up seven children through the great depression era. My father died in 1938 (age 57), so she became a single mother raising her family—at that time I was 15 and my youngest brother was only nine. After a long life for her times, mother died in 1958 (age 77).

Aviation cadet captain, 1944

The parents of my wife, Mary, were Dan Sing Mar and Poon Shee Mar. Both immigrated from Bak Sai in Toy San to America with their two daughters, Anna (age 7) and Mary (age 6 months). Mary's grandfather had provided false papers for their entrance at the Port of Seattle, Wash.; however, sister Ann's papers ap-

peared questionable and she was detained in Seattle for almost a year. The Mar family settled in Fresno, Calif. and worked in their grandfather's gambling establishment. Grandfather Mar Oak was like a respected Chinese godfather to the Mar clan."

My Early Days

My birth name was Man Teing Ng—the surname Ng from my father's immigration name. I changed my name to Ralph Fong after I received my 2nd Lieutenant commission during World War II. All my school records and passport are under Ralph Fong. My primary language is English; however, I am fluent in Cantonese. When I visited my father's village in China in 1986, I was able to converse with the villagers in their dialect.

Apart from learning the spoken language at home, there were the reading-and-writing years at Chinese school. There were four Chinese families living in Alameda, so the parents got together and hired a Chinese teacher to teach us the basics. There were 15 kids in all—six came from our family. Later, for two years, we went to a regular Chinese language school in Oakland; the hours were 5 p.m. to 8 p.m. Mondays through Fridays, and 9 am to noon Saturdays. I learned and remembered enough so that when I was in the Army, I was able to write my mother once a month in Chinese characters.

Besides Chinese school, there was time left over for American school. I went to Alameda High School and my major was pre-college. My fondest memory of high school is my participation in ROTC (the Reserve Officer Training Corp). I still have an old photo of myself in an ROTC uniform wearing my Sam Brown Belt and carrying a sword. (A Sam Brown Belt is worn from over the right shoulder to the left hip and around the waist.) After my junior year, I volunteered to go away for one month in the summer to CMTC (Citizens Military Training Camp). The camp was at Fort Ord, Calif.; however, it was known as Camp Ord then. In that short month, I qualified as an expert machine gunner.

After all the gung ho training in the American and Chinese schools, I decided to enroll in pre-medicine. I went to the University of California at Berkeley ("Cal") in the fall of 1941. Then came Pearl Harbor on December 7, 1941 and World War II began. Knowing that a machine gunner was without much future opportunity, I volunteered for the Army Air Corp (today's USAF). I left for the Army Air Corp in 1943, where I was a cadet captain during pre-flight training, and graduated as an aerial navigator. I ultimately became an instructor for aerial navigation and was selected as lead navigator. I was honorably discharged late in 1945.

Following discharge, I returned to Cal, but changed my major to civil engineering. This change would shorten my school time and get me into the work force earlier, so that Mary and I could marry in the fall of 1946. With a modest stipend under the G.I. Bill of Rights, and through Mary's moral and financial support (she worked as an auditor at the U.S. Naval Supply Depot in Oakland, Calif.,) I graduated in civil engineering in June 1949.

My wife, Mary Mar Fong, obtained her legal name through the 1956 INS instituted "confession" (hon pak) program to eliminate the paper families by Chinese im-migrants. (The purpose of this program was to permit all aliens, not just Chinese, who illegally entered the U.S., to adjust their status to that of an alien lawfully admitted for permanent residence, which in turn paved the way to naturalization. This program extended into the 1960s.) Mary came to America when she was an infant, settled in Fresno and grew up in Stockton. We met in 1943 while I was home on a weekend pass from the Presidio of Monterey. It was love at first sight. We corresponded to each other almost daily until my honorable discharge in late 1945. We were married in September 1946. We have three children, Mary Christina (Tina), Russell Curtis (with two children) and Ralph Jr. (one child). An acknowledgment: from our marriage and until the birth of our first child in July 1951, Mary was the main breadwinner for our family."

His Career

The foregoing narrative is a summary of Ralph Fong's thoughts (let's call him RF) on what were important during his formative years. Obviously, the VIPs of these years were the two grand ladies—his mother and his wife. Now that

Oil rig dollies

126

In transit from South Korea to Saudi Arabia

he was on his own, did RF do okay? Our short answer is; "you bet, big time!" (a phrase borrowed from another oil-man—Dick Cheney).

It was during his nine-year engineering phase that RF acquired his basic design skills gained from working at four different companies in the San Francisco bay area: Ellison and King, the City of Oakland, the Bechtel Corporation, and Ehrhart & Associates. Following his engineering phase, RF embarked on a 28-year project phase with the Chevron Corporation. At Chevron, RF worked in the engineering and construction of many different energy-related systems. Project locations were worldwide, from California, Texas, Mississippi, and New Jersey to South Korea, the Netherlands, and Saudi Arabia. RF's last project, from 1982 through 1985, exemplifies his expertise. At a contract value of $415 million, his Zuluf project consisted of two sets of three platforms, each processing 150,000 barrels per day of crude oil. Zuluf was designed in Houston, Texas, fabricated at the Hyundai shipyard in Ulsan, South Korea, barged to the Arabian Gulf, and installed in 150 feet of water of the Zuluf fields. RF was the on-site project manager throughout the 41 months of design, fabrication, and construction, completing a seven-year assignment as a loaned executive to the Arabian American Oil Company.

RF returned from ARAMCO to Chevron and retired in September 1985. During his 28 years, he had received numerous commendations for his organizational leadership and technical excellence. After his retirement, RF continued his memberships and pursued an even more active role in various organizations, including the American Society of Civil Engineers, the Phi Alpha Phi Fraternity, the Cal Alumni Association and the UC Chinese Alumni Foundation.

In a small but significant way, RF has made a difference in his profession, affiliations and for all energy consumers worldwide.

His Personal Side

RF is a natural and charismatic leader and is known by those beyond his profession as sociable, considerate and engaging. For example, Calvin Lee, an old friend, states, "The outstanding quality of Ralph is his thoughtfulness. For years until my mother died, she would receive a birthday card from Ralph for having entertained him at her home. He would always bring her a gift when he visited frequently, observing a long cherished Chinese tradition for visitors."

And from Wing Mar, another lifelong friend, "I remembered Ralph as an exceptionally nurturing father. Once, when they lived in Torrance, Calif., he and his son brought over to my house the biggest squash I ever saw. They did the gardening together and they both got so much pleasure in giving it to me."

Pacific Avenue to Easy Street

RF's journey from Alameda to Berkeley is but a short distance of a few miles. For Ralph Fong it was a wondrous journey around the world in 80 years. From Ng to Fong, from Chinese school pupil to American university scholar, from aerial navigator to college student, from pre-med to civil engineering, from courtship to fatherhood, from junior engineer to senior management, from South Korea to

Saudi Arabia, and from childhood to retirement.

RF is a lifelong sports enthusiast, especially for professional football and basketball. He still renews his season tickets for the Cal basketball games. His hobbies are a little gardening, a few trips a year, a little reading and some TV watching. RF plays golf once or twice a week and still scores an occasional birdie. Now, at age 80, that's big time.

William F. Chew

From Railroads to Aerospace and Back to Railroads

By Jason Jem

Wearing a black shirt and black pants, with a trim goatee, Bill Chew looks like a cool jazz musician or a wise poet. In reality, instead of being a musician or poet, Mr. Chew is the proud grandson of a Chinese railroad worker in America, an accomplished aerospace engineer, inventor and entrepreneur. Now, in retirement, he has embarked on yet another career—that of historian, writer and self-publisher of a book which illuminates the true contributions of the Chinese-American railroad workers.

The Chew Ancestry

Chew's parents were the children of Chinese railroad workers, born and reared in Winnemucca, Nev., which was a big railroad town. His paternal grandfather, Chew Wing Qui, came to America from China in 1870 and worked for the Central Pacific Railroad Company. When the railroad was completed in that region, he moved his family to San Francisco in search of work

His maternal grandfather, Woo Sing Jung, had eight children. The youngest was Bill's mother, Ida Alice Woo, (Woo Shui Hong), born in 1906, the year of the great San Francisco earthquake. Tragically, Ida's mother died unexpectedly from complications of childbirth when Ida was only six months old. Ida and her two sisters were reared in San Francisco's Gum Moon Orphanage.

The Gum Moon Orphanage was for Chinese infants and girls from destitute families. The orphanage added on to the Gum Moon Residence Hall was founded and operated by the Chinese Methodist Church in 1868. The residence hall in its early history provided shelter and education to rescued Chinese girls who had been sold into slavery and prostitution. In 1984 the organization established the Asian Women's Resource Center to expand its community outreach services.

photo by Jason Toth

During the depression years, Bill's father was superintendent at the Bayside Canning Co. At that time Bayside Canning was the third largest cannery owned and operated by Chinese Americans in the United States. His community service earned William Sr. the honor of being accepted as a Mason of the Rio Vista Lodge.

Early Years

William Chew, Jr., was born in 1931 in San Francisco during the depression. Fate dealt the Chew family another blow when his father passed away. With young Bill and his brother, Donald, his mother moved the family to Los Angeles to look for work. However, because of increasing financial hardship, she reluctantly placed her two sons in the Masonic Home for Children in Covina. There, Chew learned discipline, teamwork and self-reliance. This background instilled in him a strong work ethic. Later, as a young man in Chinatown, he was trying to come to terms with his own frustration of finding any hope for the future. He nearly dropped out of high school, but a coach and a counselor recognized his ability in academics and athletics and convinced him to persevere. He also credits his mother's words of encouragement, "You're going to make it. Be somebody. Look for opportunity and step up to it." With her words of encouragement, young Chew worked hard and studied diligently so that he did eventually succeed. "I remember working at many jobs, but I especially hated the work in restaurants. But I kept in mind that each dish that I washed took me one step closer to college."

Aim For the Stars

After high school Chew married his high school sweetheart, Dorothy Ginn. In 1950 he went to work for Douglas Aircraft Company in El Segundo, California. His position was that of a Master Layout Man and Loftsman. Here is where he discovered his love of aircraft engineering. So, working by day and attending classes at night at California State University at Long Beach, he earned his BS degree. He graduated summa cum laude, achieving the highest grades of his engineering class. All the while he and his wife were also busy raising two sons, Michael and Gregory. (Both are college graduates—one, a sports photographer and the other, a dentist.)

"I want any young person who is feeling discouraged to remember that someone like me, a starving student, can do it."

Chew's ability to foresee and solve engineering problems brought him many promotions, including positions in management. Ever ambitious and hard working, he decided to continue his education with more evening classes at UCLA where he received his Master's degree in Engineering in 1969. After graduation he received professional licenses for Mechanical and Controls Systems Engineer. His aerospace engineering career continued for 45 years with positions at Aerojet (General Tire), North American, Douglas, RCA, Northrop, TRW and GTI.

Milestones

The recent excitement of NASA's latest mission —called Spirit—provides an opportunity for historians to recall the similar emotional and educational experiences of nearly three decades ago with the landing of the Viking Mars Landers 1 and 2. In 1976 NASA assigned to TRW the building of a biological experiment to search for the existence of life on Mars. Initially TRW was having difficulty designing an "organic vapor trap" to vaporize surface material from the landing site in a matter of two minutes time and using only 60 watts of power, in a minimal space and a specified weight limit. Given this complex set of problems Bill Chew, who was working for TRW and having a reputation of being a creative trouble shooter, did the research and designed this critical unit for the Viking Mars Landers. After vigorous testing, NASA accepted the instrument that was Chew's design as working perfectly.

(However, organic compounds or evidence of microbiological life were not found in the samples obtained by the robotic arms on Mars. While most of the scientists concluded at that time that there was not any evidence of life as we know it on Earth, others challenged this view.)

In 1986, as Director of Engineering for GTI, Space division, Chew was awarded Patent #4,603,730, "The Multiple Module High Temperature System for Aerospace Experiments for Material Processing in Space."

To discover new possibilities of living and working in space was a Bill's mantra. For example, he is proud of demonstrating the concept of a renowned hematologist that certain disease states would have "fingerprint patterns" that show up in red blood cells in the space environment. Despite NASA's doubts that Bill could meet their requirements, he not only finished the experiment but also delivered it on time. The experiment was conducted on the space shuttle Discovery in 1985 and 1987.

In the 1970s, W. F. Chew Enterprises came into being. With excitement Bill said, "I was able to use my accumulated knowledge and experience in the running of my own company. I had to do everything—engineering, accounting, marketing, machining, making contracts and hiring personnel. I loved the independence." W. F. Chew Enterprises operated successfully for 25 years, nurtured by Bill's philosophy of innovation, quality, cost-effectiveness with on-time delivery.

Mr. Chew later launched another career as a historian and writer. Through his book, Chew is the first person to provide proof that there were tens of thousands of Chinese railroad workers in the United States. Armed with his laptop computer, and assisted by his wife, Natalina, he has spent considerable time over a five year period examining 142-year-old documents. He traveled through California, Nevada and Utah researching state archives, railroad museums and libraries. He has met many others who are

*Chew designed and fabricated the
A.R.C.: Aggregation of Red Blood Cells
Space Shuttle Mission 1984*

descendants of railroad workers. Their stories added valuable affirmation to Chew's own research. Tragically, his research showed that on one occasion 20,000 pounds of human bones were brought to San Francisco for transport back to China for proper burial (a Chinese tradition). Using a medical formula based on skeletal weight, Chew calculated that this was equivalent to 1,200 individuals. His book reveals that from 1864 to 1867 there were 23,000 individual Chinese workers on the payrolls of the railroads. His face lights up with an "Eureka!" expression as he says, "Look at the numbers, they were really there!" Accordingly, his book is entitled, "The Nameless Builders of the Transcontinental Railroad."

Words of Wisdom

Chew repeated many times, "I want any young person who is feeling discouraged to remember that someone like me, a starving student, can do it. By it, I am referring to getting a good education. If I could do it without much money, without any scholarships, without any student loans, plus a family to support, others can too. It was not easy but it can be done with hard work and sacrifice."

Vernon Chong

Into the Wild Blue Yonder

By Edgar Wong

"*Dear God: So far today, I've done all right. I haven't gossiped, haven't lost my temper, and haven't been greedy, grumpy, nasty, selfish, or overindulgent. I'm really glad about that! But in a few minutes, I'm going to get out of bed and from then on, I'm going to need a lot more help. Thank You! Amen.*"

Yes, this was Dr. Vernon Chong's invocation at the Western Region TRICARE Conference in August 2002. His presentation at the conference was to encourage increased collaboration and sharing of health care resources and services between the Department of Defense (DoD) and the Department of Veteran Affairs (VA). Having served with distinction in command and executive positions at both the DoD/VA, Maj. Gen. Vernon Chong, MD provided a unique blend of vision, leadership, medical expertise, institutional knowledge, and objectivity for resolving the partnership-in-healthcare organizational issues. As might be expected, Vernon Chong's two extraordinary careers have been a path of service, dedication and compassion for his fellow man—indeed, the right "stuff" about which entire books are written—but only a capsule glimpse of that story can be offered here. And so, off we go ....

The Formative Years

Vernon Chong, MD was born in Fresno, Calif. where he attended Jefferson Elementary, Longfellow Junior High, and Fresno High (the Class of 1951). An excellent and inquisitive student, who also enjoyed campus activities, he was elected student body president—both in junior high and high school. Six days a week through the fourth grade he attended Chinese school; later he took Mandarin courses in college and at Stanford. Much to his sadness, Vern has retained very little of the Cantonese learned as a child, or of the Mandarin studied as an adult.

Vern's father wanted him to become an attorney with the expectation that he would go to China and improve the political structure there. To Vern that seemed like a laudable but unrealistic goal; instead, he pursued medicine at Stanford and graduated with a bachelors of arts degree in 1955 and a doctor of medicine degree in 1958. During vacations, he worked as an orderly in the operating room at the Fresno Community Hospital, and it was there that he developed a keen interest in surgery. He went on to complete his internship and surgery residency at the General Hospital of Fresno County (now the Valley Medical Center).

Starting medical practice with the specter of being drafted into the military for two years seemed disruptive, so Vern volunteered for the U.S. Air Force (USAF) in 1963. The Vietnam War occurred shortly after this and he cared for numerous casualties from this conflict. With the many opportunities offered by the military, Vern soon found that it was a truly noble profession that offered a lifetime career of increasingly difficult challenges. It provided the opportunity to assume increasing roles of responsibility and leadership while transitioning from surgeon and teacher to the role of physician–executive.

Gen. Chong interfacing with the Romanian Surgeon General during his time as Command Surgeon of U.S. Air Force European Command.

1968, colonel in June 1973, brigadier general (one star) in October 1982, and major general (two stars) in April 1987. Vernon Chong retired from the USAF in November 1994. Over his 31 years in the Air Force, he had served 12 years as a flag officer; and, notably, he was the first Asian-American physician to serve on active duty with this rank. (An interesting statistic: only one of every 3,200 military personnel achieves major general rank or higher.)

The USAF and Major General Chong

The Department of Defense is divided into three equal branches: the Department of the Army, the Department of the Navy (which includes the Marine Corps), and the Department of the Air Force. For its mission of maintaining air and space superiority, the Air Force has a complement of 500,000 servicemen and women on active duty located globally in three principal locations: the continental United States, the Pacific and Europe. Major General Vernon Chong has served in all three theaters of operations.

Service Chronology

Following the completion of his residency in general surgery in October 1963, Vernon Chong entered the Air Force as the Chief of General Surgery Service at Scott Air Force Base in Illinois, with the rank of captain. His leadership, his team-player spirit, and his devotion to duty set the groundwork for his career to rocket upward, and he achieved the rank of major in December 1966, lieutenant colonel in August

Duty Assignments

Prior to his promotion to flag rank, Chong served seven tours of duty in various locations throughout the world, including Travis Air Force Base in California, Air Force Academy in Colorado Springs and the Tachikawa Air Base in Japan. During this period his increasing responsibilities included staff general surgeon, director of hospital services, deputy commander, and commander (chief executive officer). Upon achieving flag rank, Chong went on to serve six more tours of duty, including Randolph and Lackland Air Force bases in Texas, Andrews Air Force Base in Maryland, and Headquarters of the United States European Command in Germany. As a flag officer, he served as Commander of hospitals and as command surgeon (vice president for medical affairs) at headquarters level.

Collateral Duty

Chong was a chief flight surgeon; he was a member of the elite DoD launch-site recovery and emergency surgery teams for all 15 of the manned space-launches during the

Apollo Program (1968–1972), the Skylab project (1973–1974), and the Apollo-Soyuz test project (1975). For then—Lt. Col. Chong, the most memorable recovery team mission was the Apollo 11 lunar landing on the Sea of Tranquility by Astronauts Armstrong, Collins and Aldrin in July 1969. Indeed, it was the recovery team's great pride that President Kennedy's national commitment made in May 1961 "of landing a man on the moon and returning him safely to earth" was successfully fulfilled.

Lt. Col. Chong during training exercises in preparation of the Apollo 12 launching.

Honors and Awards

Decorations, listed in the order of precedence, include: Defense Distinguished Service Medal, Air Force Distinguished Service Medal, Legion of Merit with oak leaf cluster (the oak leaf cluster means awarded twice), Meritorious Service Medal, Air Force Commendation Medal, National Defense Service Medal, Vietnam Service Medal, Order of Merit-Brazil, and Gold Cross of Honor-Germany. Note that the first two Distinguished Service medals, from the Department of Defense and the Air Force, respectively, are the 3rd and 4th highest decorations given to an Air Force person (from a total list of 65 decorations—the highest is the Medal of Honor). Additionally, Major Gen. Chong was awarded the prestigious Order of the Sword, a high honor in recognition of support and leadership. This honor was bestowed by the enlisted personnel of the Air Training Command at Randolph AFB-TX in 1989. It is noteworthy that in the history of the Air Force, he was the first Asian American of the 133 recipients to receive this unique award.

Flight Facts

Rating: chief flight surgeon. Flight hours: more than 1,600 (roughly equivalent to more than 160 coast-to-coast roundtrips). Aircraft flown: Transports (C-141, C-130, C-5, C-21, C-12, and C-9A), search and rescue helicopters (H-53, H-3, and UH-1), trainers (T-29, T-39, T-33, and T-38), and tankers (KC-135). The KC-135 Stratotanker "flying gas station" has served in many Air Force mission roles, including a flying command post, a zero gravity simulator, and a flying hospital. A minimum of 10 flying-hours per month was required for Chong to maintain his flight status, allowing him to receive flight pay and wear wings on his uniform.

The VA and Dr. Chong

The Veterans Health Administration, under the Department of Veterans Affairs (formerly the Veterans Administration), is responsible for managing veterans' healthcare benefits throughout all 50 states and the U.S. territories. It accomplishes this through a consortium of 21 Veterans Integrated Service Networks (VISNs). A typical VISN has an annual operating budget of $900 million, a workforce of 8,000, eight VA medical centers, 30 outpatient clinics, etc., and serves over one million veterans. A critical goal of the VISN is to be accessible to 90% of their patients within 30 minutes/30 miles of a network facility. Each VISN is also dedicated to healthcare education and research by on-site residency and training, and by affiliation with medical schools and institutions at an expenditure of about 5% of its budget.

After retiring from the Air Force, Dr. Chong accepted a position at VISN 17, "Heart of Texas," in Grand Prairie, Tex., from October 1995 to October 2000. As the network director, he was faced with the challenge of serving over a million veterans residing in 134 counties stretching from the Oklahoma border to the lower Rio Grande Valley. To meet this challenge, Dr. Chong expanded the use of community-based outpatient clinics in order to bring healthcare closer to the patients, thereby meeting the stringent patient accessibility goal. Dr. Chong's astute fiscal skills in acquiring and managing DoD, VA, and civilian funds were a significant factor in achieving a marked improvement in patient healthcare, medical training and advanced research.

Dr. Chong receives the prestigious "Order of the Sword" award from the U.S. Air Force, with his family.

Dr. Chong is currently the special assistant to the network director at VISN 21, "Sierra Pacific," in San Francisco where he is developing a more customer-focused organization. He is instrumental in implementing a "culture" for all employees to govern themselves by shared values and guiding principles, rather than by rigid policy and procedures. No doubt, his Chinese heritage of family values—of personal character and respect for authority—have provided him with a special qualification to meet this task.

Chong Ancestors

Ruth Lee Chong, Vern's mother, was born in San Francisco in 1904. She was orphaned at an early age and lived with her aunt and uncle in Fresno. Seu Ling Chong, Vern's father, was born in the village of Kong To near Canton, China in

1892. He graduated from the Kwangtung Military School, immigrated to the United States in 1916 as a student, and subsequently settled in Fresno, Calif., where he married Ruth Lee in 1922. Seu Ling's principal occupations included Chinese herbalist, Chinese restaurant owner, and Chinese school principal and teacher. Though always busy, he was an activist and made time to hold offices in various Chinese organizations and family associations. During the Sino-Japanese war in China and World War II, he was very active in the Chinese War Relief, the Red Cross, Community and War Chests, and other charitable and service activities. Highly respected by the business and Chinese communities, he was a principled man who believed not only in hard work and productivity, but compassion for his fellow man.

Vern's father passed his work ethic to his eight children who worked in the various family enterprises, and both parents instilled cultural and ethical values in all the children. Citizenship, respect for authority, and personal character were stressed. Above all, the senior Chong's main goal was to assure that all of his children would have a higher education: all eight children graduated from a major college or university, and several have postgraduate degrees in the healthcare field.

The Chong Family

Vern met Ann on a blind date when Ann was working for the Social Security Administration in Fresno as a claims representative. But Vern was in his second year in medical school at Stanford (then located in San Francisco before moving to Palo Alto in 1960), so when the blind date blossomed, it became a long-distant courtship. Two years later, after Vern's junior year in medical school, he and Ann were married. They have three sons—Christopher, Gerald, and Douglas—and each adapted well to life in a military family, feeling that they were afforded many opportunities that they would not have had in a civilian family. And the children have grown into good citizens with good cultural and family ethics; each is successful in his chosen career field. The Chongs have seven grandchildren.

Vernon Chong on Success

"Success in life is a relative matter and our individual success criteria can be defined in many different ways … and not necessarily in financial terms", Chong believes. "Success is better defined in measures-of-merit that are based on contributions to one's family, community, society and country. One should be an active participant in most, if not all, aspects of one's life. It involves values and education, risk taking and venturing into new territories, and it is well worth the pursuit. There is a saying that goes: 'There are those who make things happen, those that watch things happen, and those that do not know what is happening' so be prepared for life's pursuits; let not the societal barriers stand in the way of one's higher calling and success."

Choy G. Wy

A Glimpse into an Architect's 97 Years

By Joyce Mar

韋材基

Wy designed the memorial of President John F. Kennedy, including the eternal flame and original picket fence that surrounds the gravesite at Arlington National Cemetery.

Early Years

Choy Wy was four years old when the 1906 earthquake struck in San Francisco. At that young age he could tell by the anxious faces of his mother, grandmother and brothers that there was grave danger in the city. During the chaos that prevailed, they were able to board a ferry to Oakland where, in the course of four days, there would be 4,000 Chinese looking for food and shelter. Upon arrival they had to live in crowded temporary quarters with friends until his mother's employer helped them acquire the house they would live in—on 27th Street in Oakland.

Choy was born in San Francisco in 1901. He was the second of three brothers in the Wy family. Times were difficult for the family as his father (Wy Yuen Quon, 1851-1905) had passed away leaving his mother (Lowe Ling How, 1877-1938), with three boys and her own mother. She managed to find work in a sewing factory and as an assistant to a Chinese herbalist. She was one of only a few women who worked at the San Francisco Chinatown Telephone Exchange. To be able to work there one had to be bilingual—fluent in Chinese and adequate in English— besides having to be able to remember nearly 2,500 subscribers' names and their phone numbers. She continued this work for a time when they moved to Oakland, allowing her to support her family.

While his older brother, Gay (1894-1971), also helped with supporting the family, Choy and his younger brother, Wing, (1903-1994) were able to pursue their education. Many Chinese American families followed this pattern. There were not many summer jobs available in those days to help his family but the one he remembered most was picking fruit in the countryside. He was quite proud of the free, overripe fruit he was given which he then "dragged in a sack" back home for his mother. He enrolled in Chinese school but admitted that he didn't retain much of his written Chinese. Yet he spoke both Chinese and English equally well.

Oakland High School is where he discovered the joy of drawing and drafting. His teacher recognized his talent and encouraged him to think about majoring in architecture at UC Berkeley. His mother could only think about who would ever hire a Chinese-American architect and discouraged him from studying architecture. Despite his mother's admonition, he graduated from UC Berkeley in 1923 with his degree in architecture. He recounted that there was probably only one other Chinese American who graduated with him in architecture.

Architect Years

Before long a job offer came from Washington, D.C., where he was hired by the Army Corps of Engineers, and it was there that he worked for over 40 years. When he first moved to Washington, he encountered some prejudice at the YMCA, where he was denied housing. The clerk told him it was the Y's policy not to rent to non-whites even while he was helpful in directing Choy to find housing elsewhere. (The YMCA rescinded this policy of exclusion a year later.) The clerk also invited Choy to board at his mother's home. During these early years he and one woman were probably the only registered architects employed by the U.S. government; architects were contracted out by the U.S. government prior to this time. By 1941 he was the chief of design in the Directorate of Military Construction for the Army Corps of Engineers, the highest civilian position in that branch. During Choy's career, he designed barracks and officers' quarters as well as military chapels and administration buildings. His work sometimes took him to military and airforce bases outside the continental United States. Two of his special projects not connected to the military were his designs for the memorial of President John F. Kennedy, including the eternal flame and original picket fence that surrounds the gravesite at Arlington National Cemetery, and the permanent residence for the vice president of the United States. (Later, in 1974, the grounds of the U.S. Naval Observatory was designated as the first official residence of the vice president.)

Though Wy worked full time in his government position, there were occasions—on his own—when he drew plans for more than a dozen homes in and around Washington. At one point he designed the renovation of the J.W. Marriott family home. Mr. Marriott asked Wy if he would be interested in helping him design new hotels, but Wy declined, because of his volume of work with the Corps of Engineers. It wasn't until the 1960s when he finally found time to design his own home.

Married Years and Community Participation

In 1926 Choy married Esther Chin (1907-2000), the girl who waited in California for him to be "properly employed for one year" in accordance with his mother's standards before he could return for their wedding. They were married for 72 years. To satisfy his mother in the Chinese tradition, Choy waited a week after his older brother's marriage before his own marriage took place. This seems to be the one known Chinese marriage and courtship custom that was followed in their family. All three brothers in this family went out on dates. All three brothers chose and married American-born Chinese women. They attended dances where they practiced the latest new step, the Charleston. They went to silent movies starring Rudolph Valentino or Charlie Chap-

lin. They hummed the music of Rudy Vallee, followed the acts that vaudeville brought to town and even played baseball and basketball and ran track. There were no arranged marriages, no dowries and no tea ceremonies performed by any of the daughters-in-law. This Wy family had begun at a very early period to observe Western ways that were not yet common among Chinese Americans. His mother dressed in Western clothes, usually in conservative colors and used a curling iron on her hair.

By the mid-1920s the Wy family had already been in America for more than 50 years. Choy's mother was born in San Francisco in 1877. It is unknown how her mother (maiden surname Lau) arrived in America. Choy's father was born in China where he was married, but his first wife died and he later married Choy's mother in the United States. He traveled often to Guatemala from San Francisco, presumably as a merchant. The Wy family was already uniquely American without any thought of returning to China, but, in America, the climate of prejudice against Chinese Americans was ever present. Despite embracing many American customs, Choy maintained the habit of buying fresh-killed chicken or roast duck in Chinatown and patronizing his favorite Chinese barber.

The Wy family had no ties with China until after 1980 when Choy and his wife researched and later visited his ancestral village there. His family had never found another Chinese Wy family in America. Therefore, there were no family associations to which they belonged, no letters that were ever written to China, until after the contact with the Wy clan in China after 1980.

During their years in Washington, Choy and Esther had many outside interests, including playing tennis, rooting for the local football and baseball teams, going to the opera or listening to jazz, attending horse races and hosting dinners in their home for a varied circle of friends, including overseas Chinese attached to the embassy in Washington and World War II servicemen who were told by parents or friends to "stop by to say hello to Aunt Esther and Uncle Choy." They were also world travelers. Whoever heard of Chinese Americans photographing yurts, a tent-like structure, in Mongolia back in the early 1970s? Actually, Choy's wife Esther was an accomplished photographer who was employed at Walter Reed Hospital. At 90 years old Choy took a trip to Tibet, climbing the mountains with the assistance of his cane.

Very much a part of his community, Choy contributed architectural services and funds for the expansion of the Chinese Community Church in Washington's Chinatown. He and his wife were generous supporters of Opera International, an organization that encouraged overseas Chinese and Chinese-American artists in their pursuit of music. They had no children, but their warmth and generosity toward their nieces and nephews were always apparent. After they both retired, they supported a student from China for undergraduate studies. That student went on to receive his Ph.D. and is now employed as a scientist in America.

Along with his pioneering efforts as a Chinese American architect, Choy Wy seemed quite comfortable moving seamlessly from his Chinese roots to being Chinese American during the early twentieth century. He and Esther had a good life and had many friends in the Washington community. Except for not finding a room at the Y the first day he arrived in Washington, he had not encountered any prejudice toward him (which he expressed forcefully during the oral history interviews). Ever proud of his profession, and until his death in 1998 at age 97, he still read his architectural journals and was fully aware of the events of the day.

Wy designed the memorial of President John F. Kennedy, at Arlington National Cemetery.

Jim Hong

Go East and Fly High

By Bill Chew

> They overcame hard times and adversity with determination, courage, and strength.

Ancestors

This is the story of Jim Hong, a Chinese-American aeronautical engineer who achieved the positions of chief of aerodynamics, preliminary design, advance system research and manufacturing program manager for the Lockheed Aircraft Corporation. He graduated from the University of Washington in 1941. He had to break the racial barrier to get the first job. His forefathers were also breaking barriers to settle in the north-west corner of the U.S. following the Gold Rush. The Hongs are good examples of many of the early families of Chinese Americans in the United States.

Jim Hong is a native of Pocatello, Idaho. His grandfather, Hong Kee, came to America in the mid-1850s. Record keeping was minimal prior to 1880 and immigration records were destroyed by fire in the 1906 San Francisco earthquake.

From the meager amount of information available, Jim surmised that his grandfather did his mining in Idaho to escape the onerous laws restricting Chinese miners in California. He made enough money to return to China to get married. His first son, Hong Kee "number two", was born in August, 1867. He must have returned to the States alone because the 1870 Idaho census shows a person named Hong Kee, age 35, listed as a miner in the territory of Owyhee, which included the future town of Pocatello, Idaho. It is uncertain whether he returned to China to bring his son back to the States or had his son travel by himself, because an Idaho fire destroyed the census records of 1880 and 1890. In any

event, Hong Kee #2, Jim Hong's father, came to Evanston, Wyo. at age 14, a year before the passage of the Exclusion Act of 1882. He worked for his father for a year at the Sam Kee Co. store, then left for Pocatello to work for the Oregon Short Line as a cook for the Depot Café.

The Scott Act of 1888 prohibited Chinese men working as laborers from bringing wives to America. Like his father Hong Kee "number two" returned to China to get married but had to leave his bride in China. He returned to the U.S. to start the Grand Café in 1895 and operated it until its sale in 1903. This allowed him to rejoin his wife in China to start a family. Hong Kee stayed in China for four years. He took on a younger second wife, Leung Shee, because he thought that his first wife could not bear children. With his second wife, he traveled to Vancouver to establish a business that would guarantee him merchant credentials that would allow him to bring his wife over legally to the United States.

"Number two" and his brother started the Hong Yuen Co., a mercantile store in Vancouver. Hong Kee and Leung Shee had their first child, Yen Lun (Jennie), in August 1908. A year later, the young family returned to Pocatello and bought the Wah Yuen Company, which was so successful that Hong Kee built a three-story building, the most modern in the city. The first-class U.S. Café and his mercantile store occupied the street floor. The other two floors were leased to the Crow Hotel with 35 rooms, each plumbed with hot and cold running water.

The Early Days

Hong Kee and Leung Shee had eight children. Hong Kee prospered and was eventually considered the wealthiest Chinese man in the region. James was not yet two years of age when his father died at the age of 54 on Jan. 5, 1922. He was buried in China according to Chinese tradition. Leung Shee returned to China with her eight children to provide them a Chinese education, leaving the management of all the businesses to her husband's nephew, Pak Wah, who was the most articulate in English and recently married. Unfortunately, at 23, he had no experience in business or in management. On learning her assets were almost gone, Leung Shee returned to the States with her brood in the steerage class on the SS President Jackson. The restaurant was losing money, the mercantile store was sold, and the hotel lease income barely covered the mortgage.

Leung Shee Hong was a strong disciplinarian and a survivor. She supplemented her income as a seamstress, while the children worked at whatever jobs were available, including selling newspapers and magazines. Eating homegrown vegetables also helped to save on the food bills. Jim's mother used her wisdom, courage and determination to the survival of the family.

Education, Opportunities and Marriage

In 1935 Mrs. Hong made a monumental decision to move to Seattle, Wash., because Pocatello had limited education and job opportunities. Being the only Chinese family in Pocatello, she wanted her nearly adult children to be in a Chinese social environment. James finished high school in

Seattle and enrolled at the University of Washington with the intention of becoming an aeronautical engineer. He believed that this was the way of the future and worked and borrowed money to pay for his education. At the university, all male students were required to take ROTC courses, but Jim was excused because they did not want a Chinese person in the officer corps. Just before his graduation, the school administrator told him he had insufficient credits because he had not completed ROTC. They were reminded of their actions four years earlier and told that if they kept him from graduating they would hear about it in the newspaper. This item quickly became a non-issue, and in 1941 he graduated with honors with a BS degree in aeronautical engineering.

Getting a job was foremost on Jim's mind. He contacted Boeing by phone, as his professors suggested. While impressed with his academic achievements, the Boeing personnel officer stammered out in an embarrassed voice, "I am sorry, we do not hire Chinese." This rebuff resulted in Jim sending a plethora of letters to Lockheed, Douglas, Vultee, Vega, Hughes, Consolidated, North American, Grumman, Vought, Brewster and Martin. Of the few replies he did receive, the perfunctory form letter of "no interest at this time" appeared to be engraved in stone. It became obvious that somehow or some way, a face-to-face interview was a prerequisite.

Since Southern California had the largest concentration of aircraft firms, he made plans to go to Los Angeles. Before he could do that, Jim had to report to his draft board in San

Francisco. A sympathetic draft board employee, on seeing his university transcript, stated she could not provide him with a deferment but would put him at the bottom of the list to provide him enough time to get a job that would give him the deferment legally. She felt with his education that he could better serve the country in industry than as a foot soldier.

Residing at the Los Angeles YMCA, he made many forays to the various aircraft firms. Cooling his heels and waiting an interminable amount of time to just talk to the personnel representative, who had no knowledge of aviation, to receive a "don't call us, we'll call you" was a painful experience. Finally, Fletcher Aviation, a small aircraft company in Pasadena, hired him for 65 cents an hour. By then to work at any job provided a sense of accomplishment. The hours spent, and the chores taken, including redesign, testing, flying, helping the shop building parts and even janitorial service contributed to his education. In July 1942 his boss told him that he was going to return to Vega, and asked if he would like to follow. Jim became the first Chinese engineer ever hired by a major airplane company.

On Dec. 28, 1942, he married Nellie Lee in San Francisco. At that time, it was difficult for Chinese to buy homes outside of Chinatown. In 1953, they purchased their first home in the Hollywood Hills directly from the owner. After five years, their charming two-bedroom home was too small for their four children–Michael, Jerald, Sharon and Jeffrey. When they bought a ranch-style home in Sherman Oaks, their neighbors joined forces and offered to buy them

out. When their neighbors finally got to know them, they were invited to join the homeowners association, where Jim was designated treasurer.

Meanwhile, Jim was extremely proficient and productive in his new job. His accomplishments included his first design of a new Navy P2V Neptune Anti-Submarine Warfare airplane. After completing the flight test operations phase, Jim was promoted to division chief of aerodynamics. In this position he was responsible for all the aerodynamics, flutter, thermodynamics and power plant analyses for all of Lockheed's airplanes, including the Constellation, the P-80 and F-104 jet fighters, the cargo transport C-130 Hercules, the commercial propjet Electra and a new concept for a helicopter. In 1965 he became technical director of Lockheed's Supersonic Transport Program because it represented a huge challenge. Later Jim took on the challenge of running a small manufacturing program and finally the L-1011 Tri-Star transport. He retired in 1975 after 33 years but soon after was recruited by other companies. He continued to work until 1995, when he retired for good.

Recognition and Family Values in his Life

Jim Hong's talent was recognized early on by company executives and by his peers. A paper he wrote on airplane construction technique won the Wright Brothers' Medal from the aeronautical section of the Society of Automotive Engineers (SAE). During his 33 years at Lockheed, Jim wrote reports and proposals that won many design competitions.

The Hong Kee family personifies the Chinese work ethics of hard work, frugality and honesty. They overcame hard times and adversity with determination, courage, and strength. They infused their children with values emphasizing the benefits of having a better education—a truly American Chinese mainstream value. Their children learned to be goal-oriented rather than role-oriented while being aware of the necessity to acclimate into the American mainstream. Jim's story provides a model of inspiration for future generations, truly a portrait of pride.

Jim Hong is a published author of two books, "Go East, Go East to Gold Mountain" and "If Man Were Meant to Fly."

Ruby Kwong Lee

Many Paths to Fulfillment

By Susie Ling and Wing Mar

After arriving in Guangdong, Ruby would study in Pui Ching Primary School and True Light High School for six years. She was given a scholarship to go to the high school because she was outstanding in her calligraphy class and was always tops in her classes at Pui Ching.

A Reverse Educational Experience

It was a culture shock to return to Sacramento High School in California. The standards were so different from my school in Canton. Here, in Sacramento, my high school classmates thought I was from China. They did not know I was born in Sacramento, but had left for seven years to go to school in China.

What was it about Ruby's life that had her going back and forth between the two continents? It was a combination of circumstances and the adventurous attitude of a 10 year old American girl of Chinese immigrant parents. Her father, one of the first Chinese physicians in the Sacramento valley, died in 1927 of pneumonia, before the days of antibiotics. He left his widow alone with six young children to raise. Ruby was six years old. To make ends meet, her mother, a schoolteacher, taught during the day at the Chinese language and church school and would work the night shift at the local cannery with other immigrant Chinese women. Little Ruby's paternal grandparents arrived three years later to help settle the family affairs. They offered to take two children back to China with them to lighten the burden on her mother. Ruby's brother, William, the oldest son, was chosen. Ruby—the third daughter—agreed to go when her two older sisters refused. It was 1931 and Ruby had just turned 10.

For seven years, Ruby would study in two private schools in rhe Canton area, achieving a status that was unheard

of for a girl who was from the United States. As the class valedictorian at Pui Ching Primary School, she received a scholarship to a well known Guangdong high school, True Light Middle School. As an "overseas student", it was an unusual honor to be admitted to True Light. Not only did Ruby have outstanding calligraphy skills, but she was an honor student in all her classes, played on the varsity softball team as its youngest member, joined the choir and social clubs, and was elected class president. One school activity was a yearly Olympic type athletic competition for all the high schools in the province. This is where Ruby's softball team played against a boy's team with an overseas Chinese American boy, named Mark Lee from Los Angeles. A decade later they would meet again, a continent away, and become sweethearts.

The year was 1937. Ruby was into her sixth year in China when Japanese forces start heavily bombing Guangdong and people begin to flee the city.

The train leaving Canton to Hong Kong was packed like sardines. At the terminal just before Kowloon, we had to evacuate because the wheel caught on fire probably due to the excessive weight. We could see lights flashing over Canton from the bombs. When the war threatened Hong Kong, passage was arranged for me to go home and soon. Like many other overseas kids, I was on a ship headed for California.

When Ruby returned to her hometown of Sacramento in 1938, she found her life had changed and others no longer looked at her as a local California girl.

I was very quiet at first because I had forgotten much of my spoken English. Still, I did well in class, as my educational background was very strong. I did not take shorthand, typing, or shop like the others. In fact, I was one of the few girls who took the core academic courses in science. I was the oddball. Even the girls I knew from elementary school before I left for China thought I was strange, and I was initially known as "the girl from China". But I was not completely avoided or rejected. There was this Japanese American girl who took some science classes with me. We were friends, although we were taught and expected to be enemies because of the war between China and Japan. To us, our interest and friendship as kids overrode the geopolitical concerns of the adults. Much to my distress, I later learned that she was sent to a Japanese internment camp and we lost touch.

The ethnically mixed Sacramento High yearbook shows Ruby Kwong as an active leader in many clubs as she was determined to make her mark wherever she was in school. She graduated in the class of 1940.

College, Career Choices, and Time for Family

I was ready to go to junior college and then transfer to UC Berkeley. My older brother said to me, "Don't ask Mom for any money…. She does not have any. Whatever you need, go out and earn it." I did many odd jobs like typing out menus, clerking in a dry goods store, and working in the chemistry lab at the junior college. When I transferred to UC Berkeley, I worked part-time at the Heinz 57 factory as a quality control lab tech. Life was hard, but I took the tough courses and studied when I could. Upon graduation with a

> **"Don't ask Mom for any money; she does not have any more. Whatever you need, go out and earn it."**

degree in chemistry in 1944, I pursued graduate work in biochemistry at Berkeley. I applied for medical school at UC San Francisco and also to the grad school at University of Wisconsin and was accepted to both schools. UC San Francisco Medical School only took a maximum of two girls per class. It was a great achievement for me. However, when my younger brother got accepted to dental school, I felt like the family resources needed to support him since he would be the breadwinner of his family

Instead Ruby continued at UC Berkeley doing graduate work in biochemistry.

I had met my husband-to-be, Mark Lee, briefly in Canton. Mark also returned to the U.S. in 1938 and was drafted for WWII. When he returned, he looked me up at Berkeley. We fell in love and married in 1946.

After marriage, Mark earned his M.D., becoming a family physician in Chinatown, Los Angeles. Ruby supported and encouraged her husband's education while taking care of a growing family. She had four children, three daughters and one son, over the next seven years. After the birth of her third child, Ruby resumed her science career. She first worked as a compound chemist for a pharmaceutical company, then became the production manager for the whole lab. Next, Ruby worked for the research division of Rexall Drugs as a synthetic chemist developing new drugs, including one that was patented for treatment of children with learning disabilities. She was the first woman research chemist to work in that lab. With her hard work ethic, her male co-workers soon accepted her as a colleague.

When Rexall moved to Northridge, I decided to make a career change into teaching. The kids were going to school and I wanted the same hours as my children. I went to night school at USC to fulfill my teaching credential and then I worked for Los Angeles Unified School District (LAUSD). In 1958, I got into a car accident and I was disabled, but I later went back to teach math at Berendo Junior High, as it was right in my own neighborhood. I figured it would be easy for me, especially as I didn't drive at that time; I could take a cab home for a dollar.

Actually, Ruby's accident in 1958 left her hospitalized for several months with multiple broken bones. Returning home after three months and several operations, she had to learn to walk again with crutches, then a leg brace, which she wore when she resumed teaching in Los Angeles' inner-city junior high and high schools. Eventually, she improved her strength to be able to walk unassisted. Later, she further overcame her post-accident fears, and learned to drive a car. She advanced as a teacher to become the department chair, earning teaching awards, and later pioneering a Math Lab and a new curriculum for Berendo Junior High.

After 26 years of teaching, she retired. Ruby continued to be busy at home as a grandmother of eight grandchildren a board member of the Chinatown Service Center, contributor to the Chinatown Library, as a traveler to four continents, as a manager of her investments, and as a friend. She has shared her hobbies of cooking, painting, sewing, orchid growing and flower design with many people whose lives she has touched. Her four children, who all became professionals in medicine and dentistry, credit their mother with just the right combination of discipline, unselfish love, and instruction by example.

Reflections

As a teacher, she recalls the many young students she helped in their teenage years by encouraging them to succeed, not just by arming them with strong math skills that helped them progress in the sciences. She added to their personal confidence by encouraging and counseling them to reach for higher goals and aspirations.

I am most proud of my family. My husband and I had great rapport. In our quiet way, together, we were able to help many. All our children were very good children. Two are physicians and two are dentists. They were taught early to show proper respect and I can't ask for more. When I think back, it was hard at times, but I think I did pretty well. Don't let adversity discourage you. Just stick with it and put in that extra effort and you can succeed in ways you never dreamed!

Annie Chin Siu

A First and An Original

By Susie Ling

> *"Being an orthodontist turned out to be a very good career for me. Working gives me the satisfaction that I have done something worthwhile ...."*

nnie Chin Siu was the only woman in her class at UC San Francisco Dental School. But despite her excellent educational achievements, Dr. Siu could not find someone who would hire a Chinese-American woman dental associate in the 1950s. Heedless of such prejudice, Dr. Siu opened her own practice and became one of the first Chinese-American female orthodontists.

Growing up in San Francisco's Chinatown

Annie Chin grew up in the unique world of San Francisco Chinatown, surrounded by her four sisters and two brothers. Her father was a domestic cook for the Paulson family, who owned a downtown haberdashery. Her mother had been a maid in the same household until she became pregnant:

"I was born at home in San Francisco Chinatown. My father delivered me and my siblings. My father was born in Guangdong and immigrated as a teenager. He went back to marry my mother. My father had some education but my mother had none.

My father installed some bathtubs in our basement and my mother had that business going. Ladies in the neighborhood would come for their weekly bath and mother provided towels and things like that.

There were seven children, and I was the fifth. I had one older brother but my father wanted another son. I was lucky that the third and fourth children were girls, or else I wouldn't have come along in 1929.

My father was driven. He worked long hours at his low-paying job. On Sundays, he would take us to the park. He had a 1926 Buick that he probably bought from his boss. We

youngsters were embarrassed to be seen in such an old car. Much later, we learned to appreciate his sacrifices."

Most of the Chinatown youngsters went to the all-Chinese Commodore Stockton Elementary. When they transferred to Francisco Junior High, Annie and her peers came into contact with students from the neighboring Italian community.

"All the staff were Caucasians except for two, a man and a woman. We really didn't have the right attitude towards the man. He was short and bald and we didn't look up to him. We didn't realize how much he had achieved as a Chinese-American teacher.

Francisco Junior High was in Italian town and was my first exposure to non-Asians. They had much longer names than the Chinese! A few days into school, this Italian boy came to me and said something obscene in Chinese. I looked startled and he laughed because he realized he had pronounced it right. Apparently, all the Italian boys learned the bad Chinese phrases and all the Chinese kids learned the bad Italian phrases."

Annie Chin continued at the now-defunct Commerce High School. World War II loomed in the background of her formative years.

"The war had started and we saw the Japanese Americans leaving. We had a polite, cordial relationship with some Japanese neighbors. They came over one night, apologized, and asked if we would buy their rice and other things they could not take with them. We paid them for it. Prior to Dec.7, 1941, the Sino-Japanese War had already begun. We Chinese were to avoid the Japanese. We didn't buy things that were made in Japan. We wouldn't talk to them. We would

even cross the street to avoid passing a Japanese store.

The war ended when I was still in high school. The United Nations started across the street. Some of my classmates even went over as interpreters to help people negotiate the city."

Upon graduation in 1947, Annie was uncertain about her own future. In high school, she had avoided a school counselor who systematically tracked Chinese girls into sewing courses to prepare them for work in the garment industry

Choosing a Profession

At UC Berkeley the young Chinatown girl began to define her goals.

"My brother returned from the Armed Services after World War II and asked me about my major. I didn't realize that it had to be chosen. So he said, 'What do you like?' I said, 'I like math...' He thought, 'That's dumb, what would you do with that?' Somewhere along the line, I decided on dentistry. It kind of fell in 'by guess and by gosh'. I muddled around and found my way.

When I was at Berkeley, I went to visit my major advisor. When it was my turn, the advisor asked if I was in the wrong place as he was not the advisor for dental hygiene. I told him I was pre-dental. He looked at my records and told me I would never get into dental school with the grades I had. His attitude and pronouncement was a stimulus for me; it drove me to get better grades."

Before the Civil Rights Movement, many professional schools had quotas limiting the number of women and students of color. Annie was the only woman in her class of 60 at UC San Francisco Dental School. She was the third woman ever. There were about five or six other Asian Americans when she entered in 1950.

"My family was surprised. I would not have made it if I didn't live at home. For one thing, my father could not, and would not, support my living out alone. I had also gotten accepted to University of Southern California Dental School, but I would have never made it there because the cost would have killed me."

Annie Chin graduated with the UCSF Dental Class of 1954. She served four years as the class secretary. She was accepted as one of six students to the highly regarded combined-orthodontic curriculum and graduated as a specialist in orthodontics.

Annie married Tim Siu in August of 1954. Her husband was interning at Los Angeles County Hospital and Annie moved down to Southern California. As interns were not making a living wage, Annie looked for employment.

"I had my new dental license, my new marriage license, and my new driver's license. I started driving all over the freeways looking for work. Somebody at the Dental Department had helped me write to people looking for associates, but no one replied. I admit I was 'different' as I was a young Asian woman. I probably was still wearing bobby socks and may just have started wearing lipstick. I was not sophisticated and certainly not street smart. People were nice but it was always 'no'."

Starting a practice was not easy either. Annie and her husband had to finance the risky venture by themselves. Annie scouted several communities and chose Alhambra:

"Alhambra was such a delight at that time because Garfield Avenue was tree-lined on both sides. It was a small all-American town. I found a small dental-medical duplex on Garfield we could afford, so I signed the lease and ordered equipment. I opened my office in 1955. It turned out that my new neighbor's daughter needed braces. She talked me

> **"My advice to the young women readers of this book is to pursue what you find exciting."**

down to a very reduced rate. Then she decided that I should do both her daughters for the price of one. Those were my first two patients."

In the suburban 1950s, most married women followed the norm of being stay-at-home mothers. Annie continued to listen to her own drumbeat. Her daughter, Susan, was born in 1957, followed by three younger sisters.

"I condensed my work load. I worked really hard as I reached the end of my pregnancy. For each baby, I took two months out of the office. In those days, if you took too little time, you were not considered a good mother.

Being an orthodontist turned out to be a very good career for me. When things got going, there was no reason to stop. So I stuck around so long. Usually, the patient – as well as the parents – end up happy with the results. Working gives you the satisfaction that you've done something worthwhile. Now that I'm essentially retired and although I've been busy, there are days when I still feel I haven't done something special."

Along with her practice, Dr. Siu has been a clinical associate professor at USC School of Dentistry for more than 25 years. She is a member of the USC School of Dentistry Board of Councilors and the Angle Society. In October of 2000, Annie was awarded a Fellowship in the American College of Dentists for her demonstrated leadership and contributions to the dental profession and society. In 2003, she was the proud recipient of the UCSF's Dental Alumni Assn. Medal of Honor. She was also given the Edward Angle Orthodontic Excellence Award.

Dedication to Her Community

Annie Siu is also well known for her dedication to community service. Annie chaired a committee to start a Chinese-American women's scholarship at California State University, Los Angeles. She is a past president of the Soroptimist Club of Alhambra-San Gabriel-San Marino. Annie Siu has served on the boards of the West San Gabriel Valley YMCA, the United Way and the Alhambra Community Hospital and in 1988 she became president of the Alhambra Chamber of Commerce, the first Chinese American in that capacity. She received the 2003 Woman of the Year Award for California's 29th Congressional District and the 2003 Historymaker Award by the Chinese American Museum.

"You should give back to your community. My teacher promoted that. Don't just take from your community. When United Way called, I did that. You see the good that the service clubs do. You get a lot from your participation. It's not quid pro quo, but you get different kinds of satisfaction. I don't have an agenda to do one thing or another. I just do what seems right. My Soroptimist service club is currently working on a project for six girls. That's not very many, but it is important. We also work on Reading is Fundamental with the Alhambra and San Gabriel school districts. We

Annie Chin Siu was the only woman in her class at UC San Francisco Dental School.

go into the third-grade classrooms to read to the students and bring books to them.

My advice to the young women readers of this book is to pursue what you find exciting. The times are changing and many fields are opening up for young women.

Those who are talented will be promoted and recognized. Be in a profession you are good at and one that you enjoy.

In my life, I'm most proud of my family. My four daughters are doing well and are independent. Secondly, I'm very happy that in my profession, I've tried to maintain a standard that was set before me. I'd stay with problem cases, despite my set fees. I hate to stop short of my standards."

Dr. Annie Siu: a first and an original

Annie Siu was joined in her practice by her daughter, Dr. Tina Siu. Another daughter is a dentist, while the others work as an athletic director and a registered nurse.

Julius F. Sue

L.A. Chinatown's Medical Patriarch

By Susie Ling

> "As I walked toward this jovial man, I was fully aware of what he has built in Chinatown, how far he had come in his own career and as an advocate for Asian American healthcare."

In the Chinese-American community, hundreds of men and women of all ages are proud to call themselves "Dr. Sue babies." The term conjures a sense of belonging and a history. After all, "Dr. Sue babies" were all delivered with special care.

Early Background

Julius F. Sue MD was born in southern China's Zhongshan county on Nov. 2, 1914. His father, Stephen So Chee Sue, was an herbalist who wanted his oldest son to follow in his footsteps. But his fate would not be in the village. Instead, the family migrated to the United States when Julius was 13. Father had arrived in Oregon first and established himself as a merchant and herbalist in Portland and nearby Corvallis. The herb enterprise served both a Chinese-American and a Caucasian clientele. Lum Shee-sue, Julius' mother, followed him to America with the two sons, Julius and Eugene. The youngest sister, Violet, was born in 1929 in Oregon.

Julius attended Portland's Lincoln High School. Founded in 1869 as Portland High School, Lincoln is one of the oldest public high schools west of the Rocky Mountains. Julius learned English quickly and continued to speak Zhongshan dialect, Cantonese, and a little Mandarin. The teenager worked hard and was active in the school's chess club. The family also belonged to the Chinese Christian Church.

For Julius, the dream was always to live up to his father's and his own expectations to become a doctor. He graduated from Reed College in Portland in 1938 and was subsequently accepted to the University of Oregon medical school. His father died just before Julius graduated in 1941. Those were not easy days for ambitious Asian Americans. The school had a quota on Asian students and there was only one other, a Japanese American, in his class. Still, life-long friends were made on the University of Oregon campus. For seven summers, Julius also worked at a cannery in Alaska to earn school funds.

Major Julius F. Sue
14th Air Force

With the pending war, Julius knew what he had to do. He interned at St. Catherine Hospital in East Chicago, Ind., for a few months. Then he was commissioned as a first lieutenant, in January, 1943, and he served briefly as a base surgeon at the Atlanta Army Air Base. And because few others would take the job, Dr. Sue volunteered to serve the 14th Air Force—the Flying Tigers.

Prior to World War II, retired U.S. AAF Capt. Claire L. Chennault was commissioned by Madame Chiang Kai-shek to reorganize the Chinese Air Force. When active fighting with the Japanese ensued, Chennault built the American Volunteer Group, the Flying Tigers, with an impressive record of attacking Japanese planes all over China. In 1943, President Roosevelt activated this unit as the 14th Air Force and Chennault was promoted to major general.

Julius' wife, Eleanor, remembers:

"Julius had strong feelings about the war. He was concerned about America being attacked. He was very patriotic. He felt it was his duty to serve his country so he volunteered for the U.S. Army... They needed doctors for the 14th and he volunteered. He didn't want to go to England, he wanted to go to China. Nobody else wanted to go to China as it was unfamiliar territory."

As a group surgeon, Dr. Sue attended to the medical care of seven air bases where 14th Air Force personnel operated, including Kunming, Luliang, Chanyi, Tungjin, and Chihkiang (Zhijiang). At the end of the fighting, Dr. Sue joined the U.S. Repatriation Team in Shantung, China where he gave Japanese soldiers physical examinations before they boarded ships to return to Japan. Dr. Sue did not return home until May of 1946.

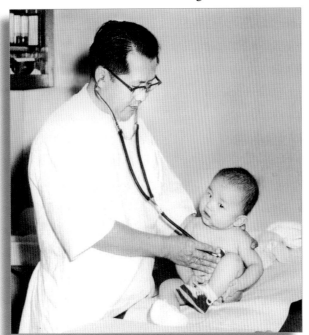

Building Roots in Los Angeles

Like so many other Chinese Americans during the war years, Dr. Sue's mother and his fiancée both relocated to California. Eleanor Young, formerly of Chicago, had met Julius while he was interning at St. Catherine Hospital. Her father had come to Chicago as a paper son (he used an assumed surname, a common immigrant practice) in 1920 without knowing a soul. He built a hardware store and restaurant in Chicago's Chinatown. During the war years, Eleanor's father moved his family to Oakland, Calif.

"I corresponded with Julius through the war years. I volunteered for the Army Signal Corps and was stationed in Ogden, Utah as a civilian. I lived on the air base. We were married in 1947."

Julius' GI patients and friends encouraged him to begin private practice in Los Angeles. Chinese-American veterans were now bringing brides and young families to the Los Angeles area and they needed a doctor. By 1946, Dr. Sue was one of the first Chinese-American doctors at French Hospital in Los Angeles' Chinatown.

Dr. Sue first opened his general practice in downtown Los Angeles at 307 South Hill Street, near Central Market. But his patients complained—especially the pregnant women—and urged him to move closer to them. At his new address at 746 North Broadway in Chinatown, Dr. Sue became a community doctor. (The clinic later moved to 711 West College Street.) Dr. Sue not only cared for pregnant women and delivered their babies, he was their pediatrician and family doctor as well. In the afternoons, Dr. Sue worked out of his office. Eleanor often accompanied her husband on late house calls:

"There would be five or six kids. Julius would check all of them but only charge for one kid. He charged about five dollars for house calls and three dollars for office visits in the 1950s. If you couldn't pay, he would forget about it. He was also very active in Chinatown. He wanted to build professional buildings and was always fundraising for the hospital. He was successful because he was kindhearted. He mentored a lot of young doctors and encouraged them to stay in Chinatown to serve the community. Chinatown needs specialists close by."

Dr. Sue was often referred to as "kai yeh" (or "godfather") by the next generation of Chinese-American medical professionals.

Building a Legacy

Dr. Tiffany Chow of Rotman Research Institute, in Toronto, Canada was a "Dr. Sue baby." She now works on neuro-imaging. She writes:

In most ways, I have never considered my parents to be very Chinese, [except when] my mother told me how she found Dr. Sue. She said, "If you were a Chinese woman, you went to see Dr. Sue. All the Chinese babies were born at the French Hospital." The office was run efficiently by his wife, Mrs. Sue, and for all I knew, there weren't any other Chinese doctors who saw Chinese people living in Los Angeles.

By the time I went to medical school myself, there were, of course, plenty of Asian American doctors in the States. On some of my application interviews, people would ask, "Would you return to 'your community' when you complete your training?" At the time, I didn't recognize the Chinese American in myself, and I found that an odd question. Nevertheless, 10 years later, my research interests came to rest on educational outreach to Chinese communities in the Los Angeles area. With some trepidation, I went to a Chinese American Medical Assn. of Southern California meeting to develop ties with physicians serving the Chinese community. Not speaking Cantonese or Mandarin fluently and being very junior to the members of the association, I wasn't sure how welcome I might be.

But Dr. Sue was there. He made it a point to attend each of these meetings, in support of all the Chinese physicians who had come up behind him. As I made my way over to his table, I considered the impressive and inspiring history of the jovial man sitting with old friends, enjoying a collegial evening. I was fully aware of what he had built in Chinatown, how far he had come in his own career and as an advocate for Asian American health care. I introduced myself to him as one of his babies, and I was bowled over by his warmth, enthusiasm, and immediate acceptance into the

fold. He took it upon himself to endorse me to the rest of the group. And despite the fact that there were surely hundreds of us "Dr. Sue babies," from that point on, he never forgot my name, our brief meeting on my first day out of the womb, or my research project. Needless to say, I have been grateful for that welcome, but it also serves as an example of the grace with which great things can be built. His was the kind of grace that earns a patient's trust, helps people through tragic events, mentors budding professionals, builds teams, and makes positive differences on all levels. He has had a meaningful impact on the community, but also on individuals, as a truly special contributor. We owe it to him to continue the momentum he began.

Speaking five Chinese dialects, Eleanor Sue did more than help her husband at his practice. She taught at Washington Junior High School, Bellflower High School, and Cal State Dominguez Hills. She and Julius raised another generation of Sue doctors: Jeffrey (radiologist in Honolulu), Darryl (internal medicine at Harbor General/UCLA), and Gregory (orthodontist). Dr. Julius F. Sue retired in August 2002 and passed on later that year. The "Dr. Sue babies" still abound.

Choh Hao Li

The Master Chemist of the Master Gland

By E. Leong Way with introduction by Wing Mar

Dr. Li contributed to scientific research by demonstrating the structure and then the isolation of the Growth Hormone in 1956 enabling endocrinologists to treat exceptionally short stature people with commercially produced products.

Introduction

In this book, we sought to bring interesting life stories of under-recognized Chinese Americans to a generally unaware public. And yet, this story is about a man who is still remembered worldwide for his lifesaving pioneering work in discovering hormones. The reason for this exception is that the editors wanted to broaden the recognition of Choh Hao Li not only for his acomplishment of isolating six out of eight hormones from the pituitary glands, but also for his multifaceted and collegial approach to his science. From a historical point of view, the protein chemist Choh Hao Li led an adventurous life finding the secrets of the hormone in living and functioning mammalian brains. But he did not do this in isolation but with many team members whom he mentored. We hope people, especially the young, will appreciate him for some very important scitentific discoveries.

Emeritus Prof. E. Leong Way was a friend and colleague of Choh Hao at the UC San Francisco Medical Center. In 1988, he coauthored—with Leslie L. Bennett, David Chung and Harold Papkoff—the University of California Memoriam to Choh Hao Li; excerpts from this memorial follow. I added some information from articles written by other authors.

The Productive and Adventurous Years

The death of Professor Choh Hao Li in Berkeley, Calif., in November, 1987, brought to an end an intimate 52-year association with the University of California. In 1938, when he began his research on the isolation and purification of the anterior pituitary hormones, none of the six then known had been identified chemically. The following years brought unparalleled advances in the isolation and chemical assessment of a large group of pituitary protein and peptide hormones. The following paragraphs can only offer a glimpse of his extraordinary accomplishments

In the early 1940s, Li obtained a highly purified and potent preparation of bovine (cattle) growth hormone. Li wanted to use this specimen to learn the composition (amino acid sequence) of growth hormone from cattle and other species. Of prime importance was his isolation of human growth hormone in 1956. Thus ended a protracted period of research into the mystery of these amino acid linkages. From his determination of the structure of the human growth hormone, the ability to synthesize human growth hormone, both by chemical means and also by recombinant DNA technology, was made possible. This was important clinically to the endocrinologist since it was known that humans do not respond to growth hormones from other species except from human or the higher primates. Now an exceptionally short stature person can be treated with the synthetic hormones. Not to rest on his laurels, Li found another vista to study when he discovered b-endorphin, a protein substance in brain tissues that was tested to be several times more active than morphine as a pain reliever.

By the time of Li's death, all of the original six anterior pituitary hormones had been chemically identified, their amino acid sequences determined. One of them, human growth hormone, was being sold for clinical usage.

Li was generous in providing hormone preparations he

had made to fellow workers worldwide. He was especially generous in acknowledging the contributions of his students, post-doctoral fellows, and laboratory staff. In surveying his bibliography it is not unusual to find laboratory technicians among the co-authors of many papers. With the establishment in 1950 of his own laboratory—the Hormone Research Laboratory in Berkeley and later in San Francisco—Li nurtured an environment that in many respects was very much like a family. The family, representing senior staff, post-doctoral scientists, students, and technical staff, numbered 200 or more over the years. These people came not only from the United States, but from every continent in the world.

Becoming an emeritus professor and retiring as director of the Hormone Research Laboratory in 1983 was not an occasion for his becoming inactive. Rather, he established yet another laboratory, the Laboratory of Molecular Endocrinology at UCSF, where he could continue his hands-on research style with somewhat fewer administrative duties.

Many awards and honors came to C. H. Li for his scientific work. He was the recipient of 10 honorary degrees from universities both in the United States and abroad. He received 28 honors and awards, among which was the Koch Award from the Endocrine Society, the Luft Medal from the Swedish Society of Endocrinology and the Lasker Award. He was a fellow or a member of 14 societies and he was a sought-after visiting professor. Prominent among his teaching positions were the first Herbert M. Evans Memorial Lectureship, the

Faculty Research Lectureship at UC San Francisco, and the first Geschwind Memorial Lecturer at the UC Davis.

Li was on numerous advisory boards for a wide variety of activities such as the Sloan Kettering Institute for Cancer Research, the International Symposia on Growth Hormones, the 8th International Congress of Endocrinology held in Kyoto, Japan in 1988 and the Advisory Board of the Chinese University of Hong Kong as well as Academia Sinica and the National Science Council of Taiwan. He published over 1,000 scientific papers through 1980, averaging 50-60 papers per year and was editor of many specialized books and journals.

The Early Years

Choh Hao Li was born in Canton, China (Guangzhou), the fourth of 14 children of Kan Chi Li and Mew Shing Twui. He graduated from Pui Jing High School in Canton and then attended the prestigious University of Nanking, where he received a B.S. degree in chemistry in 1933. From that year until the summer of 1935 he was the instructor of chemistry and during these years he conducted research leading to his first scientific paper, published in 1935.

Li received the Nichols Medal from the American Chemical Society in March 1979. In his acceptance speech entitled, "Faith and Fate: My Personal Experiences," he recounted briefly how he applied for graduate work in the United States at the University of California and at the University of Michigan. Enroute to Michigan, he stopped in Berkeley to visit his older brother, Choh Ming Li, who was then completing his Ph.D. in economics. His brother insisted that Choh Hao should see Prof. G.N. Lewis, dean of the College of Chemistry. Choh had brought with him a reprint of his article in the Journal of American Chemical Society of which Prof. Ward V. Evans of Northwestern University was senior author. Since Lewis knew Ward Evans, Lewis decided to accept Choh Hao as a graduate student on probation for one semester. Thus began his long association with the University of California.

Choh Hao Li met Annie S. H. Lu of Nanchang in China's Jiangxi Province, in the fall of 1931 when both were students at the University of Nanking. Annie Lu was a freshman in the Department of Economics in the School of Agriculture. They dated until 1935 and then kept in touch through correspondence during Choh Hao's graduate years in Berkeley, while she stayed at Nanking completing her B.S. degree. In 1938 she was admitted for graduate work at both Cornell and UC Berkeley. She chose Berkeley, and they were married in October of that year.

Annie Lu Li received an M.A. degree in agricultural economics. Although she was not a scientist they were full partners in his research. He would show her the draft of his papers for her to read the introductions and the conclusions. He also discussed titles of papers with her and briefed her about happenings in the laboratory.

The couple had three children, Wei-i Li, a cardiac surgeon, Ann-si Li, a veterinarian, and Eva Li, an architect. Choh Hao and Annie built their final home in Berkeley near Arlington Circle and it was here that their children matured. Later they built a small retreat on the shores of Bodego Bay. They were among the most gracious of hosts in their home, at dinners arranged by them for visitors at local restaurants, or at formal banquets for international meetings. Their aesthetic tastes were cosmopolitan and both their home and Dr. Li's university office pleased the eye with

fine examples of artwork from both East and West. Choh Hao himself did things with his hands other than building scientific equipment or things for his home. He liked classical music and took cello lessons from one of the premier teachers of the East Bay.

The C. H. Li Legacy

Prof. Li left an enormous legacy of accomplishments in the world of science as well as a standard of discipline and hands-on personal involvement in research. As a friendly, humane person of wide interests, he is remembered by his family, his students, his colleagues and his associates throughout the world.

Keh-Ming Lin

Journey to the West

A biographical sketch as told to
Margaret Lin and Wing Mar

> ...I tried to become more like the American colleagues in my new environment. Interestingly, despite all the confusion and pressure to assimilate, the sense of pride in my Taiwanese and Chinese heritage grew stronger, as was the calling for me to serve the Asian Americans by conducting research to better understand their needs, and by setting up services and training programs focusing on Asian American mental health issues. These passions became the compass that set the course for my journey from that point on.

Dr. Keh-Ming Lin interviewed me (Margaret Lin) when I first came to Harbor-UCLA Medical Center to begin my residency training in psychiatry. In the last five years, Dr. Keh-Ming Lin has become my revered mentor. Our weekly supervision not only consisted of discussions about research topics but more significantly, about personal journey in the context of the rich cultural confluence in which we live. As an immigrant scholar from Taiwan, Dr. Keh-Ming Lin's story of career and personal development reflects a lifelong struggle that every immigrant person goes through— the task of searching for one's identity. I have learned from Dr. Lin that our cultural origins make us unique, both as individuals and pharmacological subjects in terms of drug response. However, I have also realized through Dr. Lin's mentorship that the discoveries in scientific research also bring us closer to each other as knowledge dispels myths about different cultures and diffuses the misconceptions of stereotypes.

businessman who ran a family-operated grocery store. His father was a banker. Dr. Lin was the first-born child, followed by two sisters and one brother. His parents named him Keh-Ming, which had its origin in the Four Books of the famed ancient Chinese classics. Keh-Ming means to "be able to understand." This expressed their unspoken wish for him to become a virtuous scholar. As the first-born son, Dr. Lin was brought up with the expectation to be a high achiever to bring honor to the family's name. Because life was difficult in general, in the years growing up in the post-Japan occupation era, Dr. Lin's family went through several years of economic hardship. Having been afflicted with polio at the age of five, Dr. Lin had some motor difficulties and often felt different from the other children. However, he was encouraged by his parents to study hard to persevere and succeed. Thus, even early on, his identification of himself with the poor and the weak already set the roots for his career path later on.

Dr. Lin's remarkable journey from the East to the West is told in a series of personal interviews. This biographical summary will hopefully stir in readers a sense of pride in the achievement and struggle of an Asian-American scientist.

Upbringing

Dr. Keh-Ming Lin was born in 1946 in a small village called Po-Zi west of the Chia-I Province in the Southern part of Taiwan. His ancestors came to Taiwan from Fujian in the Southeastern part of China in the early 1700s. His great-grandfather was a teacher and his grandfather was a

Career

Choosing psychiatry as a career became a natural and inevitable course of action for Dr. Lin as he went through adolescence and college. His obligation to fulfill the family's unspoken expectation for him to succeed in life through the understanding of scientific knowledge clashed with his desire to accept human mortality while transcending the injustices he saw around him. He finally found a balance in the art of medicine. The study of the human mind presented to him a world of unanswered scientific and spiritual challenges worthy of a lifetime's devotion.

After completing two years of residency in psychiatry in Taiwan, the political atmosphere in Asia and America presented an unexpected opportunity for Dr. Lin to come to the United States. He was admitted as a first year resident, at the University of Washington and later completed his clinical psychiatry training in. In the first year, overcoming the language barrier was a difficult but existentially crucial process for Dr. Lin. Through these processes and experiences, he naturally formulated his identity with the Asian immigrants in Seattle. He successfully initiated a study looking at the impact of the immigration process on the mental health of the Vietnamese refugees in Seattle. The findings of this study contributed toward his being awarded the prestigious Robert Wood Johnson Clinical Scholarship at the conclusion of his residency training and provided him the infrastructure to build a solid foundation in research methodology. During this time, his research focus also began to take shape based on his observation that Asian patients appeared to respond to smaller doses of antipsychotic medications compared to Caucasian patients and also experienced more side effects at smaller dosages. Never conforming to conventions, Dr. Lin bravely ventured into cross-cultural research at a time when speaking to minority patients in their own languages was an unusual practice and even considered by some as being politically incorrect.

> *Like the curious Monkey King who journeyed to the West, I see myself continuing on a path of endless discoveries each day.*

In 1979, Dr. Lin came to Harbor-UCLA Medical Center upon the calling of his revered mentor, Dr. Milton Miller, and his own desire to merge research with clinical application. In 1990, in his pioneering spirit, Dr. Lin uniquely established the Research Center on the Psychobiology of Ethnicity in order to provide a site for academic research examining the differences and similarities across ethnic groups in their response to psychotropic medications. Over the past decade, the psychobiological ethnic research center has been the site of nationally and internationally-funded research projects and has produced many important findings in the field of ethno-psychopharmacology.

Recognition and Awards

Aside from devoting his time to writing grants and conducting clinical trials, Dr. Lin has also become an important mentor and role model to residents, students, and other mental health professionals in the local and international communities. He is also a prolific writer with more than a 100 first-author journal publications and numerous other book chapters and editorials. He is a popular guest lecturer at many university campuses and residency training programs.

Many renowned establishments have recognized Dr. Keh-Ming Lin's dedication to cross-cultural research and to improving the quality of minority mental health care. In 2002, he was awarded the Kung-Po Soo Award by the American Psychiatric Association for excellent achievement in cross-cultural research. He was also a guest lecturer at the Royal College of Psychiatrists in London in 2000. The list of accolades is too long to mention, but what perhaps best speaks to who he is and what he has accomplished is indeed the recognition he has received repeatedly over the past years from the local communities as well as the appreciation of his mentees and patients, whose lives he has made a significant impact on.

Dr Lin's Retrospective

I was a nerd extremely wary of losing myself due to conformity; yet at the same time, I also craved for others' approval. I was five years old when I was afflicted with polio. Although the illness did not leave me with much motor deficit, I was often teased and felt different from others. This unique experience shaped my character early on and established in me a need to search for my own identity.

College was a time of seemingly endless energy, intellectual curiosity, and idealisms. I recall attempting to translate some of the classics done by the forefathers of psychiatry, such as the writings of Freud and Menninger. A work of translation on a series of writings about human sexuality written by Freud almost got me arrested in the traditionally conservative Taiwanese society at the time.

In medical school, I read voraciously and devoted much time to writing but it was not until I began my residency training that I felt like a physician for the first time. That realization was so powerful and unforgettable that it still carries me through most of the day now in my attempt to balance the academia and the clinical aspects of my career.

Coming to America was a life-changing experience for me. My personal identity as a Taiwanese person was challenged as I became more aware of the truth about the political chaos between Taiwan and China and also as I tried to become more like the American colleagues in my new environment. Interestingly, despite all the confusion and pressure to assimilate, the sense of pride in my Taiwanese and Chinese heritage grew stronger, as was the calling for me to serve the Asian Americans by conducting research to better

understand their needs, and by setting up services and training programs focusing on Asian American mental health issues. These passions became the compass that set the course for my journey from that point on.

While in Seattle during my training years, I had the good fortune of having the privilege to work with the first waves of Vietnamese refugees, right after their arrival to this new homeland of theirs. We established a free clinic, offered counseling and visited them at home. A longitudinal research project evolved from these experiences that vastly enriched my understanding of the profound impact that trauma has on people's mental health, as well as the complexity of the process of adjustment to new cultural environments.

Seemingly paradoxically, one of the greatest shocks that confronted me professionally after my cross-Pacific translocation was the way medications were used. These impressionistic observations led to a series of studies examining the extent of ethnic variations in psychotropic responses and reasons for such differences. They led to increasingly sophisticated approaches to tease out the genetic and environmental (i.e., cultural) factors that determine how an individual might respond to therapeutic interventions. These efforts culminated in the establishment of the Research Center on the Psychobiology of Ethnicity at the Harbor-UCLA Medical Center, where I have been a faculty member since 1979. Blessed with continuing support from federal and other major funding agencies, my colleagues and I hope to continue to contribute towards making the use of psychotropics and other medications increasingly more rational and individually tailored. At the same time, such pursuits also enriched my understanding, and deepened my conviction, of the interconnectedness between biology and culture, and of the artificiality of certain scientific efforts to separate nature from nurture, or vice versa.

In yet another study conducted during those formative years, I was surprised at how excruciatingly long a wait and torturous it was for almost any psychiatric patient to reach the mental health care system. An "average" patient suffering from schizophrenia, irrespective of ethnicity, typically took more than one year from the onset of their psychotic symptoms to finally come face-to-face with a psychiatrist. Shocking but as expected, this delay doubled in African Americans, and tripled in Asian Americans. Speculation on the reasons for such delays (and the ethnic contrasts) aside, a practical challenge is *to remove potential roadblocks and bring services closer to the communities. Years later, my colleagues and I finally had the opportunity to establish two community mental health centers, serving specifically the needs of thousands of Asian Americans and Pacific Islanders in the South Bay and Long Beach areas. It has been extremely satisfying for me to watch these programs evolve from storefront, makeshift operations to become mature, sophisticated organizations. Today, these clinics are among those at the forefront providing mental health services to the rapidly expanding Asian and Pacific Islander populations in California.*

I have had the good fortune throughout my career of meeting people who also passionately care about the role of culture in medicine; some of them became lifelong friends. The desire to better educate providers about Asian mental health gave birth to the Consortium on Asian American Mental Health Training nine years ago. Now into the planning for the 10th Annual Training Conference, the Consortium committee members continue to volunteer their time and effort for the organization of training workshops for providers specifically about mental health issues pertinent to Asians.

Like the curious Monkey King who journeyed to the West, I see myself continuing on a path of endless discoveries each day. The process of the search for my identity defines who I am. The more I study about the human condition and our sufferings, the more I realize how different and yet how similar human beings can be. I learn to appreciate how vulnerable and resilient human nature is. I thank the many people who have left their impression in my heart. As I continue to journey into the West and back to the East, I realize the path has been a full circle.

Philip P. Choy

An Architect's Passion for Design and Preservation

By Emma Louie and Wing Mar

> *I felt that knowing about Chinese-American history in its full context would offer hope and optimism for all Chinese Americans…. It was the compilation of negative experiences that propelled me into lecturing and sharing with students the authentic history of the Chinese in America and not necessarily the politically correct version.*

On Feb. 16, 1974 the first academic conference on the history of the Chinese in Southern California was held at the auditorium of the Department of Water and Power building in Los Angeles. The main speaker was Philip Choy who was invited by Paul Louie, one of the organizers. Philip was a lecturer on Chinese-American history at California State University at San Francisco. He was also a past president of the Chinese Historical Society of America (CHSA) in San Francisco. Two hundred people attended that conference, and the Chinese Historical Society of Southern California (CHSSC) in Los Angeles was created with the assistance of the volunteers from San Francisco. A member of the State Historical Resources Commission, Philip Choy was also recently appointed to the San Francisco Museum and Historical Society Advisory Committee.

The Curious Boy and His Family

As a child, I wondered why we had a Chinatown and why we had to live there. It has been a life-long journey for me to find understanding and a satisfactory answer. For my family was not only living in San Francisco Chinatown by choice, but they were also being required to live in that circumscribed "ghetto area" shrouded under a dark cloud of illegitimacy and rejected by a white America. Yet my family did well being part owner of a meat market business on the north end of Grant Av-

enue and hiring an Italian driver who delivered to Italian sausage factories in North Beach. The paradox of being forced to live there by restrictive property covenants outside of Chinatown and then be able to hire white people to work was confusing to me as a child.

Philip Choy's father ran a Western style meat butchering business. Chinatown customers were most likely purchasers of pork. In Chinatown there was a niche, the butchering meat business, which seemed occupationally prescribed for the men of the Gow Gong area of Namhoi County of Guangdong Province, China.

I grew up in San Francisco Chinatown living at 714 Pacific Avenue until I was 22 years old. I was No. 4 in a family of five children; three older sisters and a younger brother. No. 1 sister, whom I never knew, died at an early age. The mortality rate of infants in Chinatown was high partly due to the dense population and the lack of pediatric care for infectious diseases. (My mother was born in 1903 in San Francisco and at age three was sent to China by my grandfather to be a companion for his first wife there. Having two wives in two continents was often practiced by men who then had the responsibility to support both families—one in China and one in the United

States.) *My mother was married to my father at age nine-
teen, by proxy, then returned to the United States.*

*My father came to the United States as a "paper son" so
he could claim American citizenship. To be consistent with
the "papers," we took on the family name of Choy while in
reality, our surname is Woo. Father worked as a butcher
while my mother worked nine hours in the sewing factory
by day and usually brought work home. My sisters worked
their way and I went under the G.I. Bill through college.
However, the influence of attending Chinese school in the
evenings and being exposed to our Chinese heritage helped
to give us a strong identity and probably helped to compen-
sate for some of the prejudices that many of us encountered
as children. In my school the Chinese teachers were filled
with the spirited fervor of nationalism toward China. History and geography of China were taught and gave us a
lasting appreciation of our background, even though we
were born in America. As we got older the lessons were
more current and the wish was to win the Sino-Japanese
War and help the Chinese people. I had even considered
going to China to be helpful when I reached adulthood.
Those lessons in Chinese school left a lasting impression
on me.*

*I attended kindergarten as "Poon Choy" at Jean Parker
School. In the third grade, my teacher, Mrs. Wramp, called
me to her desk and gently said, "Go home and get yourself
an American name." My father had a customer named
Philip so I became Philip, but in Chinese school I was still
Woo Poon Quon.*

*During high school I enlisted in the Army Air Corps. I
attended San Francisco City College during World War
II until called to active duty for basic training in Biloxi,
Mississippi. There, in the South, I witnessed the unjust
reality of segregation. Every public facility was labeled
for black or for white—even the drinking fountains. Not
knowing where I belonged in the South, I, at first, didn't
dare drink any water; I rode in the middle of the bus and
voided behind a tree. Returning from military service I entered the University of California at Berkeley and studied
architecture. I had previously studied engineering at City
College and found out that did not suit me. I worked as an
architect for over 50 years designing homes, office buildings
and restaurants in the San Francisco Bay Area. I have
been married to Sarah for 52 years and I have three adult
children: Randall, Brian and Stephanie.*

A Preservationist at Heart

*After World War II, U.S.-China relations deteriorated
with the ascension of the People's Republic of China in late
1949. I embraced the PRC as the legitimate China. My
original idealism of working for the salvation of China
diminished as the door to mainstream America began to
open up after World War II. However, it was the 1960s
Civil Rights Movement that inspired me to exert my rights
as an American born of Chinese descent. I became aware
of my roots, which are planted in America, not in the land
of my grandparents. It was an emotional as well as an intellectual transformation in finally feeling that I belonged
here.*

*I was president of the Chinese Historical Society of
America (CHSA) during the Civil Rights Movement.
There was a growing frustration and anger among Chinese American students then. Demand for information
on Chinese Americans from teachers throughout California poured in. CHSA held a seminar on the history of
the Chinese in America. Representatives of school districts
throughout California attended. The interest shown was
surprising. The next day one of the attendees, Prof. Ches-
ter Cheng of California State University at San Francisco
(formerly known as San Francisco State College), called
and asked for someone who would teach the subject at the
college. Another fellow Chinese-American historian, Him
Mark Lai, and I took up the challenge. I felt that knowing
about Chinese-American history in its full context would
offer hope and optimism for all Chinese Americans. Our
class was the first course ever taught in any college or uni-*

versity specifically on the Chinese in the United States. The course taught by us was named History of the Chinese in America. The time was September 1969.

After CHSSC was formed, Philip Choy participated as a speaker at its first seminar on April 5, 1975 at the Rest-haven Hospital near Los Angeles Chinatown. His subject was "A History of the Chinese in California." Him Mark Lai was the other speaker.

As president of CHSA I was given the responsibility to correct 100 years of oversight on the role of the Chinese in the building of the first Transcontinental Railroad. In 1969 we wrote to the centennial commissioner and requested to be placed on the national ceremony to dedicate a plaque in recognition and memory of the Chinese railroad workers. Instead we were placed in a secondary minor program. The disappointment was a bitter moment for me and served as one of my rallying points to promote knowledge of our history here in the United States. More recently other members of the Chinese-American community were again represented at a ceremony in Utah. This time those pioneer railroad workers were honored and recognized. Some in attendance could trace back to members of their families who had worked for the railroad.

My involvement in the preservation of Angel Island, where so many Chinese immigrants were detained, and other facilities in our state as historic and cultural sites offer a closer look at important history lessons about the early Chinese pioneers. The old YWCA building designed by architect Julia Morgan in San Francisco's Chinatown is now the home of the Chinese Historical Society of America. It houses materials for exhibits. Visitors will be inspired to study more about the Chinese in America. I, among others, will continue preserving and interpreting the history of Chinese Americans for future generations.

I do not wish to be portrayed as a success story. It was the compilation of negative experiences that propelled me into lecturing and sharing with students the authentic history of the Chinese in America and not necessarily the politically correct version.

We are indeed indebted to Philip Choy for preserving the history of the Chinese American experience in the consciousness of all students he has taught.

Joyce Mar and Gilbert Hom
assisted in the writing of this story.

Luther Lee, Jr.

From Restaurants to Aerospace in Three Generations

As told to Wing Mar and Joyce Mar

> *"When Charles Lindbergh flew across the Atlantic Ocean to Paris in 1927, my father bought me an aviator's outfit with goggles. My fifty years of a love affair with aeronautics and spaceships began."*

The Lee Ancestry

My grandfather, Wong Lee, opened a restaurant in Philadelphia Chinatown in the 1870's called Mei Hong Low. By 1899 grandfather returned to China to marry my grandmother, Wong Su. In 1900 my father was born, the first Chinese male born in Philadelphia. The Baptist Mission School on Cherry Street gave my father's name, Luther, to him. The Chinese population then was very small. Many who settled there had come from New York as my grandfather had when he arrived there from China; he was 15 years old then.

And so it was in Philadelphia that Luther grew up, the eldest of seven children, and where I, Luther, Jr., would grow up also.

There were 137 Chinese Americans in the North Atlantic Area in the 1870s and only 1,165 by 1890. In Philadelphia, by 1920, the population of Chinese Americans was at an all time low of 869.

Luther, Sr., was sent to China in 1910 to attend school. When he returned to the United States in 1915 he was held at Angel Island for seven months. Even though Luther was a U.S. citizen, the immigration officials required more proof of his citizenship. He was told that they had to secure more documentation from Philadelphia to prove further that indeed he was a citizen of the United States. For those documents to arrive from the East to the West Coast took many

months. This extraordinary delay kept Luther, Sr., at Angel Island. Arriving home in Philadelphia, my father helped in the restaurant and went to school until he entered the U.S. army in the infantry in World War I. After being discharged from the Army, my father was sent back, again, to China to be married, a tradition followed by many Chinese Americans. My father was nice looking, a good dresser and a sociable chap who liked to sing. These were qualities my mother, Kim Goon Jin, would appreciate. She was born in San Francisco in 1899 but left for China to attend school just before the 1906 San Francisco earthquake. My mother was pretty, loved to read, followed Chinese customs and liked music. My parents returned to the United States and settled in Philadelphia in 1920. My sister, Florence, was born in 1921. She became an artist and a teacher. I was born in 1922 and was given the name of Luther Lee, Jr. When I reached my midteens, I was called "Luke."

Young Adult

My father, in 1925, opened several large restaurants outside of Philadelphia Chinatown. American and Chinese food was served. In those days lunch was 25 cents and dinner was 50 cents for a complete meal. Several of the restaurants provided entertainment that included floorshows, live bands, and dancing. After prohibition was lifted, liquor was served. Luther, Sr. later opened several smaller restaurants in Philadelphia. By then I was old enough to work, first as a pantry boy, a dishwasher, a bar boy, and finally, as waiter. My typical schedule was to work 12 hours per day, seven days a week, when school was not in session. Trays were made of steel then and were carried by one hand at shoulder height. This was no easy task since the kitchen was located nearly two blocks away from the dining room. As a waiter I would be responsible for about 10 tables, seating from two to 10 people per table. No bus boys were used in those days, so my tips which amounted to about $3.00 per day were well earned and considered pretty good.

Tragically, my father lost all the restaurants during the years after the Depression. It was heart wrenching to see this happen after more than 60 years of toil by our family. Luther, Sr. went to New York Times Square and opened a cafeteria called Shang Way (my father's Chinese name), which eventually failed. Later, he, with partners, started a large restaurant called New Fulton Royal, in Brooklyn. This restaurant was similar to his earlier restaurants in Philadelphia. He served as manager and the restaurant prospered. He became the president of the Chinese American Restaurants Assn. of Greater New York. He was there until he retired in 1962, when my parents moved to Oakland.

I stayed in Philadelphia to be with my mother when my father was in New York, but when I was old enough I worked during my vacations and holidays at the family restaurants. My father would come home to Philadelphia to see the family and to look in on the restaurant. There was little time for interaction with my classmates, who were mostly from immigrant families and who had come to America from Germany, Poland, Italy and Eastern Europe. Essentially I had few close friends but I did enjoy sports and I gained a spot on the varsity soccer team. I was vice president in student government when I was the only Chinese American boy in high school. I joined the Boy Scouts and became the camp bugler. Because of our family business there was little time for a social life while in high school or college. I do remember feeling strange when during prom time my classmates would come to our restaurant as customers and I was their waiter.

Aeronautics to Astronautics

When Charles Lindbergh flew across the Atlantic Ocean to Paris in 1927, my father bought me an aviator's outfit with goggles to wear. I started to go to airports to watch airplanes taking off and landing. I also saw the large blimps and dirigibles at the U.S. Navy base in Lakehurst. In 1937, on a day of thunder and lightning, I watched a dirigible fly so low over our house that I could read the word, Hindenburg. Shortly after it flew out of sight, I heard on the radio that it had crashed and exploded. The dirigible was inflated with hydrogen, as helium was not available then. The explosion was reported widely in the news and the cause is still debatable—whether the lightning storm or something else caused the disaster.

I earned my C.A.A. (now F.A.A.) license and worked in flight-testing on various experimental airplanes in research and development. Later I received my bachelor's degree in mechanical engineering from Drexel University in Philadelphia and, later, my master's degree in education from the University of San Francisco. It took me 10 years to earn the two degrees since I was working full time and raising a family. I took the necessary courses at night and weekends.

My father did not want me to "waste my time" by going to college. He noted that many Chinese-American graduates from college could not find a job and that I would eventually have to work at the restaurant as a waiter anyway.

I left flight-testing in 1942 and enlisted in the U.S. Army Air Corps in World War II. At first I was going to join the Marines but was told "no Chinks." I eventually became a sergeant in the Air Corps, assigned as flight chief in the 306th Fighter Squadron that consisted of P40 and P51 airplanes. (Upon my discharge four years later, I noticed that the U.S. Marines began to enlist Chinese Americans.)

After my discharge I returned to flight-testing. I was Chief Flight Test Inspector for the Navy. During that time I was responsible for the airworthiness of the Piasecki production helicopters for the navy fleet and for experimental helicopters. As an engineer in management I was responsible for various phases of design, development and tests on different types of aerospace vehicles. In 1957 the Russian Sputnik flew into space and the national priority changed to space exploration. Subsequently, I was responsible for the reliability of the Gemini and the Apollo rocket engines at Aerojet General in Sacramento. The project I enjoyed the most was the Nuclear Rocket Nerva, which was designed to obtain maximum data in one trip, when all the planets would line up exactly, which is a-once-in-a-lifetime experience.

After Neil Armstrong landed on the moon in 1969, I accepted a position teaching engineering, aeronautics, and technology at Sacramento City College. I was the Asian Student Club adviser on campus. During summers, I gave lectures at various symposiums on aeronautics and space. For contributing 50 years to aeronautics and space technology, I received various awards from the F.A.A, the Navy, academic institutions and many engineering societies.

Lee Legacy

I married Ming Wong from Cincinnati, Ohio. Ming was a lovely lady, well mannered, and very kind. We both came from similar childhood experiences having worked hard during Depression times. After 44 years of marriage she passed away. Our daughter, Kim, teaches at San Francisco City College. Since retirement I now live in Oakland, where I am able to enjoy her family. In retrospect, I am proud to be a Chinese American. While I may have been a pioneer in my field and reached what has been known as the glass ceiling, I am hopeful that I helped pave the way for others to advance to their fullest potential. Professionally, I feel lucky to have lived in the period where, in engineering, we started from subsonic, supersonic to hypersonic and that I was able to be part of that for over 50 years. Also I am indebted to Carolyn Gan for encouraging me to document my experience in aerospace as a Chinese American.

Timothy C. Chew

A Man of All Seasons

Interviewed by Lily Wu Moffly
Written by Randy Bloch

CIA Operative, Entrepreneur and Venture Capitalist

To Gold Mountain

Tim Chew is that rarest of people who, drawing on a vast reservoir of inner strength and resolve, sees each challenge as an opportunity for growth and every obstacle as a springboard for personal development. Tim, a third generation Chinese American, born in 1924, faced polio when he was a year old and lost his father at the age of seven. His family faced more ups and downs in the course of their lives than most other people. Notwithstanding the travails which might have defeated the most exceptional individual, Tim shone ever more brilliantly in each of his subsequent careers. He, with an entrepreneurial spirit and winning personality, like his grandfather and father before him, ventured into careers as an industrial engineer, a CIA agent, a businessman, a banker and a manufacturer at a time when his friends and classmates were looking for a steady and secure profession.

Tim's grandfather, Sai Yen Chew, arrived in California in 1895 from Guangdong Province. Those early Chinese immigrants were largely miners, domestic servants and agricultural workers. A degree of personal wealth allowed Sai Yen to avoid the permanent yoke of physical labor and he founded a can-

nery in the heart of the agricultural area of Alviso, Calif. Thomas Foon Chew, Tim's father, took over the cannery's operation in 1912. Tim has sweet memories of sitting on his father's lap, driving down the main street of Alviso with the townspeople waving to them. When Thomas passed away in 1931 at age 42, Bayside Canning was the third largest cannery (behind Del Monte and Libby) in America, employing thousands of workers in three plants throughout California. But with the loss of Tim's father, the business did poorly; because of the Great Depression and mismanagement it ultimately went bankrupt. Lacking a formal education, Thomas' widow was forced to raise her seven children, the youngest being Tim, by moving to San Francisco and by using her sewing skills to earn a living. But Tim's father and grandfather had demonstrated that during the era of fierce anti-Asian discrimination, they were able to build a successful business empire, if only for a time. Tim internalized his father's admonition, "Be honest and value your reputation above all; the Chews have a good name." In 2003 the City of Alviso named a street in honor of Tim's father: "Thomas Foon Chew Way".

School and Leadership

In San Francisco, Tim quickly rose to the top of his class at Francisco Junior High School and assumed leadership roles as well. At Galileo High, which was one-third Chinese American, he was president of both his sophomore and junior classes. Then, as America entered World War II, Tim's carefree years camping and playing sports at the Flying Eagle Boys Club at the Chinese Methodist Church abruptly ended. He dropped all extracurricular activities in his senior year to contribute to the war effort, working full-time on the graveyard shift in the shipyards.

Tim then entered UCLA in 1943, when the university offered only freshman and sophomore engineering classes. Tim next matriculated to UC Berkeley, graduating with an industrial engineering degree in 1947. Though challenged physically from childhood polio with his affected foot and special shoe, he earnestly pursued athletics, joining the varsity boxing team at both universities. His disability never hindered his participation in sports or social activities, including dancing. Fresh from college, Tim became the first Chinese American salesman for a large San Francisco real estate concern, Baldwin & Howe. Next followed a four-year stint for the state of California as an industrial safety engineer. At the same time he established and operated the first Chinese takeout restaurant in San Mateo, Calif. with his childhood friends from church as partners. These invaluable experiences helped shape his future, but Tim yearned for a greater sense of purpose. That was just what beckoned in 1951.

A CIA Operative and More

In the post-WWII years, the Central Intelligence Agency needed Asians in the field for intelligence gathering and covert operations. China had been "lost" to the Communists in 1949 and Washington feared regimes in Southeast Asia would fall to the Communists like dominoes. Distinguished by his high social profile and college academic record, Tim caught the eye of CIA recruiters. Being unable to serve militarily due to his polio, Tim jumped at the opportunity to travel abroad in service of his country. He was a true patriot. After four months training as a covert agent in Baltimore, Md., Tim was dispatched to Bangkok, Thailand, to collect intelligence on the country's Communist insurgency. Not surprisingly, Tim distinguished himself both as an agent and as the general manager of Robert Reed Hospital Supplies, the CIA straw company he managed.

Tim's years spent making Robert Reed Hospital Supplies profitable were pivotal and would shape his future. The lack of capital and the consumer shortages he saw in Asia opened Tim's eyes to business opportunities. He wanted to make a difference as a businessman in Asia. Despite being born and raised in the United States, Tim found himself comfortable living in Asia. He also met his first wife, Carol Cummings— a Bostonian who was visiting her father, a UN official—in Thailand. They were married in 1952 in a ceremony hosted by Thailand's Prime Minister Pibunsonggram.

Entrepreneur and Venture Capitalist

After his contract with the CIA expired, the Chews returned to America. Increasingly, Tim was becoming a liaison between American and Asian business interests. American brand names had a cachet in Asia and were seen as a guarantee of quality. But many American companies considered Asia too risky to make capital investments. In 1955, Tim helped launch Allied Biochemical Laboratories, a San Francisco pharmaceuticals operation marketing penicillin, hormones, vitamins and related products to Korea, Taiwan and Thailand. Allied aggressively targeted the Asian pharmaceuticals market. The company opened a four-story factory in San Francisco's Chinatown manufacturing ointments, pills, capsules, injectables and elixirs. The company's meteoric success, however, was relatively brief due in part to Asian protectionism, and by 1962, its fortunes were waning. Tim sold his interest in the company and began to seek new business opportunities.

Return to Asia

Though deeply patriotic and an American first and foremost, he was nevertheless a businessman in the global sense. He renewed his Asian business connections and prepared for a possible relocation to the other side of the Pacific. Pi Alpha Phi fraternity brother Paul Louie had recently founded the Bank of Trade, the first Chinese-American bank in California. The Bank of Trade was focused on trade and financing. Tim was asked to join the bank in 1964. He learned the banking business from the ground up, quickly rising to vice-president and later establishing the bank's Sacramento branch. During the merger mania of the time, the Bank of Trade was taken over. Fortuitously, Tim was asked by a mining professor turned entrepreneur to be a venture capitalist for an industrial explosives company in Taiwan. As an industrial engineer Tim had experience with industrial explosives and knew its potential. In 1969, Timothy C. Chew became president of Jupiter Explosives, manufacturing industrial explosives in Taiwan. But, in 1973, because of his background in finance, he was invited to establish a branch of Thailand's Asia Trust Bank in Hong Kong. Over the next two decades, Tim's experience as a liaison between American and Asian businesses reached its apex as he helped fund entrepreneurs and venture capitalists in the dynamic Hong Kong business climate of the 1970s and 1980s.

Fulfillment

Being managing director of Asia Trust Bank Finance Ltd, Hong Kong was a time of fulfillment and security for Tim. During these years the life cycle of three generations of the Chew family had truly come full circle. Tim's grandfather, Sai Yen Chew, had traveled to America from a homeland diminished by years of decadent dynastic rule. Sai Yen and his son, Thomas, thrived in their new home, creating new opportunities with every challenge. Finally, a full century after Sai Yen's departure from China, his grandson Tim, with American sensibilities and can-do spirit, tempered by the ideals of Chinese tradition, had returned to Hong Kong, a few miles from his ancestral homeland, to participate in the bustling economy.

Contentment – A Life Well-Lived

Today, Tim and his second wife, Sally, live a somewhat quieter lifestyle in Tim's hometown of San Francisco. Sally Grimsey, a native of Australia, met Tim in Hong Kong. They travel extensively, dabble in venture capital opportunities, and visit with Tim's son and daughter, Tom and Robyn, and three grandchildren who live nearby. Upon reflection, Tim has never felt any discrimination toward him during his lifetime although he never looked for it. His ease with mingling with all people was his natural personality.

Joyce and Wing Mar, who are among Tim's oldest friends, provided first hand knowledge of Tim Chew.

Paul Louie
&
Emma Woo Louie

Something About Our Lives

By Jason Jem and Wing Mar

Cancer research Epidemiologist and Onomastician.

Co-founder of the Chinese Historical Society of Southern California.

Both Paul and Emma were born in Seattle into Chinese-American families that were among the first to settle in the Pacific Northwest. Coincidentally, their fathers came as young men to America the same year—in 1882. Paul grew up in the heart of Seattle Chinatown, in Canton Alley, while Emma grew up in San Francisco's Chinatown.

Paul was an ordained minister in the American Baptist church when, in an act of providence, he met Emma at a Sunday service in the Presbyterian Church in San Francisco Chinatown. Married for more than a half-century, they celebrated their 55th wedding anniversary in 2003 with their four children, seven grandchildren, and an eighth grandchild-in-waiting. Paul and Emma retired in the late 1980s. After working and living in Los Angeles for nearly four decades, they moved back to the San Francisco Bay Area to be closer to the children and their families.

About Paul Louie

Paul was born in 1918 into a family of 11 children. He recalls his humble upbringing in small Seattle Chinatown: "It was a circumscribed environment and I did not have real contact with the outside world." Nonetheless, he was appreciative of his intimate world: "I had the good fortune to receive the kindnesses, caring, and opportunities from the Baptist Church people, especially the home missionaries and youth workers."

After high school, Paul received a scholarship from Linfield College in McMinnville, Ore., which he attended from

photo by Jason Jean

1938 to 1942. It was his first exposure to life in a small American town. He majored in philosophy and religion and nostalgically recalls his mental and spiritual growth in college. Influenced by the home missionaries at the Seattle Chinese Baptist Church and his role models at Linfield, Paul decided to enter the ministry.

A scholarship from Harvard University's Divinity School enabled him to obtain a Science of Theology Master's degree in 1945. While still in seminary, Paul and his friends, George Kan and Eddie Leong Way, along with Rev. Edwar Lee, founded the Chinese Christian Youth Conference (CCYC), which met the summer of 1943 at Silver Bay, N.Y. It was the first of many conferences before disbanding in the 1960s. The parent CCYC conference was held at Zephyr Point, Lake Tahoe, Calif. for many years before Paul and his friends were commissioned to establish the East Coast conference.

After a brief Seattle homecoming, Paul moved in 1947 to San Francisco, where he worked at the Chinese YMCA as program director. His fondest memory was of forming the Public Affairs Committee with a small group of young men that included Ed Cheng and George Wee. Its purpose was to bring speakers to discuss current events and other topics of interest, such as marriage. The YMCA, at that time, did not admit women as members but the discussion group welcomed them as guests.

After Paul and Emma had been married for two years, he returned to the ministry to serve as pastor of the Chinese Presbyterian Church in Oakland from 1950 to 1955. To expand his spiritual reach, he furthered his education in order to specialize as a minister of Christian education. As a result Paul served in several mainstream Presbyterian churches, where he was their first non-Caucasian minister. These were enriching experiences for both Paul and Emma as the members of each church warmly welcomed them and their children.

In 1971, Paul was offered a position with the Los Angeles County Human Relations Commission. He, like other ministers, left the active pastorate to continue helping people in what the church called "the special ministries." The 1960s were a time of much turbulence in the church, when some members were not comfortable with the changing society. Yet it was a time when anti-discriminatory laws had been enacted and when government agencies were established to help solve or alleviate social problems. "It was a time of great social unrest and much remedial work was needed" says Paul.

His first assignment was to work in the Chinese community. There he met Bill Mason and Paul deFalla, who had written articles on the history of the Chinese in Los Angeles. The three men were inspired to establish an organization with the purpose of disseminating information about Chinese-American history, specifically in Southern California, and encouraging more research on the subject. At that time, even Chinese Americans knew little about their own history in this country. The three men invited Philip Choy and Him Mark Lai of the Chinese Historical Society of America, based in San Francisco, to speak about the history of the Chinese in America. As a result, many in the appreciative audiences became charter members of the newly formed Chinese Historical Society of Southern California (CHSSC), founded in 1975.

In 1975, Paul worked with the Vietnamese and Cambo-

dian refugees who had fled to this country at the end of the Vietnam War. He recalls taking great satisfaction in helping to organize the Protestant Refugee Committee which was set up to aid the refugees in their transition to life in America and to acquaint Americans with their new Southeast Asian neighbors. Paul also helped in the organization of other groups while living in Los Angeles, such as the Asian Business Association, the National Asian Presbyterian Conference, and the Los Angeles Asian Education Commission. He has long believed that organizations lay a strong foundation when writing down its bylaws and goals.

About Emma Woo Louie

Born in 1926, Emma also grew up under the nurturing influence of the Protestant church. By the seventh grade she wanted to become a nurse—perhaps being tested skin-positive for tuberculosis as a child influenced this early career decision. The nurse-in-charge at the Public Health Clinic in Chinatown was Eunice Gibson, daughter of Rev. Otis Gibson, the founder of the Chinese Methodist Episcopal Church in 1873 (now the Chinese United Methodist Church), where she was baptized. In the 1930s and 1940s, densely populated Chinatown had the highest rates of TB incidence and deaths from this highly communicable disease. The problem was so acute that Wednesdays at the main Public Health Department were designated as "Chinese Day" for seeing Chinese patients.

Emma attributes her interest in nursing to a more practical reason: to prepare for the uncertainties of life. When she was growing up, women were expected to get married, have children, and stay at home while the husband was the sole wage earner. But she knew that many women in Chinatown worked to supplement the husband's income, while others had to find work because they were divorced or the husband had died or was too sick to work.

In 1948 Emma received her nursing degree from Santa Clara County School of Nursing in San Jose. In 1971, she accepted the offer to work as a 'nurse epidemiologist' for a cancer research project at the University of Southern California. This was a new type of position which appealed to her because the goal of the three-year project was to examine the high incidence among Cantonese Chinese of nasopharyngeal cancer, a disease that occurs at the back of the throat area—that the incidence rate decreased with each generation born in this country was of great significance. Analysis of the data collected by Emma and colleagues at the California Tumor Registry in Berkeley validated the Hong Kong studies showing that a diet of certain salted fish fed to weaning babies and young children may be a cancer source. The link of cancer to foods is always of universal interest.

Because some ethnic groups have a predilection for certain cancers, investigators often used surnames for ethnic identification. This led Emma to renew her interest in Chinese-American names. Such use of surnames, however, was becoming less meaningful because of interracial marriages and name commonality between racial groups. For example, the surname Louie may belong to a person of Chinese or European origin. In her spare time, she began applying her data-collecting skills to learn about the evolution of surnames. She wanted to understand how Chinese Americans came by their surnames—the spelling and Chinese character. She wanted to share this information with her family and others so that Americans who possess a surname of Chinese origin could appreciate its rich legacy.

What began as a hobby slowly turned Emma into a serious student of the origins and forms of proper names (an onomastician to etymology buffs). Consultations with family and friends, especially Ruby Ling Louie, encouraged her to write the book "Chinese American Names: Tradition and Transition." Published in 1998 by McFarland & Company, it tells the history of family names and naming customs in China; the creation of new name styles through angliciz-

ing or Americanization; the influences on spelling and the correlation to Chinese-American history. "Having a sense of history—through names—can help people understand themselves and each other better," says Emma.

As Paul and Emma later confided, the interview made them reflect anew on the many good and positive things that have happened in their lives. They felt fortunate to be born in this country despite the terrible hardships suffered by their parents in the early years. They are indebted to the church for its guidance and influence during their formative years, thankful for their career opportunities and, most of all, grateful for good relationships with family and friends.

Edgar Wong edited this story

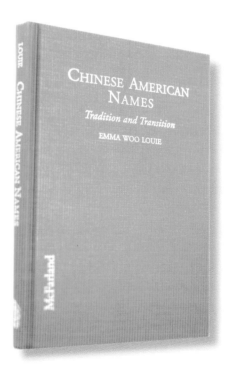

William Y. Fong

A Medical Visionary

By Gladys Ikeda and Wing Mar

> **Dr. William Fong is most proud of having "raised eight kids and . . . no one is in jail."**

Physician/Medical Director

I (Wing Mar) got to know Dr. William Fong in the 1980s when he was Chairperson of the medical advisory committee of the Asian Community Nursing Home in Sacramento. Dr. Fong joined the community center board in 1983 and chaired the finance committee, raising funds for the nursing home's construction. This new nonprofit nursing facility for Asians, particularly the elderly, opened in 1987 under the auspices of the Asian Community Center on land donated by a benefactor. In the 18 months after it began accepting patients, the nursing home experienced the usual startup problems of a new facility with complex operations. In 1989, Dr. Fong elected to assume the day-to-day role of the home's medical director—its fourth—to execute the needed operational turn-around. To gain greater insight on elderly healthcare, he joined the California Association of Medical Directors (CAMD). It was in this voluntary organization of physicians experienced in the treatment and care of acute and chronic diseases of the disabled and elderly that Dr. Fong learned more about the complexities of nursing home care and administration.

Under Dr. Fong's tenacity and leadership, and with the changes he effected by the dint of his personality, persuasiveness, new knowledge and personal example, he improved the nursing home's quality of care and its administrative practices. The facility overcame its early marginal grading by the health department to become an outstanding facility. Dr. Fong credited the success to the team that worked hard to understand the cultures of the patients and learned to better communicate with them. The facility recently scored first among all California nursing facilities, receiving a Golden Survey rating by the California Department of Health Care Services, and a commendation from then Gov. Gray Davis. To this day, he continues to serve as the Asian Community Nursing Home medical director. Dr. Fong's life story will give a glimpse of his character, along with an overview of his unique organizational contributions and his dedication to the remarkable transformation of this key healthcare asset for the elderly.

The Fong Ancestry

The year 1906 was important in California history; in April, the Great Earthquake rocked San Francisco and demolished much of the city's downtown. That same year, William Fong's father set foot on U.S. soil for the first time. As a teenager, William's father bypassed the post-earthquake turmoil of the largest Chinese enclave and traveled to Merced in California's Central Valley, where he found work in a local restaurant. Later, he moved to Sacramento, where he eventually opened a grocery store with a personal nest egg scrimped from his hard work, self-sacrifice and thrift. Following the pattern of many men in the early era of Chinese immigration to California, the elder Mr. Fong eventually returned to China to bring back a wife and raise a family. "My father did not talk much about those early years," William Fong remembered. "It must have been hard for all the early immigrants—but he never complained."

There were 10 Fong children, and as they grew up, each worked in the store, stocking shelves, sweeping, cashiering, bagging groceries and performing other tasks needed in the family business. As someone with a knack for organization and record keeping, William, the third child in the family, became the store's bookkeeper at an early age. Mr. and Mrs. Fong inculcated a work ethic and a cooperative spirit in each of their children to make the store a success and enable them all to get an education. Based on these lessons from his parents, the siblings developed the personal attributes that made William Fong a responsible individual and a successful physician—a warm and caring person.

Medical School and Internship

Fong enrolled in Sacramento City Junior College to study business administration and law. With an associate of arts degree in hand in 1943, he transferred to University of California, Berkeley. By then, World War II was well underway, and the U.S. government was granting deferments to collegians studying engineering, medicine or dentistry. This gave Fong an incentive to switch to a science curriculum and enroll in a pre-med program; he received his B.A. from UC Berkeley in 1945. His academic success in physics, chemistry and life science courses resulted in his acceptance into the accelerated wartime medical education program at University of California, San Francisco Medical School (UCSF). The program enabled him to complete his academic studies for a medical degree in 36 months instead of the usual four years. Despite the busy academic years, Fong found time to pursue other aspects of campus life. He was president of the Chinese Student Club and was a member of the Pi Alpha Phi fraternity, an all-Chinese fraternity.

His post-graduate training took him to medical internships and residencies in San Francisco, St. Louis, and New York City. Interested in chest and infectious diseases early in his career, Dr. Fong spent more than the usual amount of required intern time in numerous county facilities with tuberculosis and infectious disease departments. "Tubercu-

losis was rampant in Asian communities at that time and many Asians were hospitalized in sanitariums," he recalled. "Now discredited treatments like pneumothorax and thoracoplasty to rest the lungs were used then to treat pulmonary tuberculosis. The more effective drug, streptomycin, was just introduced." Dr. Fong remembers children, hospitalized for months and years in sanitariums, gaining weight on diets rich in dairy products without really effectively treating their disease. "Given our knowledge of cholesterol and coronary artery disease nowadays, the diet would be different," he said.

Besides gaining more experience in treating pulmonary diseases, Dr. Fong also decided to study internal medicine as well. He completed a three-year internal medicine residency at St. Louis City Hospital of Washington University. Dr. Fong hoped at the end of the three-year period to return to UCSF to work with and study under the renowned Dr. Seymour M. Farber, one of the country's leading authorities on chest diseases. That plan was interrupted by an opportunity to study in the pinnacle of the emerging specialty of pulmonary medicine at Columbia University's Bellevue Hospital in New York City. Calling it a "professional life-changing opportunity," Dr. Fong states simply, "I had to go."

Practitioner and Organizer

He practiced as a medical chest disease specialist at the Veteran's Hospital in West Haven, Conn., before joining the United States Air Force in 1955. Honorably discharged as a captain two years later, Dr. Fong, now a husband and father, returned to Sacramento where he founded an internal medicine and pulmonary disease practice. A visionary, he recognized the advantages of group practice for both the patient community and physicians. He thus established Sacramento Internal Medicine Group and is now associated with the Midtown Internal Medicine Group. No doubt, his organizational skills, honed as a youngster at his parents' grocery store, had helped in these new endeavors.

One of the earliest Chinese-American graduates of the UCSF medical school, he racked up other pioneering achievements by obtaining fellowship training in the sub-specialty of pulmonary medicine, becoming the first person of Chinese descent to become president of the local medical society as well as the local hospital system in Sacramento. By devoting time in extra training in chest medicine and infectious diseases, he has served his patients well during the course of his distinguished career. He helped found the California Association of Long Term Care Medicine (CALTCM) and wrote the bylaws for the organization, whose mission is improving care in the state's chronic care facilities.

In the late 1980s, Dr. Fong served on a California Medical Association committee on the topic of minority student admission into medical schools. Reflecting on his own experience, Dr. Fong said he experienced no racial discrimination in college or medical school. "The times were such that the Chinese were allies in the war against Japan. We were also few in numbers, and thus did not present overwhelming competition in schools or for jobs. The media was friendly; China and U.S. relations were good; Madame Chiang (Kai-Shek) was a goodwill ambassador for all Chinese in the U.S.; the movie, "The Good Earth," based on the book by Pearl Buck, elicited a lot of sympathy for the Chinese people," he recalled. This benign attitude was not the case in the early 20th century when there was overt discrimination. Dr. Fong suggests that these days, with the continued educational successes of Asian students and a larger Asian population, there might well be a backlash of racial animosity in the future. "We need comparative studies for the sake of learning and to help maintain a balance," he opines. "Each of our input—those who lived through those years—is very important."

Career Recognition

In 2003, the County of Sacramento's Board of Supervisors and the Organization of Chinese Americans issued a resolution honoring Dr. William Fong and his wife Ruby as

Outstanding and Pioneering Chinese Americans in Health Care Fields. Earlier in his career, his peers in the Sacramento-El Dorado Medical Society bestowed on him the Golden Stethoscope Award in 1988 in recognition of his dedication to his community and patients in his long and distinguished career. Honoring him for his uncompensated service to Sacramento County's indigents and his teaching of young physicians, the county hospital (Sacramento Medical Center) awarded him its Outstanding Medical Service Award in 1969. Dr. Fong has also served on the boards of and held offices in the area's Heart Association, Tuberculosis and Health Association, Medical Foundation and Blood Bank, Mercy Hospital Foundation, Sutter Health Systems, California Association of Long Term Care Medicine, California Association of Medical Directors, and other professional organizations. He was president of the local medical society, held various posts in the California Medical Association and the Sacramento Asian Community Center, and for 42 years was a medical consultant to the California Youth Authority. Twice he received the Sacramento Asian Physician's Society's Outstanding Achievement Award, and in 1990 he was honored for his legacy of outstanding service by the Asian Community Center.

The Fong Legacy

William Fong was equally dedicated and successful in his personal life. He married Ruby Yee of Hawaii in 1955. They settled in Sacramento and raised a family of seven boys and one girl. Each of the children graduated from college and has a professional career in business, science, education or law. William and Ruby are the proud grandparents of 18. Growing up in his father's family of 12, William Fong learned the importance of individual character and of family unity. Regarding his own family of 10, he remarked that what gives him the most pride is having "raised eight kids ... and no one is in jail ... I am so proud of them." In addition to being successful in their professions, they are also a musically talented clan. At a recent event celebrating the anniversary of an uncle and aunt, several of the Fong offspring, with some of their children, entertained the guests with a Fong family concert.

As a child Dr. William Fong was restless, curious and competitive. As an adult he has been thoughtful, dedicated, visionary, and, at the same time, humble. Dr. Fong has been a role model for the many lives he has touched—indeed a Chinese American for the ages.

Roots, Challenges & Fullfilment

by Joyce Mar

About the Stories

Many readers may now reflect upon their own families and lives and can find themselves mirrored in the similar experiences portrayed in these 35 stories. Those who are discovering for the first time the Chinese-American experience of this particular time in history, have been introduced to some wonderful stories of family, loyalty, hard work and perseverance along with personal achievements. We have come to appreciate and to be inspired by these pioneers for sharing their stories with us all.

More discussion will continue concerning the Chinese-American experience. For newcomers to Chinese-American history, we hope your appetite will grow for more materials to read. The men and women in Portraits of Pride give us a glimpse of themselves so that we can have the benefit of

their stories before they are gone. Americans, especially new immigrants, can learn to understand the cultural and historical significance of what it means to become American.

About Him Mark Lai

We are pleased that Him Mark Lai has offered his words of reflection to Portraits of Pride. Mr. Lai has written extensively on the Chinese in America. In 1969 he co-taught the first college level course on Chinese American history. *Chronicle of Higher Education* recognized him as "the scholar who legitimized the study of Chinese America." His personal collection on Chinese-American history is one of the richest and most extensive collections of its kind.

About the Appendix

To give the reader a sense of how the laws, acts, events and rulings in courts impacted Chinese Americans, an appendix follows for reference. Nearly all the laws restricted the lives of Chinese Americans and certainly influenced the immigration of the Chinese to America, particularly the Exclusion Act of 1882 that is printed in its entirety. (The mentality of "the Chinese must go!" was prevalent during this period.) Succeeding laws and acts continued to discriminate against Chinese immigrants and even American-born Chinese until they were lifted many decades later. Though restrictions have been repealed or rescinded for Chinese Americans and other Asian Americans, there are stereotypes that continue. Attitudes change slowly.

Him Mark Lai

Preeminent Chinese-American Historian

CHINESE HISTORICAL SOCIETY OF AMERICA

965 Clay Street • San Francisco, CA 94108-1527 • tel 415-391-1188 fax 415-391-1150• www.chsa.org

The experiences of the Chinese American middle class that emerged and developed during the Chinese exclusion era and the immediate post-exclusion years probably constitutes one of the more inadequately chronicled sectors of Chinese American history. Portraits of Pride promises to fill part of this void with a collection of biographic sketches of representative personages who grew up and began to build careers during this period. The overwhelming majority were professionals in scientific, technological and medical fields, with a scattered few in education, business, the military, and other fields. This phenomenon did not merely happen by chance, but was a reflection of the limited career choices these individuals faced when they began to break out of the confines of the Chinese community and staked out careers as integral parts of mainstream America. Their successful careers without a doubt paved the way and helped guide decisions on career goals for a generation of Chinese Americans.

Portraits of Pride was a collective effort by volunteers connected with the Chinese Historical Society of Southern California. Dr. Wing Mar and his colleagues have worked hard during the past four years to gather material through interviews and correspondence, as well as conducting literature and Internet searches in order to compile and edit this volume recording the experiences of these individuals. In addition, the work also includes appendices presenting historical documents and a historical timeline to provide background information enabling the reader to understand the biographies in the proper context.

Shared in common among these pathfinders was a tenacity of purpose based on a deep abiding belief in the value of education and the work ethic. Strong family support was often another important factor. Although many among this group frankly discussed encounters with discrimination and institutional racism, the overall mood projected in these accounts was upbeat and the outlook optimistic. For certain these portraits of pride will long serve as positive role models to guide and inspire present and future generations even though the Chinese American career horizon has now been considerably broadened.

Him Mark Lai

Him Mark Lai

Appendix:
Historical Material
Compiled by Edgar Wong

Knowledge of American history and Chinese culture is helpful in understanding the Portraits of Pride's World War II generation. The scope and content of the Appendix is self-explanatory. Each descriptive text is followed by a referenced website for supplemental reading. For readers with access to a computer, why not pop the enclosed CD into the tray and enjoy the surfing. You might be surprised to discover your own family history listed in the National Archives Records Administration website (see Part 2).

Cultural Topics
Part 1. 'Documented' Aliens – with two entries
Part 2. General Reading – with eight entries

Historical Periods
Part 3. Open Immigration (Pre 1924) – ten decades with 37 entries
Part 4. Closed Immigration (1924-1965) – five decades with 18 entries.
Part 5. Preferential Quota System (1965-Present) – five decades with 13 entries

Historical Documents
Part 6. Text of the Chinese Exclusion Act (1882)
Part 7. Text of California Constitution, Article XIX (1879)

A note on the CD version of this book: the referenced websites (underlined text) are hyperlinks to sites of interest. They were compiled in the spring 2004 and some sites might be unavailable today. If so, please use your search engine to find comparable websites for the topic of interest.

Part 1. 'Documented' Aliens
(False papers – forerunners of the 'gray' Green Cards)

Paper Children (False citizenship claims after the lost-documents in the 1906 earthquake fires)
http://oldworld.sjsu.edu/asiangate/angel_island/paper_children.html

Paper Sons (False identity papers in common usage after the 1882 Chinese Exclusion Act)
http://www.pacificnet.net/jue/docs/paperson.html

Part 2. General Reading
(Cultural topics – relevant to the Chinese experience)

Bound Feet (In China, the "ideal" length, called the "Golden Lotus," was three inches long)
http://www.anomalies-unlimited.com/OddPics/Bound.html

Chinese Holidays and Festivals (Listing of official and traditional holidays)
http://www.index-china.com/index-english/chinese_holidays.htm

Flying Tiger (Famed American Volunteer Group and on their fighter planes with the Tiger Shark Mouth)
http://thevanguard.bizland.com/squadron_news.htm

Immigrant Records Search (Helpful hints on immigrant "Case File" search by UC Berkeley)
http://groups.haas.berkeley.edu/iber/casefiles/chinese_immigrants_question_how_do_i_search_for_someones_case_file.cfm

National Archives Records Administration (NARA's Pacific Region – immigration records repository)
http://www.archives.gov/facilities/ca/san_francisco.html

Shee: The Name (Married women may use their maiden names and add "Shee")
http://policy.ssa.gov/poms.nsf/lnx/0200307388

Women in Aviation (Two Chinese-American women served as pilots in World War II)
http://www.wai.org/resources/100womenscript.cfm

Yin Yang (Characterized by some as the foundation of Chinese philosophy)
http://www.friesian.com/yinyang.htm

Part 3. Open Immigration (Pre-1924)

1839-1844
Trading conflicts between China and Britain started the Unequal Treaties. These conflicts became known as the first Opium War (1839-1842). The conflicts stopped in 1842 with the Treaty of Nanking, which stated that China would pay the British an indemnity, gave British control over Hong Kong, and to establish a fair tariff. Then in 1844, China signed the Treaty of Wanghia with the United States and the Treaty of Whampoa with France. Both of these treaties expanded the extraterritorial rights and allowed these nations to maintain a separate legal, judicial, police, and tax system in the treaty ports.
http://home.sandiego.edu/~pbugler/page1.htm

1848

Gold discovered in Sutter's sawmill in Coloma (50 miles northeast of Sacramento), California. Chinese begin to arrive. The Chinese who found their gold and wanted to return home knew they were popular targets of thieves. They solved the problem by melting the gold and forming it into ugly cooking utensils. When they got home, they melted the utensils and had their gold.

http://www.geocities.com/terriebittner/goldtext.htm

1850

California imposes Foreign Miner's Tax and enforces it mainly against Chinese miners, who often had to pay more than once. This tax required a payment of three dollars each month at a time when Chinese miners were making approximately six dollars a month. Chinese American population in U.S. was about 4,000 out of a population of 23.2 million. [See the year 2000 census for today's population data]

http://www.museumca.org/goldrush/curriculum/gamsaan/foreigntax2.html

1854

People v. Hall rules that Chinese cannot give testimony in court. The California Supreme Court decided that a state law prohibiting "Blacks, Mulattos, or Indians" from testifying for or against a white criminal defendant should be interpreted to include Chinese. In the court's view, an opposite conclusion would produce an "anomalous spectacle." After all, the court reasoned, Chinese were "a race of people whom nature has marked as inferior, and who are incapable of progress or intellectual development beyond a certain point … between whom and ourselves nature has placed an impassable difference."

http://www.cetel.org/1854_hall.html

1858

California passes a law to bar further immigration of Chinese and "Mongolians."

http://www.chiamonline.com/Laws/state.html

1862

California passes a "police tax" of $2.50 a month on every Chinese. An act to protect free white labor against competition with Chinese coolie labor and to discourage the immigration of the Chinese into the State of California.

http://www.cetel.org/1862_tax.html

1863-1865

Chinese men served and many died in the armies and navies during Civil War (Union and the Confederate army), along with German, Irish, French and African American soldiers. Ironically enough, they even served under the "Color Troops" division of the armies.

http://hometown.aol.com/gordonkwok/accsacw.html

1864-1869

Central Pacific Railroad Company recruits Chinese workers from Kwantung (now Guangdong) Province for the first transcontinental railroad. 10,000 workers were hired, of which 9,000 were Chinese—1,000 workers died on the job. Leland Stanford, president of the Central Pacific Railroad, reported that not less than 15,000 Chinese laborers could be procured the next year—enabling the push on the work so as not only to complete it far within the time required by the Acts of Congress, but so as to meet the public impatience.
http://cprr.org/
http://www.nps.gov/gosp/
http://cprr.org/Museum/Chinese.html
http://us_asians.tripod.com/timeline-1600.html

1868

China and U.S. sign Burlingame–Seward Treaty: United States and China agreed to trade, travel, and residence rights for each other's citizens; still prohibited naturalization.
http://academic.udayton.edu/race/02rights/treaty1868.htm

1870

California passes a law against the kidnapping and importation of Mongolian, Chinese and Japanese females, for criminal or demoralizing purposes.
http://www.sanfranciscochinatown.com/history/1870antiprostitutionact.html

1872

California's Civil Procedure Code drops 1854 law barring Chinese court testimony.
http://us_asians.tripod.com/timeline-1600.html

1875

U.S. Congress passed first law–The Page Law–excluding certain categories of aliens (e.g., convicts and prostitutes); declared all earlier state laws regarding immigration unconstitutional.
http://www.cetel.org/1875_page.html

1878

In re Ah Yup: rules Chinese not eligible for naturalized citizenship. A federal judge in California ruled that naturalization laws that were limited to aliens of African descent and "free white persons" should not be interpreted to include persons of the "Mongolian race." So, Ah Yup, the first Chinese immigrant who applied to be a citizen, should be denied. In so ruling, the judge relied heavily on the hysteria raised by one U.S. Senator who warned against changing the citizenship laws to include Chinese: "This amendment involves the whole Chinese problem ... the country has just awakened to the question and to the enormous magnitude of the question, involving a

possible immigration of many millions, involving another civilization; involving labor problems that no intellect can solve without study and time. Are you now prepared to settle the Chinese problem, thus in advance inviting that immigration?"
http://www.chiamonline.com/Chronology/1850.htm

1879

Californians led the way in anti-Chinese nativism. Numerous state and local laws were passed to limit Chinese economic activity. Denis Kearney organized his Workingmen's party to make anti-Chinese sentiment a partisan political issue. The Workingmen succeeded in including numerous anti-Chinese articles into a revision of the California State Constitution in 1878. California's second constitution prevents municipalities and corporations from employing Chinese. California state legislature passes law requiring all incorporated towns and cities to remove Chinese outside of city limits, but U.S. circuit court declares the law unconstitutional. Repealed in 1952. [See text of the California Constitution of 1879 in Part 7 below.]
http://www.chiamonline.com/Laws/state.html

1880

China and U.S. sign treaty giving the U.S. the right to limit but "not absolutely prohibit" Chinese immigration. Section 69 of California's Civil Code prohibits issuing of licenses for marriages between whites and "Mongolians, Negroes, mulattoes and persons of mixed blood."
http://members.aol.com/wdwylie/1880-1889.htm

1882

Chinese Exclusion Law suspends immigration of laborers for ten years; subsequently renewed; prohibited naturalization. The Chinese Exclusion Act was subsequently repealed in 1943. [See complete text of the Chinese Exclusion Act of 1882 at the end of this Appendix A—after the year 2000 entry.]
http://www.cetel.org/1882_exclusion.html

1884

The 1882 Chinese Exclusion Law amended to require a certificate as the only permissible evidence for reentry; wives barred; anti-miscegenation laws.
http://academic.udayton.edu/race/02rights/immigr05.htm

1886

Chinese laundrymen win case in Yick Wo v. Hopkins, which declares that a law with unequal impact on different groups is discriminatory.
http://www.cetel.org/1886_yickwo.html

1888

Scott Act renders 20,000 Chinese reentry certificates null and void; prohibited immigration of virtually all Chinese, including those who had gone back to China to visit.
http://immigrants.harpweek.com/ChineseAmericans/2KeyIssues/ScottAct.htm

1889

Chinese exclusion case Chae Chan Ping v. United States: Supreme Court ruled that an entire race that the government deemed difficult to assimilate might be barred from entry regardless of prior treaty; upholds constitutionality of Chinese exclusion laws. The court upheld a law that cancelled the validity of return certificates for Chinese laborers who had left the United States for visits to China, and also upheld the racist Chinese Exclusion Act.

In the process, the language of the court reveals the acceptance of stereotypical views of Chinese at the time. Chinese were "industrious and frugal." Without families, "their expenses were small; and they were content with the simplest fare, such as would not suffice for our laborers and artisans." Chinese "remained strangers in the land, residing apart by themselves, and adhering to the customs and usages of their own country. It seemed impossible for them to assimilate with our people, or to make any change in their habits or modes of living. As they grew in numbers, each year the people of the coast saw, or believed they saw, in the facility of immigration, and in the crowded millions of China, where population presses upon the means of subsistence, great danger that at no distant day that portion of our country would be overrun by them unless prompt action was taken to restrict their immigration."
http://www.augustana.edu/Users/Podehnel/cases/CHINEXCL.htm

1892

The Geary Act required Chinese living in the United States to carry a certificate of residence, without which they were subject to deportation or imprisonment and a year of hard labor. It denied bail to Chinese and prohibited them from from appearing as witnesses in court.
http://www.geary.com/The_Geary_Act_of_1892

1893

Fong Yue Ting v. United States: Supreme Court declared Congress had the right to legislate expulsion through executive orders; Chinese community had raised money to bring this before the Court to test the Geary Act. Congress amended the Geary Act to make it more difficult for Chinese businessmen to enter this country.
http://caselaw.lp.findlaw.com/scripts/getcase.pl?navby=case&court=us&vol=149&invol=698

1894

Gresham–Yang Treaty: China accepted total prohibition of immigration to the United States in return for readmission of those back in China on a visit; did away with Scott Act of 1888.
http://www.epcc.edu/ftp/Homes/monicaw/borderlands/19_chinese.htm

1898

United States v. Wong Kim Ark: Supreme Court rules person born in the United States of Chinese parents is of American nationality by birth—that Chinese born in the U.S. can't be stripped of their citizenship.
http://www.cetel.org/1898_wongkim.html

1900

United States v. Mrs. Cue Lim: Supreme Court ruled wives and children of treaty merchants were entitled to come to the United States. Bubonic plague scare in San Francisco—Chinatown cordoned and quarantined.
http://academic.udayton.edu/race/03justice/aspilaws.htm

1902

Chinese Exclusion Act extended for another ten years. An Act To prohibit the coming into and to regulate the residence within the United States, its Territories, and all territory under its jurisdiction, and the District of Columbia, of Chinese and persons of Chinese descent.
http://www.sanfranciscochinatown.com/history/1902exclusionactextension.html

1904

Chinese exclusion made indefinite. All Chinese excluded from the United States, Washington, D.C., and all U.S. territories.
http://www.cetel.org/1904_extension.html

1905

Section 60 of California's Civil Code amended to forbid marriage between whites and "Mongolians."
http://www3.niu.edu/ptaa/history.htm

1906

The 1906 San Francisco Earthquake devastated Chinatown, and many of the survivors fled to other parts of the San Francisco Bay Area, but about 500 out of 5,000 remained. A handful of city planners and local politicians considered the earthquake both an opportunity and a great blessing to be rid of the Chinese in a prime real estate area, and move them to Hunters Point.
http://www.pandanet.co.jp/English/art/sfchinatown/sfchinatown.html

1910

Angel Island opens as an official immigration station.
http://www.cetel.org/angel_poetry.html

1911

On October 10, the Manchu rule was overthrown in China. Sun Yat-sen was declared president of the new Republic of China in 1911. His leadership of the Nationalist Party, or Kuomintang, lasted only 2 years. In 1913, he stepped down and retreated from the political spotlight under pressure from the military leader Yuan Shi-kai. Yuan's death in 1916 plunged China into the warlord era, which was to last until 1927. Sun Yat-sen returned to politics during this time to form a southern Kuomintang government, which exercised nominal control over parts of the south in the 1920s.

http://www.thecorner.org/hists/china/chin-revo.htm

http://www.chinaetravel.com/china/history2.html

1913

California passes alien land law prohibiting "aliens ineligible to citizenship" from buying land or leasing it for longer than three years.

http://www.santacruzpl.org/history/ww2/9066/land.shtml

1918

Servicemen of Asian ancestry who had served in World War I receive right of naturalization. Prior to and during WWI, the US Navy allowed Filipino enlistees to serve under a range of military occupational rating such as petty officer, band master, musician, coxswains' mates, seamen, machinist, fireman, water tender, commissary stewards, officer's stewards, and mess attendants. After World War I, the United States Navy issued new rulings restricting Filipinos, even those with college education, to the rating of officer stewards and mess attendants. These military occupational discrimination practices were stopped in the 1970s when there was a senatorial investigation of the use of stewards in the military due to pressure from the civil rights movement. During World War I (1917-1918) 2,666,867 men were drafted, about 1,300,000 actually were deployed in Europe. All males between the ages of 21 and 30 were required to register for military service.

http://us_asians.tripod.com/timeline-1910.html#servicemen-naturalized

1920

Initiative in California ballot plugs up loopholes in the 1913 alien land law. Repealed in 1956.

http://www.pbs.org/race/000_About/002_03_d-godeeper.htm

1921

National Origin System – Immigration Act (Johnson Act): used the country of birth to determine whether an individual could enter as legal alien, the number of previous immigrants and their descendants used to set the quota of how many from a country could enter annually—basis of immigration system until 1965. Washington and Louisiana pass alien land laws.

http://www.maltamigration.com/history/exodus/chapter4-3.shtml

1922

Cable Act declares that any American female citizen who marries "an alien ineligible to citizenship" would lose her citizenship.

http://college.hmco.com/history/readerscomp/gahff/html/ff_029900_cableact.htm

1923

Chinese student immigration ended because of strict requirements for having the funds necessary to return to China.

http://www.celt.sunysb.edu/angel/newmedia.html

Part 4. Closed Immigration (1924-1965)

1924

Immigration Act (Johnson–Reed Act) restricted all Asians from coming into the United States.

http://www.washington.edu/uwired/outreach/cspn/curaaw/aawdoc02.html

1925

Chang Chan et al. v. John D. Nagle: Supreme Court ruled Chinese wives of American citizens not entitled to enter the United States.

http://academic.udayton.edu/race/02rights/immigr05.htm

1927

Weedin v. Chin Bow: Supreme Court ruled persons born to American parents(s) who never resided in the United States are not of American nationality, thus not eligible for entry.

http://supreme.lp.findlaw.com/constitution/article02/03.html

1928

Lam Mow v. Nagle: Supreme Court ruled that a child born of Chinese parents on American vessels on high seas was not born in the United States, therefore not a citizen.

http://caselaw.lp.findlaw.com/data/constitution/amendment14/01.html

1931

Amendment to Cable Act declares that no American-born woman who loses her citizenship by marrying an alien ineligible to citizenship can be denied the right of naturalization at a later date.

http://www.h-net.msu.edu/~women/threads/marr.html

1938

150 Chinese women garment workers strike for three months against the National Dollar Stores (owned by a Chinese).

http://ark.cdlib.org/ark:/13030/ft7v19p1vp/

1942

Executive Order 9066, signed by President Roosevelt on February 19, 1942, was the instrument that allowed military commanders to designate areas "from which any or all persons may be excluded." Under this order all Japanese and Americans of Japanese ancestry were removed from Western coastal regions to guarded camps in the interior.
http://www.cetel.org/1942_9066.html

1943

The Chinese Exclusion Repeal Act of 1943 repealed the Chinese Exclusion Act of 1882; token 105 Chinese immigrants allowed to enter the United States annually, selected by U.S. government. War Brides Act: Admission to the United States for spouses and children of U.S. armed forces members included 722 Chinese.
http://www.cetel.org/1943_repeal.html

1944

GI BILL Act of June 22, 1944: The Servicemen's Readjustment Act of 1944 put higher education within the reach of millions of veterans of World War II and later military conflicts.
http://fcis.oise.utoronto.ca/~daniel_schugurensky/assignment1/1944gibill.html

1946

The number of Chinese women in Los Angeles begins to increase largely because of the passage of the 1945 War Brides Act, the 1946 Fiancées Act, and the enactment of Public Law 713 in 1946, as well as by immigration from other U.S. Chinatowns.
http://www.gaeleire.freeservers.com/custom4.html

1947

Amendment to 1945 War Brides Act allows Chinese American veterans to bring brides into the U.S.
http://us_asians.tripod.com/timeline-1940.html

1948

The Displaced Persons Act allowed for admission of many refugees displaced by the war and unable to come to the United States under regular immigration procedures. This act gave permanent resident status to 3,465 Chinese students, visitors and seaman who didn't want to go back to China.
http://uscis.gov/graphics/aboutus/history/articles/oview.htm

1949

U.S. breaks off diplomatic ties with newly formed People's Republic of China—5,000 highly educated Chinese in the U.S. granted refugee status after China establishes a Communist government.
http://web.mit.edu/21h.153j/www/chrono.html

1950

Second Displaced Persons Act further helped Chinese in the United States to change their status (due to communist takeover in China).
http://academic.udayton.edu/race/02rights/immigr05.htm

1952

Immigration and Nationality Act (McCarran–Walter Act) removed total ban of Chinese immigrants but upheld national origins quotas. It somewhat liberalized immigration from Asia, but increased the power of the government to deport aliens suspected of Communist sympathies.
http://modelminority.com/modules.php?name=News&file=article&sid=73

1952

Repeals Article XIX of California Constitution, as adopted in 1879, which directs Legislature to prescribe laws imposing conditions on residence of certain aliens and to provide for their removal from the State; which prohibits Chinese employment by corporations and on public works; which directs passage of laws providing for removal of Chinese from cities or their restriction to certain portions of cities, and adoption of laws to prohibit Chinese from entering State.
http://lalaw.lib.ca.us/ballot-1950.html

1953

Refugee Relief Act: 2,800 places allotted to Chinese out of total 205,000 people to be admitted; law expired in 1956. Included for the first time, refugees of Chinese origin, as long as the Nationalist Chinese government vouched for them.
http://www.ed.uiuc.edu/courses/eps300/Asianimmigration.html

1956

Repeals inoperative law of 1920 that formerly denied aliens ineligible to citizenship the right to hold real estate in California.
http://lalaw.lib.ca.us/ballot-1950.html

Part 5. Preferential Quota System (1965-Present)

1962-1965

Attorney General allowed 15,000 Chinese to enter as parolees due to refugee situation in Hong Kong.
http://academic.udayton.edu/race/02rights/immigr05.htm

1965

President Lyndon Johnson signed a bill that has dramatically changed the method by which immigrants are admitted to America. This bill is the Immigration Act of 1965. This act, also known as the Hart-Cellar Act [1],

not only allows more individuals from third world countries to enter the US (including Asians, who have traditionally been hindered from entering America), but also entails a separate quota for refugees. [2] Under the Act, 170,000 immigrants from the Eastern Hemisphere are granted residency, with no more than 20,000 per country. One hundred twenty thousand immigrants from the Western Hemisphere, with no "national limitations," are also to be admitted. [3] The significance of this bill was that future immigrants were to be welcomed because of their skills/professions, and not for their countries of origin.
http://campus.northpark.edu/history/WebChron/USA/ImmigrationAct.html

1972

President Richard M. Nixon traveled to China. Nixon: "…we simply cannot afford to leave China forever outside the family of nations …"
http://www.pbs.org/wgbh/amex/china/peopleevents/pande01.html

1975

Operation Frequent Wind—US government evacuated U.S. and Vietnamese people from Saigon. More than 130,000 refugees enter the U.S. from Vietnam, Kampuchea, and Laos as Communist governments are established there.
http://www.cnn.com/ALLPOLITICS/time/2000/04/17/ladders.html

1975

The Chinese Historical Society of Southern California is founded. The Historical Society is the publisher of this book—Portraits of Pride. See website for ongoing Society activities.
http://www.chssc.org

1976

President Gerald Ford rescinds Executive Order 9066—the Internment of 110,000 Japanese Americans in 1942.
http://www.thesurvivorproject.org/pdfs/section_v_japanese_american.pdf

1979

Resumption of diplomatic relations between the People's Republic of China and the United States of America reunites members of long-separated Chinese American families.
http://usinfo.org/docs/basic/prc_e.htm

1981

Taiwan and Mainland China each allowed 20,000 immigrants.
http://www.maxwell.syr.edu/maxpages/classes/soc248/Asianas%20Post%20WWII%204-24-00%20.html

1982

Vincent Chin, a Chinese-American draftsman, is clubbed to death with a baseball bat by two Euro-American men. The jobless automobile workers reportedly mistook him for a Japanese and blame him for their plight. In 1984 Ronald Ebens was convicted on one count of civil rights violations and sentenced to 25 years in prison; Stepson Michael Nitz was acquitted. Ebens was instructed to undergo treatment for alcoholism but was freed after posting a $20,000 bond. Neither he nor his stepson ever spent a day in jail. And, soon afterwards, the conviction was overturned due to a legal technicality, and a retrial was ordered. In 1987 a jury in Cincinnati cleared Ebens, stating the attack was not racially motivated. Later that year a civil suit against Ebens was settled by a court-approved agreement whereby Ebens agreed to pay, over time, $1.5 million to Chin's estate. But the laid-off 47-year-old does not have a steady job, and the chance that he will ever pay the maximum amount seems extremely unlikely.

http://www.mindspring.com/~louve/vinchin.html

1986

Immigration Reform and Control Act imposes civil and criminal penalties on employers who knowingly hire undocumented aliens.

http://www.usda.gov/oce/oce/labor-affairs/ircasumm.htm

1990

Immigration Act increased number of immigrants admitted because of skill level; Immigration Act continued priority for skilled workers and family reunification.

http://uscis.gov/graphics/shared/aboutus/statistics/legishist/568.htm

1996

Illegal Immigration and Responsibility Act of 1996, Pub. L. No. 104-208, 110 Stat. 3009; People who have been in the United States longer than six months after their visas expired can be deported. They will also be barred from returning to the United States for three years. And those who have been in the United States illegally for more than a year will have to wait 10 years before they will be allowed to return legally.

http://uscis.gov/graphics/publicaffairs/factsheets/948.htm

2000

According to the U.S. 2000 Census (*see next page*) , there were 2,432,585 Chinese Americans under One Race Category in the United States. They constituted 0.9% of total population. That is, in every 100 Americans, there is a Chinese American. If Chinese under two or more races are included, there are 2,879,636 Chinese Americans.

http://members.aol.com/chineseusa/00his.htm (History of Chinese Americans in the U.S.)
http://members.aol.com/chineseusa/00cen1.htm (Chinese American Population: U.S. Census 2000)

(continued on page 215)

United States 2000 Census

Rank	State	Chinese American Population	Total Population	Chinese American Population %
	United States	2,879,636	281,421,906	1.02%
01	California	1,122,187	33,871,648	3.31%
02	New York	451,859	18,976,457	2.38%
03	Hawaii	170,803	1,211,537	14.10%
04	Texas	121,588	20,851,820	0.58%
05	New Jersey	110,263	8,414,350	1.31%
06	Massachusetts	92,380	6,349,097	1.46%
07	Illinois	86,095	12,419,293	0.69%
08	Washington	75,884	5,894,121	1.29%
09	Florida	59,280	15,982,378	0.37%
10	Pennsylvania	56,831	12,281,054	0.46%
11	Maryland	55,139	5,296,486	1.04%
12	Virginia	43,532	7,078,515	0.61%
13	Michigan	38,149	9,938,444	0.38%
14	Ohio	35,043	11,353,140	0.31%
15	Georgia	31,976	8,186,453	0.39%
16	Oregon	27,145	3,421,399	0.79%
17	Arizona	26,521	5,130,632	0.52%
18	North Carolina	22,156	8,049,313	0.28%
19	Connecticut	21,963	3,405,565	0.64%
20	Colorado	20,278	4,301,261	0.47%
21	Minnesota	19,369	4,919,479	0.39%
22	Nevada	19,043	1,998,257	0.95%
23	Missouri	15,881	5,595,211	0.28%
24	Indiana	14,703	6,080,485	0.24%
25	Wisconsin	13,385	5,363,675	0.25%

Part 6. Text of the Chinese Exclusion Act (1882)

Preamble.

Whereas, in the opinion of the Government of the United States the coming of Chinese laborers to this country endangers the good order of certain localities within the territory thereof: Therefore,

Be it enacted by the Senate and House of Representatives of the United States of America in Congress assembled, That from and after the expiration of ninety days next after the passage of this act, and until the expiration of ten years next after the passage of this act, the coming of Chinese laborers to the United States be, and the same is hereby, suspended; and during such suspension it shall not be lawful for any Chinese laborer to come, or, having so come after the expiration of said ninety days, to remain within the United States.

SEC. 2. That the master of any vessel who shall knowingly bring within the United States on such vessel, and land or permit to be landed, and Chinese laborer, from any foreign port of place, shall be deemed guilty of a misdemeanor, and on conviction thereof shall be punished by a fine of not more than five hundred dollars for each and every such Chinese laborer so brought, and may be also imprisoned for a term not exceeding one year.

SEC. 3. That the two foregoing sections shall not apply to Chinese laborers who were in the United States on the seventeenth day of November, eighteen hundred and eighty, or who shall have come into the same before the expiration of ninety days next after the passage of this act, and who shall produce to such master before going on board such vessel, and shall produce to the collector of the port in the United States at which such vessel shall arrive, the evidence hereinafter in this act required of his being one of the laborers in this section mentioned; nor shall the two foregoing sections apply to the case of any master whose vessel, being bound to a port not within the United States by reason of being in distress or in stress of weather, or touching at any port of the United States on its voyage to any foreign port of place: Provided, That all Chinese laborers brought on such vessel shall depart with the vessel on leaving port.

SEC. 4. That for the purpose of properly identifying Chinese laborers who were in the United States on the seventeenth day of November, eighteen hundred and eighty, or who shall have come into the same before the expiration of ninety days next after the passage of this act, and in order to furnish them with the proper evidence of their right to go from and come to the United States of their free will and accord, as provided by the treaty between the United States and China dated November seventeenth, eighteen hundred and eighty, the collector of customs of the district from which any such Chinese laborer shall depart from the United States shall, in person or by deputy, go on board each vessel having on board any such Chinese laborer and cleared or about to sail from his district for a foreign port, and on such vessel make a list of all such Chinese laborers, which shall be entered in registry-books to be kept for that purpose, in which shall be stated the name, age, occupation, last place of residence, physical marks or peculiarities, and all facts necessary for the identification of each of such Chinese laborers, which books shall be safely kept in the custom-house; and every such

Chinese laborer so departing from the United States shall be entitled to, and shall receive, free of any charge or cost upon application therefore, from the collector or his deputy, at the time such list is taken, a certificate, signed by the collector or his deputy and attested by his seal of office, in such form as the Secretary of the Treasury shall prescribe, which certificate shall contain a statement of the name, age, occupation, last place of residence, personal description, and fact of identification of the Chinese laborer to whom the certificate is issued, corresponding with the said list and registry in all particulars. In case any Chinese laborer after having received such certificate shall leave such vessel before her departure he shall deliver his certificate to the master of the vessel, and if such Chinese laborer shall fail to return to such vessel before her departure from port the certificate shall be delivered by the master to the collector of customs for cancellation. The certificate herein provided for shall entitle the Chinese laborer to whom the same is issued to return to and re-enter the United States upon producing and delivering the same to the collector of customs of the district at which such Chinese laborer shall seek to re-enter; and upon delivery of such certificate by such Chinese laborer to the collector of customs at the time of re-entry in the United States, said collector shall cause the same to be filed in the custom house and duly canceled.

SEC. 5. That any Chinese laborer mentioned in section four of this act being in the United States, and desiring to depart from the United States by land, shall have the right to demand and receive, free of charge or cost, a certificate of identification similar to that provided for in section four of this act to be issued to such Chinese laborers as may desire to leave the United States by water; and it is hereby made the duty of the collector of customs of the district next adjoining the foreign country to which said Chinese laborer desires to go to issue such certificate, free of charge or cost, upon application by such Chinese laborer, and to enter the same upon registry-books to be kept by him for the purpose, as provided for in section four of this act.

SEC. 6. That in order to the faithful execution of articles one and two of the treaty in this act before mentioned, every Chinese person other than a laborer who may be entitled by said treaty and this act to come within the United States, and who shall be about to come to the United States, shall be identified as so entitled by the Chinese Government in each case, such identity to be evidenced by a certificate issued under the authority of said government, which certificate shall be in the English language or (if not in the English language) accompanied by a translation into English, stating such right to come, and which certificate shall state the name, title, or official rank, if any, the age, height, and all physical peculiarities, former and present occupation or profession, and place of residence in China of the person to whom the certificate is issued and that such person is entitled conformably to the treaty in this act mentioned to come within the United States. Such certificate shall be prima-facie evidence of the fact set forth therein, and shall be produced to the collector of customs, or his deputy, of the port in the district in the United States at which the person named therein shall arrive.

SEC. 7. That any person who shall knowingly and falsely alter or substitute any name for the name written in such certificate or forge any such certificate, or knowingly utter any forged or fraudulent certificate, or falsely personate any person named in any such certificate, shall be deemed guilty of a misdemeanor; and upon conviction thereof shall be fined in a sum not exceeding one thousand dollars, an imprisoned in a penitentiary for a term of not more than five years.

SEC. 8. That the master of any vessel arriving in the United States from any foreign port or place shall, at the same time he delivers a manifest of the cargo, and if there be no cargo, then at the time of making a report of the entry of vessel pursuant to the law, in addition to the other matter required to be reported, and before landing, or permitting to land, any Chinese passengers, deliver and report to the collector of customs of the district in which such vessels shall have arrived a separate list of all Chinese passengers taken on board his vessel at any foreign port or place, and all such passengers on board the vessel at that time. Such list shall show the names of such passengers (and if accredited officers of the Chinese Government traveling on the business of that government, or their servants, with a note of such facts), and the name and other particulars, as shown by their respective certificates; and such list shall be sworn to by the master in the manner required by law in relation to the manifest of the cargo. Any willful refusal or neglect of any such master to comply with the provisions of this section shall incur the same penalties and forfeiture as are provided for a refusal or neglect to report and deliver a manifest of cargo.

SEC. 9. That before any Chinese passengers are landed from any such vessel, the collector, or his deputy, shall proceed to examine such passengers, comparing the certificates with the list and with the passengers; and no passenger shall be allowed to land in the United States from such vessel in violation of law.

SEC. 10. That every vessel whose master shall knowingly violate any of the provisions of this act shall be deemed forfeited to the United States, and shall be liable to seizure and condemnation on any district of the United States into which such vessel may enter or in which she may be found.

SEC. 11. That any person who shall knowingly bring into or cause to be brought into the United States by land, or who shall knowingly aid or abet the same, or aid or abet the landing in the United States from any vessel of any Chinese person not lawfully entitled to enter the United States, shall be deemed guilty of a misdemeanor, and shall, on conviction thereof, be fined in a sum not exceeding one thousand dollars, and imprisoned for a term not exceeding one year.

SEC. 12. That no Chinese person shall be permitted to enter the United States by land without producing to the proper officer of customs the certificate in this act required of Chinese persons seeking to land from a vessel. And any Chinese person found unlawfully within the United States shall be caused to be removed therefrom to the country from whence he came, by direction of the United States, after being brought before some justice, judge, or commissioner of a court of the United States and found to be one not lawfully entitled to be or remain in the United States.

SEC. 13. That this act shall not apply to diplomatic and other officers of the Chinese Government traveling upon the business of that government, whose credentials shall be taken as equivalent to the certificate in this act mentioned, and shall exempt them and their body and household servants from the provisions of this act as to other Chinese persons.

SEC. 14. That hereafter no State court or court of the United States shall admit Chinese to citizenship; and all laws in conflict with this act are hereby repealed.

SEC. 15. That the words "Chinese laborers", whenever used in this act, shall be construed to mean both skilled and unskilled laborers and Chinese employed in mining.

Approved, May 6, 1882.
http://www-marine.stanford.edu/HMSweb/cea.htm

Part 7. Text of California Constitution, Article XIX (1879)

SECTION 1. The Legislature shall prescribe all necessary regulations for the protection of the State, and the counties, cities, and towns thereof, from the burdens and evils arising from the presence of aliens who are or may become vagrants, paupers, mendicants, criminals, or invalids afflicted with contagious or infectious diseases, and from aliens otherwise dangerous or detrimental to the well-being or peace of the State, and to impose conditions upon which persons may reside in the State, and to provide the means and mode of their removals from the State, upon failure ore refusal to comply with such conditions; provided, that nothing contained in this section shall be construed to impair or limit the power of the legislature to pass such police laws or other regulations as it may deem necessary.

SEC. 2. No corporation now existing or hereafter formed under the laws of this State, shall, after the adoption of this Constitution, employ directly or indirectly, in any capacity, any Chinese or Mongolian. The Legislature shall pass such laws as may be necessary to enforce this provision.

SEC. 3. No Chinese shall be employed on any State, county, municipal, or other public work, except in punishment for crime.

SEC. 4. The presence of foreigners ineligible to become citizens of the United States is declared to be dangerous to the well-being of the State, and the Legislature shall discourage their immigration by all the means within its power. Asiatic coolieism is a form of human slavery, and is forever prohibited in this State, and all contracts for coolie labor shall be void. All companies or corporations, whether formed in this country or any foreign country, for the importation of such labor, shall be subject to such penalties as the Legislature may prescribe. The Legislature shall delegate all necessary power to the incorporated cities and towns of this State for the removal of Chinese without the limits of such cities and towns, or for their location within prescribed portions of those limits, and it shall also provide the necessary legislation to prohibit the introduction into this State of Chinese after the adoption of this Constitution. This section shall be enforced by appropriate legislation.
http://class.lls.edu/~manheimk/cl1/chinese.htm

INDEX